D0086236

# Joining a Community of Readers

# Joining a Community of Readers

## A THEMATIC APPROACH TO READING

**Roberta Alexander**
*San Diego City College*

**Jan Lombardi**
*San Diego City College*

LONGMAN

An imprint of Addison Wesley Longman, Inc.

New York • Reading, Massachusetts • Menlo Park, California • Harlow, England
Don Mills, Ontario • Sydney • Mexico City • Madrid • Amsterdam

PE
1122
.A36
1997

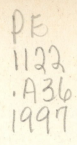

Associate Editor: Lynn M. Huddon
Developmental Editor: Melody Davies
Acquisitions Editor: Steven A. Rigolosi
Marketing Manager: Ann Stypuloski
Supplements Editor: Donna Campion
Project Management and Text Design: Ruttle, Shaw & Wetherill
Cover Illustration: Tina Vey
Cover Designer: Kay Petronio
Photo Researcher: Karen Koblik
Electronic Production Manager: Christine Pearson
Manufacturing Manager: Willie Lane
Electronic Page Makeup: Ruttle, Shaw & Wetherill
Printer and Binder: R. R. Donnelley & Sons Company
Cover Printer: The Lehigh Press

For permission to use copyrighted material, grateful acknowledgment is made to the copyright holders on pages 336–339, which are hereby made part of this copyright page.

Library of Congress Cataloging-in-Publication Data

Alexander, Roberta [date]
    Joining a community of readers : a thematic approach to reading /
Roberta Alexander, Jan Lombardi.
        p.   cm.
    Includes bibliographical references and index.
    ISBN 0-321-01181-3
    1. College readers.    2. Reading comprehension.    I. Lombardi, Jan.
    II. Title.
    PE1122.A36   1997
    808´.0427—dc21                                                          97-29538
                                                                            CIP

Copyright © 1998 by Addison-Wesley Educational Publishers Inc.

All rights reserved. No part of this publication may be reproduced, stored in a retrieval system, or transmitted, in any form or by any means, electronic, mechanical, photocopying, recording, or otherwise, without the prior written permission of the publisher. Printed in the United States.

ISBN 0-321-01181-3 (Student Edition)
ISBN 0-321-40099-2 (Instructor's Edition)

345678910—DOC—009998

To Ethel & Hursel Alexander
and
Veronica & Francis Ryan

403944

# CONTENTS

# Reading, Vocabulary, and Study Skills in *Joining a Community of Readers*

*Joining a Community of Readers* is organized in five theme-based units, each with two chapters. Each unit focuses on the development of certain skills, building on the skills learned in previous units.

- **Reading, vocabulary, and study strategies** are integrated with the themes throughout the text. Once a strategy, such as identifying main ideas, is introduced and learned, it is reinforced many times in succeeding chapters.

- **Language Tips** are designed for non-native speakers of English and other beginning college students.
- At the end of each chapter, **Applying Your Skills** sections give students the opportunity to review appropriate strategies and apply them to additional readings.

# TO THE INSTRUCTOR

Organized around high-interest, motivational, and contemporary themes relevant to the lives of all students, *Joining a Community of Readers* provides guided instruction in the reading and learning process and abundant practice of the basic reading and study skills. The first level college reading text in the two-book series, *Joining a Community of Readers* follows the same integrated, holistic approach and thematic organization as its successful companion text, *A Community of Readers*. However, this text focuses more on basic reading skills, such as finding the main idea and identifying supporting details, and provides greater accessibility for students from various language and academic backgrounds.

The first unit focuses on strategies for becoming a successful student and learning the PRO reading process for becoming an active reader. Each of the following units presents a contemporary issue—learning and expectations, our environment, our changing families, and our communities and work—and challenges students to employ their reading and related skills to individually and collaboratively understand the themes and to think about them. As students progress through the chapters, they learn, practice, and recycle the reading/learning skills required to succeed in their college courses. Because each unit of the text builds on a single theme, students have the time to develop schema and exchange knowledge on a particular topic.

## SPECIAL FEATURES

The success of this book, and its unique value as an introductory college reading text, is based on the following features:

- **Holistic approach to reading:** Reading skills are presented in the context of the study of real-life issues to provide students with the skills needed to successfully adapt the reading and study strategies to their academic courses and to work situations.
- **Thematic organization:** Each unit focuses on one theme so that students can work with the ideas long enough to begin to understand and use the material in its complexity. Readings and examples used for skills explanations are connected and related to the chapter theme, therefore the skills themselves become more accessible.
- **Abundant examples and practice:** Each skill is introduced with clear explanations and examples. The theme-based content of the practices within

the chapters progresses from paragraphs to longer passages with exercises tailored to reinforce skills through application to longer readings. The application of skills, especially finding the main ideas and support, is emphasized throughout the text.

- **High-interest readings from various sources:** The selections are from various sources to encourage students to read and enjoy reading. They have been carefully chosen for their accessibility and high interest level.
- **Integration of essential reading skills with vocabulary and study strategies:** Integrated with the reading skills throughout the text, instruction on main ideas, supporting details, vocabulary, and study skills leads to problem-solving exercises. The successful integration of these skills provides students with an understanding of the relevance of the skills and a means of applying them to their academic and career needs.
- **Language Tips:** To provide nonnative speakers of English and other beginning college students with strategies for better understanding their reading, instructional sections and exercises on issues of language such as word forms, forming complete sentences, and paraphrasing are integrated into the chapters.
- **Critical thinking skills:** By focusing on one theme at a time, students have the opportunity to understand the topic and its context in more depth and can apply critical thinking skills more effectively in class discussions, assigned writings, and collaborative activities. Exercises throughout the text lead students to apply their background knowledge to evaluate issues and make connections among various points of view.
- **Focus on the reading process:** The essential steps to teaching reading—*prereading activities, active reading, and postreading tasks*—are built into each chapter. Students are led to apply the new skills learned within the context of the reading process.
- **Collaborative work:** Exercises throughout the text encourage students to collaborate with their peers. Collaborative skills reviews and problem-solving tasks will help students in their academic work as well as in their future careers.

## ORGANIZATION

The chapters are designed to teach specific reading skills as they lead students through the steps of learning about a theme, reflecting on that theme, and generating possible responses to the theme. To accomplish this progression, each unit contains the following features:

- **An opening illustration and quotation** introduce the theme of the two-chapter unit and provide prereading questions that ask students to explore their background knowledge and opinions on the topic.
- **Unit Objectives** are listed to provide an overview of the reading skills and topics that the unit addresses.

- **Raising Issues** presents a reading selection on the issues of the unit in easily accessible ways: autobiographical essay, introductory explanation, a newspaper or magazine article, a short excerpt from a book.
- **Skills instruction** is carefully interwoven with readings about the theme of the chapter itself and examples in the pedagogy are taken predominantly from content-related material.
- **Working with Words** presents and reviews vocabulary skills with particular emphasis on understanding words in context, dictionary skills, and developing a personal vocabulary system.
- **Organizing to Learn** introduces strategies and exercises on topics such as marking texts, mapping and outlining, and making time lines and charts to help students understand and retain what they have learned in their reading.
- **Language Tips** help students better understand their reading by addressing special problem areas, such as understanding word forms, understanding what makes a sentence complete, and paraphrasing.
- **Applying Your Skills** provides students with a longer reading for practicing the skills they have acquired in the chapter, as well as skills learned in earlier chapters.
- **Chapter Reviews** provide an innovative format for students to collaboratively or individually organize and review the skills of the chapter, postreading extension activities for collaborative group work, and writing assignments that are based on the chapter content.
- **Unit Reviews** provide an opportunity for student self-assessment or for instructor assessment of student achievement using a longer passage relating the theme to which students *apply* the skills they have learned in the unit and review skills they have learned in earlier chapters. The exercises in the Unit Reviews provide the opportunity for students to practice answering objective questions as well as open-ended, short-answer questions.

## SUPPLEMENTS

*Joining a Community of Readers* comes with a complete instructor support package.

- **An Instructor's Manual** provides teaching suggestions for each chapter and ideas for introducing students to the PRO reading system, using collaborative groups in class, promoting critical thinking, and teaching non-native speakers. It also includes writing assignments, additional reading lists, and an answer key.
- **A Test Bank,** by Laura Headley, offers suggested teaching and testing techniques for each chapter, as well as a variety of multiple-choice, true/false, short-answer, and interactive exercises. An answer key is also provided.

## ACKNOWLEDGMENTS

We are grateful to our families—Laura, Christina, Paul-Vincent, and Chuck; and Elena, Paul, Marley, Margarita, and Andrei—for their patience and help. They endured our late night and early morning sessions, and our giggles. We are also grateful to Dennis Howard who has been a friend throughout and piloted early manuscripts of our texts in his classroom.

Thank you to Ellen Schatz for her constant cheer and encouragement, and to Patricia Rossi, Lynn Huddon, Ann Stypuloski, and Tom Conville, who have helped in ushering our book through its final stages of the production and marketing processes. We owe a very special thank you to Melody Davies, whose diligence, perseverance, editorial insights, and gentle sense of humor helped us to complete the text so successfully.

Thank you to our reviewers around the country: Linda Arnold, University of Central Arkansas; Janet E. Barrows, Cosumnes River College; Tamara Brawner, Thomas College; Jessica Carroll, Miami Dade Community College; Laura De-Marais, University of St. Thomas; Cathlene S. Denny, St. Johns River Community College; Mary Dubbe, Thomas Nelson Community College; Jeannine Edwards, The University of Memphis; Dennis Gabriel, Cuyahoga Community College; Mary Holdway, College of DuPage; Charles Hunter, San Jose City College; Linda Lane, Foothill College; Linda W. LaRou, Duchess Community College; Carolyn Lewis, West Valley College; Patricia Malinkowski, Finger Lakes Community College; Margaret Ann Maricle, Questa College; Jeanne Mauzy, Valencia Community College; Janice McIntyre, Kansas City Community College; Donna Richardson, Mercer County Community College; Theodore Ridout, Bunker Hill Community College; Mary Lee Sandusky, Kent State University; Jacqueline Stark, Los Angeles Valley College; Dr. Sharon A. Swallwood, St. Petersburg Junior College; Barbara VanDusen, Guilford Technical Community College; and Suzanne Weisar, San Jacinto College South.

# To the Student: Welcome to *Joining a Community of Readers*

You have probably bought this book because you need to strengthen your reading skills and strategies to be ready for the demands of college reading. If you are prepared to take responsibility for your own learning, and if you are prepared to commit yourself to the work involved, you will learn the strategies and skills you will need to become an effective, thoughtful reader. You need these skills not only to pass this course, but for success in college, and, even more importantly, for success in the workplace of the twenty-first century.

## WHY IS READING SO IMPORTANT?

Read any newspaper today, talk to any employers or human resource managers, and you will realize that the demands of today's society—not only of college study—require that you are always able to learn new skills and even new jobs or professions. During your lifetime, you will probably be faced with the need to change jobs or professions three, four, or more times. And even if you are one of the lucky few who stay in one position or who are successful at creating your own business, you will constantly face the need to upgrade your skills. Professionals of all kinds must stay up to date in their field. This is true of office professionals, medical professionals, teachers, engineers, auto mechanics, managers, computer programmers, and industrial workers.

Learning cannot stop when you get your degree; learning is a lifelong process. But, there is one ability that will not become outdated and that can serve you for the rest of your life—the ability to *know how to learn and grow*. In writing this text we have addressed the basics that will help you become a strong reader and student, be prepared for the challenges of lifelong learning for the workplace, and be effective, fulfilled adults and citizens of the modern world.

The skills and strategies that you will need to use to become effective readers and students are the same skills that you will need in the workplace. A recent survey of major businesses and industrial firms (The Secretary's Commission on Achieving Necessary Skills, U.S. Department of Labor, 1993) concluded that the workplace basics to learn in school are:

1. *Learning to learn: Joining a Community of Readers* will show you how to become active in your own reading and learning process (Chapters 1 and 2). You will learn how you study best and how to put your study time to good use.
2. *Listening and oral communications:* As a college reader, you will learn that reading is reinforced and made more meaningful when you listen to other people's ideas about a subject, and when you orally express your own ideas to your classmates (all chapters).
3. *Competence in reading, writing, and computation:* As you work through this course, your reading competence will constantly improve. You will learn, review, and practice all the basic skills necessary to be a strong reader: the reading process (Chapter 2), main ideas (Chapters 3 and 4), understanding details (Chapters 5 and 6), recognizing patterns of organization (Chapters 7 and 8), and organizing what you read so that you can retain information and understanding for tests and future needs (all chapters).
4. *Adaptability based on creative thinking and problem solving:* As a member of your classroom and of a community of readers, you will be involved in bringing what you already know and what you learn through reading and discussion to a variety of issues, and you will practice thinking creatively and problem solving (all chapters), making inferences (Chapter 9), and recognizing facts or opinions (Chapter 10).
5. *Group effectiveness characterized by interpersonal skills, negotiation skills, and teamwork:* You will learn to work with your classmates sharing your strengths and learning from each other (all chapters).
6. *Organizational effectiveness and leadership:* You will develop your organizational and leadership skills in the process of working with classmates toward a common goal.

## Are You Ready?

If you are ready to tackle the material of this course, you will be taking a big step towards a successful college career. Can you answer "Yes" to the following key questions?

- Is learning and practing college reading skills a priority for you at this time?
- Are you willing to make the effort to be *actively* involved in your learning?
- Have you decided that you can and will succeed, one small step at a time?
- Do you have the time to commit to being a student? Remember that as a student, you have a job. The payoff may seem to come with passing grades and a degree, but most importantly, the payoff of developing your reading and learning skills is for yourself and your future.

- Are you willing to share ideas and to work together with other students to reach your goals?
- Are you willing to learn new reading strategies and to apply them not just to pass this class but to anything new that you must learn?
- Are you willing to open your mind to new ideas and ways of thinking?
- Are you willing to think about ideas and arguments and to form opinions for yourself and with others?

Did you answer "Yes" to all or most of the questions above? If so, we will help you reach your goals by assisting you to become a lifelong reader and learner. Welcome to *Joining a Community of Readers!*

# Becoming a Successful Student

## *Goal Setting and Reading Skills*

*Step by step. I can't see any other way of accomplishing anything.*

Michael Jordan

### Preparing to Read

1. Describe what is happening in the picture on the previous page. Can you imagine yourself in their place in a few years?
2. Read the quotation. What does it mean to you?
3. What are your goals for the next two or three years? What steps do you need to take to prepare yourself to accomplish your goals?

## UNIT OBJECTIVES/SKILLS TO LEARN

In this unit you will learn how to

- Manage your time effectively
- Set short- and long-range goals
- Use PRO, a reading system that will help you be a stronger reader in college

In the process of acquiring these skills, you will read and use information about

- The importance of self-esteem in becoming a successful person and student
- The art of active reading
- Maxine Kingston and Malcolm X's experiences—learning to read
- Effective speaking and listening
- Benjamin Carson and several Latina women who faced challenges and succeeded in reaching their personal and academic goals

### Key Terms and Concepts

**setting goals**    deciding what you want to accomplish
**short-term goals**    goals for the day, the week, the month, or the semester
**long-term goals**    goals for years from now, or even for your life
**positive self-esteem**    feeling good about yourself
**time management**    using your time wisely

• • • • • • • • • • • • •

## Raising Issues

### Setting Your Goals and Reaching Them
• • • • • • • • • • • • • • • • • • • • • • • • • • • • • • • • •

Everyone who goes to college faces the challenge of learning to adapt to a new environment and learning to balance personal concerns and work with the demands of studying. Different demands are placed on each of you:

Some of you may be responsible for children and spouses. Others may be working full-time or may be struggling to master English as a second language. Perhaps you have to deal with a disability. You have already faced and overcome challenges in your life just to become a college student. Each of you has unique life circumstances, but you are in college now and you can succeed.

## *I Can't Accept Not Trying*

### MICHAEL JORDAN

*Michael Jordan, the world-famous basketball star, has clearly been successful in choosing and accomplishing both personal and professional goals. In his book he writes about how he approached the challenges he faced. As you read this excerpt, think about how his book's title,* I Can't Accept Not Trying, *applies to his experiences.*

1    I always had the ultimate goal of being the best, but I approached everything step by step. That's why I wasn't afraid to go to the University of North Carolina after high school.

2    Everyone told me I shouldn't go because I wouldn't be able to play at that level. They said I should go to the Air Force Academy because then I would have a job when I finished college. Everyone had a different agenda for me. But I had my own.

**agenda** plan

3    I had always set short-term goals. As I look back, each one of those steps or successes led to the next one. When I got cut from the varsity team as a sophomore in high school, I learned something. I knew I never wanted to feel that bad again. I never wanted to have that taste in my mouth, that hole in my stomach.

4    So I set a goal of becoming a starter on the varsity. That's what I focused on all summer. When I worked on my game, that's what I thought about. When it happened, I set another goal, a reasonable, manageable goal that I could realistically achieve if I worked hard enough.

5    Each time I visualized where I wanted to be, what kind of player I wanted to become.

**visualized** pictured

6    I guess I approached it with the end in mind. I knew exactly where I wanted to go, and I focused on getting there. As I reached those goals, they built on one another. I gained a little confidence every time I came through.

So I had built up the confidence that I could compete at North 7
Carolina. It was all mental for me. I never wrote anything down. I
just concentrated on the next step.

I think I could have applied that approach to anything I might 8
have chosen to do. It's no different from the person whose ultimate
goal is to become a doctor. If that's your goal and you're getting Cs
in biology then the first thing you have to do is get Bs in biology
and then As. You have to perfect the first step and then move on to
chemistry or physics.

Take those small steps. Otherwise you're opening yourself up 9
to all kinds of frustration. Where would your confidence come from
if the only measure of success was becoming a doctor? If you tried
as hard as you could and didn't become a doctor, would that mean
your whole life was a failure? Of course not.

All those steps are like pieces of a puzzle. They all come to- 10
gether to form a picture.

If it's complete, then you've reached your goal. If not, don't get 11
down on yourself.

If you've done your best, then you will have had some accom- 12
plishments along the way. Not everyone is going to get the entire
picture. Not everyone is going to be the greatest salesman or the
greatest basketball player. But you can still be considered one of
the best, and you can still be considered a success.

That's why I've always set short-term goals. Whether it's golf, 13
basketball, business, family life, or even baseball, I set goals—realistic goals—and I focus on them. I ask questions, I read, I listen. I did
the same thing in baseball with the Chicago White Sox. I'm not
afraid to ask anybody anything if I don't know. Why should I be
afraid? I'm trying to get somewhere. Help me, give me direction.
Nothing wrong with that.

Step by step, I can't see any other way of accomplishing 14
anything.

---

**Exercise 1**    **Discussion Questions**

1. How did Jordan go about setting realistic goals for himself?
2. What do you think Jordan means when he says, "Each time I visualized where I wanted to be . . . ?"

---

**Exercise 2**    **Making Connections**

1. How do you visualize yourself at the end of this semester? What goals do you plan to accomplish by then?

# 1

# *Joining a Community of Readers*

## GETTING STARTED

Starting college is very similar to starting a new job. You've assumed new responsibilities and accepted new challenges. One of the major challenges facing you as a new college student is that of entering a new community, an *academic community*, with ease. The first step you need to take to feel comfortable in your new college environment is to *get to know your fellow students*. The most successful college students are those who know their classmates. If you get to know other students in your classes, you can help each other by working together: sharing notes, phoning each other for information if you are absent, and preparing for exams together. Plan on making new friends and choose people who are also serious about school.

| Exercise **3** | Introductions/Collaborative Activity |
|---|---|

Think about your answers to the following questions. When you finish, introduce yourself to your class group by discussing your answers. Be prepared to introduce the members of your group to the whole class.

1. What is your name and can you give us some ways to remember it? (Does your name have a special meaning? Does it sound like a word that could be used to describe you?)
2. Why are you going to college? What is your major? What is your career goal?
3. What is one of the special accomplishments you have achieved in your life so far? (Be specific. Select something that you do, or have done, especially well.)

## *Positive Self-Esteem*

### DENIS WAITLEY

*One of the most important abilities that we each need to develop is the ability to value who we are, to realize that we deserve to have a good life and that we can create that life for ourselves. This recognition of self-worth, or positive self-esteem, will help you work your way through college and toward the goals you have set for yourself. In the following reading, Denis Waitley discusses the importance of beliefs of self-worth and then outlines a way to put his advice into practice with ten habits that will help you improve your self-esteem. Before you read the following selection, think about (1) how you felt when you have been successful at something and (2) how you felt if you have ever doubted your ability to achieve your goals. Why do you think it's important to believe in yourself?*

1   *Positive self-esteem* is one of the most important and basic qualities of a winning human being. It is that deep down, inside the self, feeling of your own worth.

2   "You know, I like myself. I really do like myself. Given my parents and my background, I'm glad I'm me. I'd rather be me than anyone else, living at any other time in history."

3   This is the self-talk of a Winner . . . and positive self-talk is the key to developing Positive Self-esteem.

4   Winners have developed strong beliefs of self-worth and self-confidence. They weren't necessarily born with these good feelings, but as with every other habit, they have learned to like themselves through practice. . . .

5   Confidence is built upon the experience of success. When we begin anything new we usually have little confidence because we have not learned from experience that we can succeed. This is true with learning to ride a bicycle, skiing, figure skating, flying a high performance jet aircraft, and leading people. It is true that success breeds success. Winners focus on past successes and forget past failures. They use errors and mistakes as a way to learning—then they dismiss them from their minds.

6   Yet, what do many of us do? We destroy our self-confidence by remembering past failures and forgetting all about our past successes. We not only remember failures, we etch them in our minds with emotion. We condemn ourselves. Winners know that it doesn't matter how many times they have failed in the past. What matters is their successes which should be remembered, reinforced and dwelt upon.

7   To establish true self-esteem, we must concentrate on our successes and look at the failures and negatives in our lives only as

corrective feedback to get us on target again. . . . Instead of comparing ourselves to others, we should view ourselves in terms of our own abilities, interests and goals. We can begin by making a conscious effort to upgrade our lifestyle and pay more attention to personal appearance and personal habits.

## Take Action Today for More Positive Self-Esteem

1. *Dress and look your best at all times* regardless of the pressure from your friends and peers. Personal grooming and lifestyle appearance provide an instantaneous projection on the surface of how you feel inside about yourself.

   **peers** people in the same position (age, grade, rank, status)

2. *Volunteer your own name first* in every telephone call and whenever you meet someone new. By paying value to your own name in communication, you are developing the habit of paying value to yourself as an individual.

3. *Take inventory of your good reasons for self-esteem today.* Write down what your "BAG" is. Blessings—who and what you are thankful for. Accomplishments—what you have done that you're proud of so far. Goals—what your dreams and ambitions are.

4. *Respond with a simple, courteous "thank you"* when anyone pays you a compliment for any reason.

5. *Sit up front in the most prominent rows* when you attend meetings, lectures and conferences. Your purpose for going is to listen, learn and possibly exchange questions and answers with the key speakers.

6. *Walk more erectly and authoritatively in public* with a relaxed but more rapid pace. It has been proven that individuals who walk erectly and briskly usually are confident about themselves and where they are going.

7. *Set your own internal standards* rather than comparing yourself to others. Keep upgrading your own standards in lifestyle, behavior, professional accomplishment, relationships, etc.

8. *Use encouraging, affirmative language* when you talk to yourself and to others about yourself. Focus on uplifting and building adjectives and adverbs. Everything you say about yourself is subconsciously being recorded by others and, more importantly, by your own self-image.

   **affirmative** positive

9. *Keep a self-development plan ongoing at all times.* Sketch it out on paper—the knowledge you'll require, the behavior modification you'll achieve, the changes in your life that will result. Seek out the real winners in life as friends and role models. Misery loves company, but so does success!

   **modification** change

10. *SMILE!* In every language, in every culture—it is the light in your window that tells people there's a caring, sharing individual inside and it's the universal code for "I'm O.K.—You're O.K., too!"

| Exercise **4** | Discussion Questions |
| --- | --- |

1. What is positive self-esteem?
2. Why do you think self-esteem is an important quality for students to possess?
3. Why should people focus on successes rather than failures?
4. What are some of the steps people can take to gain more positive self-esteem?

| Exercise **5** | Making Connections/Collaborative Activity |
| --- | --- |

Think about and discuss the list entitled "Take Action Today for More Positive Self-Esteem." Then interview each other, asking the following questions and taking time to briefly discuss each other's answer. Fill out the following chart. One example has been done for you.

**Interview questions:**
- What blessings have you had in your life?
- What accomplishments have you achieved so far?
- What goals do you have?
- What actions from the list "Take Action Today for More Positive Self-Esteem" do you already take?
- What additional actions from the list do you think you should take to help you achieve your goals?

| | Student 1<br>Name _____ | Student 2<br>Name _____ | Student 3<br>Name _____ |
| --- | --- | --- | --- |
| **Blessings** | a supportive family | | |
| **Accomplishments** | graduated high school<br><br>doing good job raising child as single mother | | |
| **Goals** | to become a dental assistant | | |
| **Actions you already do** | dress well (1)<br>say "thank you" to compliments (4)<br>walk erectly (6) | | |
| **Actions you think you should do to succeed in college** | remember BAG (3)<br>sit in front (5)<br>Set own standards (7) | | |

| Exercise **6** | **Writing** |

Write a paragraph in which you explain your blessings and accomplishments. Then describe the actions from the Waitley list that you already take and explain the additional actions you can take to succeed in college.

## MANAGING YOUR TIME

> *Doust thou love life, then do not squander time,*
> *for that's the stuff life is made of.*
>
> BENJAMIN FRANKLIN

Being a full-time student is a full-time job. You must learn how to find the time to be a student—to attend classes regularly and to study—as well as to do everything else that you need to do in your life. Once you have found the time for your classes and your study, you must use your time effectively.

To accomplish everything you want to do in the time you have available, you must learn how to *manage* your time. Time management involves three essential steps.

1. *Assess your time commitments:* Figure out what your commitments are now and how much time you have for your studies. Decide what is most important for you at this time. You may have to make decisions about what you can and cannot do.
2. *Get organized:* Prepare a time management plan. Establish a monthly calendar and a daily to do list. Put this plan into action.
3. *Check yourself:* At the end of each day, review your goals and accomplishments. If you are not following your plan, or if there are some problems with your plan, make the necessary adjustments.

| Exercise **7** | **Assessing Your Commitments** |

1. *Student responsibilities:* Your role as a student is like having a job. If you are to be successful, you will need to plan to spend a certain amount of time on school responsibilities each week. Calculate the amount of time you need to be a student by adding up the number of hours you are in class per week and then adding to that two additional study hours for every hour in class. For example, if you are taking two 3-unit classes (that meet for 3 hours a week), you need to plan on spending 9 hours per week for each class, 18 hours per week for both classes. If you are taking 12 units, you should plan 36 hours of class attendance and study time. Based on this formula, how many hours per week do you need to dedicate to school? _____

2. *Extracurricular responsibilities:* Are you involved in some school activities? Are you a member of an organization? How many hours per week do you spend on these activities? _____

3. *Work responsibilities:* How many hours per week do you work? _____

4. *Family and community responsibilities:* Are you responsible for other people? Are you married? Do you have children or brothers and sisters that you take care of? Do you attend church or do any volunteer work in your community? Estimate how many hours per week you need to spend on these responsibilities: _____

5. *Personal responsibilities:* Remember, you cannot take care of all the people in your life or meet all of your goals if you do not take care of yourself. Be sure to schedule some time for yourself, for some socializing (_____), some exercising (_____), and some relaxation (_____). And don't forget sleeping. You need eight hours of sleep per night (_____). Now total up the hours you wrote down in parentheses to determine the number of hours per week you need to take care of yourself: _____

6. *Miscellaneous time:* Don't forget that you need to set your time allotments realistically. How about little things like shopping and household chores? Also, transportation to and from the places you have to go takes time. Estimate how many hours per week you need for miscellaneous things: _____

7. Now, total up all of your time entries: _____ There are 168 hours in a week. If you are like many students, your total time entries add up to more than 168 hours!

**Exercise 8**    **Picture It**

Now, check the accuracy of your estimates and get a more graphic picture of where your time goes. Look at the model weekly schedule on page 11 and then fill in the chart on page 12 with your own information. Be realistic with your time allotments and do not underestimate the time it takes to do things. Fill in your class hours, your work hours, your family and community responsibility hours, your personal hours, and your miscellaneous time requirements. Then, mark off the hours that are open for study.

## Your Study Times

Take a careful look at the times you have identified for studying. Have you scheduled time so you can prepare for each class meeting? Have you scheduled time to review regularly, so that you don't have to waste time relearning information? Also, remember that sometimes small amounts of time can pay off in a big way. One such example is reviewing right before you attend a class. Either the night before or the day of the class, or even five minutes before the class begins, take time to re-

| Weekly Schedule | | | | | | | |
|---|---|---|---|---|---|---|---|
| | Sunday | Monday | Tuesday | Wednesday | Thursday | Friday | Saturday |
| 6:00 A.M. | | | | | | | |
| 7:00 A.M. | | | | | | | |
| 8:00 A.M. | | Exercise | | Exercise | | Exercise | Study |
| 9:00 A.M. | Church | Biology | P.E. | Biology | P.E. | Biology | |
| 10:00 A.M. | ↓ | Reading | Bio Lab | Reading | Bio Lab | Reading | ↓ |
| 11:00 A.M. | | Study | → | → | → | → | |
| 12:00 P.M. | Relax-movie | Lunch | Lunch | Lunch | Lunch | Lunch | |
| 1:00 P.M. | | Speech | Study | Speech | Study | Speech | Volunteer |
| 2:00 P.M. | | Study | Math | Study | Math | | |
| 3:00 P.M. | ↓ | ↓ | ↓ | ↓ | ↓ | | ↓ |
| 4:00 P.M. | Open | | | | | | Grocery Shopping Laundry |
| 5:00 P.M. | | Work | | Work | | Dinner w/ Friends | |
| 6:00 P.M. | | | | | | | |
| 7:00 P.M. | | ↓ | | ↓ | Choir Practice | ↓ | ↓ |
| 8:00 P.M. | | | | | ↓ | | Relax |
| 9:00 P.M. | | Study | Study | Study | Study | Study | |
| 10:00 P.M. | ↓ | ↓ | ↓ | ↓ | ↓ | ↓ | ↓ |
| 11:00 P.M. | | | | | | | |

view your notes from the last class session and to review the reading. This way, you will be alert and involved when the class begins. You will remember where you left off, and if there is a quiz you will be much more likely to remember the answers. If you have some questions about the reading or the lesson, plan to ask the instructor.

| Weekly Schedule | | | | | | | |
|---|---|---|---|---|---|---|---|
| | Sunday | Monday | Tuesday | Wednesday | Thursday | Friday | Saturday |
| 6:00 A.M. | | | | | | | |
| 7:00 A.M. | | | | | | | |
| 8:00 A.M. | | | | | | | |
| 9:00 A.M. | | | | | | | |
| 10:00 A.M. | | | | | | | |
| 11:00 A.M. | | | | | | | |
| 12:00 P.M. | | | | | | | |
| 1:00 P.M. | | | | | | | |
| 2:00 P.M. | | | | | | | |
| 3:00 P.M. | | | | | | | |
| 4:00 P.M. | | | | | | | |
| 5:00 P.M. | | | | | | | |
| 6:00 P.M. | | | | | | | |
| 7:00 P.M. | | | | | | | |
| 8:00 P.M. | | | | | | | |
| 9:00 P.M. | | | | | | | |
| 10:00 P.M. | | | | | | | |
| 11:00 P.M. | | | | | | | |

## How Is Your Energy?

Look at the boxes that you highlighted for hours devoted to your studies. Think about your own habits: are you a morning or a night person? When are your study times scheduled? If you are a morning person and your study hours are blocked off at 3 P.M., you may have designated poor hours to devote to school. You might be more ready to take a nap at this time than to "crack the books." As you look over your chart, you may decide that you are going to have to adjust your schedule so that you can study during your peak hours. Other chores or responsibilities may not require the intense focus needed for studying, so you might consider doing other things—shopping, cleaning the house, cooking, or even going to work—during those hours when your ability to think clearly is not at its peak.

## Can You Concentrate?

Once you designate the times of the day when you are full of energy for your studies, you need to consider whether or not you will be able to concentrate to your fullest during these times. If you are distracted, you will not be able to use your study time well. There are two basic kinds of distractions: environmental and mental. *Environmental distractions* are things such as children playing, a noisy work space, a television program in the background, or the telephone ringing. Set up your study time and location when and where you won't have to struggle with so many environmental distractions. Perhaps there is a quiet room in your house or maybe you could study in the library.

*Mental distractions* are all the things you think about while you are trying to study, such as the bills you need to pay, the argument you had with your spouse or friend, or your vacation plans. To help yourself overcome these distractions, take care of these problems as best you can before you sit down to study. Sometimes it helps if you put these problems and their possible solutions on a to do list so that you know you will not forget to follow up on them. Then you can stop worrying about them and get back to studying.

| Exercise **9** | **Think About Your Use of Time** |

1. When you totaled up your estimates (Exercise 7), was your total less than 168 hours?
2. When you look at your chart, do you have enough time to devote to your studies (on the average of two hours outside of class for every hour in class)?
3. Are your designated study times scheduled at a time when you are at your peak, when you can focus clearly on your work?

If you answered "No" to any of the above questions, think about your situation, take another look at your priorities, and make the necessary adjustments. But remember: try to decide how you spend your time yourself and base those choices on what is important to you at this point in your life. If you are a full-time student, doing well in school may be your highest priority. If you are a parent, taking care of your children may take priority and being a good student might have to take second place.

Be creative in your thinking. Maybe you will have to reduce or cut out the time that you spend hanging out in the cafeteria or the student union.

Maybe you can decrease the number of hours you work, or maybe you can find an on-campus job that could save you the commute. Maybe you should consider dropping a class or reducing the number of other commitments that you have.

Write out your plan to focus on what is important to you now and to reduce your commitments or activities to things that are not your current priorities.

I will focus on _____

_____

I will cut back on _____

_____

## Getting Organized

You need to think about two basic levels of organization when you are planning to use your time.

**Monthly Calendar.**    First, you need to establish a calendar for yourself in which you record all of your long-range assignments. When your instructors pass out the course syllabi and announce long-term assignments such as the dates of final exams and papers, write down this important information on your calendar. When you make other appointments for yourself or if you have school activities or community meetings, be sure to write them down on the *same* calendar. Use the sample semester calendar on page 15 as a guide.

**To Do List.**    Second, at the end or at the beginning of each day make yourself a to do list (see page 16). Write down your specific goals for the day and exactly what you plan to do with your time. Be sure to check your monthly calendar so that you don't forget the upcoming big assignments, tests, or appointments. It is very important to check your to do list during the day to be sure that you are not forgetting something, and at the end of the day you should cross or check off the things that you did. Write anything you weren't able to do on the following day's list. Remember to always prioritize your lists. You might not get around to something but decide that it is okay. Try to do those things that are most important to you first. For example, if you have an exam in biology, be sure to give yourself the time to review your biology notes, even if it means putting off that trip to the laundromat for a day. (Or maybe you could remember to take your biology book and notes to the laundromat and do both tasks at the same time!)

## Check Your Time Management Plan

It takes approximately three weeks to establish a new habit. Commit yourself to working on your time management every single day for the next several weeks. Hopefully, you will establish a habit that will serve you well through school and for the rest of your life.

## Semester Schedule  Fall 2000

### Month September

| Sunday | Monday | Tuesday | Wednesday | Thursday | Friday | Saturday |
|---|---|---|---|---|---|---|
|  |  |  |  | 1 | 2 | 3 |
| 4 Church | 5 Classes begin | 6 | 7 | 8 Choir | 9 | 10 Volunteer |
| 11 Church | 12 | 13 Campus newspaper | 14 | 15 | 16 | 17 |
| 18 Church | 19 | 20 | 21 | 22 Choir | 23 | 24 Volunteer |
| 25 Church | 26 | 27 Campus newspaper | 28 | 29 Bio Lab  30 Math Test | 30 Rdg Test | 1 October |

### Month October

| Sunday | Monday | Tuesday | Wednesday | Thursday | Friday | Saturday |
|---|---|---|---|---|---|---|
| 2 Church | 3 | 4 | 5 | 6 Choir | 7 | 8 |
| 9 Church | 10 | 11 Campus newspaper | 12 | 13 Bio report | 14 Rdg test | 15 Volunteer |
| 16 Church | 17 | 18 Short speech 5 min | 19 | 20 Math test / Choir | 21 | 22 |
| 23 Church | 24 | 25 Campus newspaper | 26 | 27 Choir | 28 Bio test | 29 Volunteer |
| 30 Church | 31 |  |  |  |  | Jogathon Balboa Park |

### Month November

| Sunday | Monday | Tuesday | Wednesday | Thursday | Friday | Saturday |
|---|---|---|---|---|---|---|
| Church picnic |  | 1 | 2 | 3 | 4 Bio test | 5 |
| 6 Church | 7 | 8 Campus newspaper | 9 | 10 Choir | 11 | 12 Volunteer |
| 13 Church | 14 | 15 | 16 | 17 Math Test / Choir | 18 Rdg Test | 19 Scholarship applic due |
| 20 Church | 21 Beach party | 22 Short speech 5 min newspaper | 23 | 24 | 25 | 26 |
| 27 | 28 | 29 | 30 |  |  |  |

### Month December

| Sunday | Monday | Tuesday | Wednesday | Thursday | Friday | Saturday |
|---|---|---|---|---|---|---|
|  |  |  |  | 1 Choir | 2 | 3 Mom's birthday |
| 4 Church | 5 Campus newspaper | 6 | 7 Speech due (10 min) | 8 Math test | 9 | 10 Volunteer |
| 11 Church | 12 9:00-11:00 Bio am Final | 13 12-2 Math Final | 14 10:00-12:00 RDG Final / 1-3:00 Speech Final | 15 Choir | 16 | 17 |
| 18 Church | 19 Newspaper party! | 20 | 21 | 22 | 23 | 24 |
| 25 Church | 26 | 27 | 28 | 29 | 30 | 31 |

**To Do List**

Date _____

| | | Priority<br>(a, b, or c) | Completed |
|---|---|---|---|
| 1. | Prepare for tomorrow's biology test | (a) | X |
| 2. | Do the laundry | (b) | X |
| 3. | Call parents | (b) | X |
| 4. | Plan Johnny's birthday party | (a) | X |
| 5. | Begin notes for English 101 paper | (a) | X |
| 6. | | | |

After you work with your calendar and to do lists for a week or so, take some time to make sure it is working for you. Are you able to keep up with all the activities that you schedule? Are you making sure that nothing is falling through the cracks by writing down everything that you need to do in the appropriate places? Are you alert and able to concentrate during the times that you have set aside for your studies? And, most important of all, does your allocation of time correspond to your priorities?

Exercise **10**   **Making Decisions**

Let's begin this decision-making process with a short exercise.

List all the "roles" you have right now as an individual. Who are you, as defined by the different roles, responsibilities, or jobs you fill? Each role you list must be a noun, or a name, of a role or job in your life. For example, are you a father? an employee of Sears? a tennis player? a TV viewer?

1. List below as many roles as you can identify. (You don't have to limit yourself to six.)

   A. _____

   B. _____

   C. _____

   D. _____

E. _____

F. _____

2. Next, write these roles again in the order of their *importance* to you. Letter A should be the most important role or responsibility in your life. Then list B, etc.

A. _____

B. _____

C. _____

D. _____

E. _____

F. _____

3. Last, because you're more conscious of how you spend your time now, it should be easy to list the roles you fill in the order of the *amount of time* you spend on each. Letter A should be the role in which you spend the most time on the average. Letter B should be the role in which you spend the next greatest amount of hours. Caution: answer this with the *actual* way you spend your time, not how you would like it to be.

A. _____

B. _____

C. _____

D. _____

E. _____

F. _____

As you completed this exercise, did you discover any conflicts between where you spend your time and what you think are your most important roles, your priorities, in life? Most of us can notice numerous conflicts when we complete an exercise like this, so don't be surprised. Complete the following "reflection" questions before we continue our discussion of choosing goals.

**Exercise 11**   **Making Connections**

Answer these questions based on your reflections on your answers to Exercise 10.

1. Do you need to make changes in your priorities? Explain.
2. Do you need to make changes in your current use of time? Explain.
3. How possible is it for you to make the changes, if any, that you've indicated in 1 and 2?

## Short- and Long-Term Goals

Choosing goals is not an easy job. The decisions we make influence our lives in both small and large ways.

Goals can be broken into different categories based on when and how easily they can be achieved. There is an old Chinese saying, "The longest journey begins with a single step." This certainly is true when we think of our life's goals. When you write your own goals, you need to think about both short- and long-term goals. Short-term goals can be accomplished in a limited period of time, such as daily, weekly, monthly, or semester goals. State your goals very specifically, so you can determine whether you achieve them or not. For example, one of your goals for next week might be to complete a complicated biology lab assignment on time and earn a grade of C or better on it. It will be easy to tell whether you achieve that goal or not and to analyze why you did or why you did not achieve it. Long-term goals take more time to achieve. For example, your long-term goal might be to become a research biologist with three children and a house on the beach. In this case, the biology lab assignment goal might have been one small step towards accomplishing the larger goal. While our life goals cover all categories—personal, social, economic, academic, etc.—our focus in this chapter's exercises is to ask you to examine your goals related to this course and to your future as a student.

**Exercise 12**    **Setting Short Term Goals**

1. The theme of Unit 1 is "becoming a successful student." In order to meet this goal, you learned how to manage your time and read how Michael Jordan chose goals and worked to achieve them. Now it's time for you to make some decisions about goals (if you haven't done so already).

2. Write at least three goals that you plan to achieve this semester. Be specific in your wording so that you can tell at the end of the semester whether you have achieved your goals or not. For example, if your goal is to improve your English skills and to get a B or better in this class, you won't simply write *"I will study harder this semester"* because it is too vague. It's better to write something like *"I will study English at least six hours a week for this class this semester."*

| **Specific Semester Goals** | **Steps to Accomplish Them** |
|---|---|
| A. *Improve English skills. Get a B in this class.* | A. *Study and review six hours per week. Never miss class.* |
| B. _____ | B. _____ |
| C. _____ | C. _____ |

# Organizing to Learn

## Using Campus Resources

Many studies have been done about which students are most successful meeting their college goals. The results show them to be students who get to know the campus services and those who develop relationships with other students and faculty. Begin this process by familiarizing yourself with the types of services and organizations available at your campus. If you do this early in your college career, you will be able to find the support you need when you need it later. The following list mentions some of the most important resources offered on most campuses.

**Student Newspaper.**    This is a good place to find out what is happening on campus. Pick up a copy and read it. It will often have information on scholarships, housing, campus club meetings, and special cultural and sports events that your college is sponsoring.

**The College Catalog.**    The catalog provides you with information such as the majors offered by your college, the requirements for the majors, class add and drop policies, and the on-campus resources available to you. Be sure you have the most recent copy of the college catalog and check it for official information.

**Student Counseling Office.**    The academic advisers or counselors can help you decide which courses you need to take to reach your goals as quickly as possible. It is a good idea to talk to an academic counselor during your first semester at college. Usually counselors are also available to help you deal with more personal problems. If there aren't any such counselors on your campus, the academic counseling office can suggest where to find additional help.

**Student Government and Student Associations.**    Joining student government activities or a club with students who share your interests is a good way to network—get to know people—on campus. Most campuses have a wide variety of organizations, such as language clubs, political clubs, and women's support groups. Find one that interests you, check out the meeting schedule in the newspaper, and visit a few of the meetings. You may decide you want to participate!

**Tutoring Programs and Learning Centers.**    Don't wait until you're behind to go visit these places. Locate your tutoring programs and begin to use them early in the semester. Some of these resources might help you turn a good paper into a great one or can offer help if you have trouble with an assignment.

**Job Placement Offices and Career Centers.**   Here you can find information on which careers best match your interests. Very often you can take an interest inventory, and a counselor will help you match your future career to your interests and aptitudes.

**Financial Aid Office.**   Even if you didn't get financial aid during your first semester, visit this office early so that you can apply for assistance for next semester. The staff can explain the variety of possibilities that exist to help you put together the financing you need to pay for your education. They will give you information on scholarships, loans, and work/study programs that are available to you.

**Student Health Center.**   Visit this center to find out what services they offer. Most campuses provide appointments with a doctor, HIV and TB tests, and routine care. Some campuses even have an infirmary where you can stay if you are sick.

**Library.**   Your college library is often the best place to find a quiet area to study and to do research required for your classes. If you are not familiar with the library, ask the librarians for assistance. They are experts at finding information, and if you describe your assignment to them, they can show you where to begin and how to use the library.

**Exercise 13**   **Getting to Know Campus Resources**

Choose two of the above resources. Find out where they are located on campus, visit them, and ask what services they provide for students and what their hours of operation are. Write down the information and bring it back to share with the rest of the class.

• • • • • • • • • • •

# Working with Words
## Your Personal Vocabulary Plan
• • • • • • • • • • • • • • • • • • • • • • • • • • • • • • • • • • • • • • •

Having a good vocabulary is one of the most important factors in becoming a strong reader. Probably the best way to improve your vocabulary is to develop your own system or vocabulary plan to learn new words. There are two basic techniques for improving your vocabulary: (1) reading more, and (2) developing a system for learning general vocabulary.

## Reading Itself Improves Vocabulary

Probably the one activity that will most improve your vocabulary is reading. The more you read, the more words you will learn. It's as simple as that. The more words you know, the easier it is for you to read, and the more you will enjoy reading for its own sake. So, maybe instead of watching a rerun of a TV program, try to set aside about half an hour a day to read for fun. Pick anything that you enjoy reading—sports magazines, women's magazines, mystery novels, the newspaper—it doesn't matter what you read at first, as long as you get into the habit. Then, eventually try to push yourself to read material that is a little more challenging and that expands the type of reading you do. But remember, you want to enjoy this reading, so pick things that interest you.

## Developing a System for General Vocabulary

It is important to start your own list of words that you need to learn. Choose carefully the words you want to add to your list. They should be terms that you have encountered more than once, words that are important and useful and that are fairly common in the English language. *Do not look up a new word in the dictionary as soon as you see it.* This technique will simply distract you from your reading. If you look up five words on a page (which is really not all that many), by the time you get to the end of the page you will not remember what you have read. Instead of going straight to the dictionary put a *small check in pencil* by the word; when you finish the page or the section of the text and you still want to know that word and you cannot figure it out, then go to the dictionary. *Do not highlight or underline all the words that you do not know as you read.* Highlighting's purpose is to help you remember the main ideas or the important details of a passage. If you highlight all the words that you do not know, when you look back at a page or a chapter, all you will see is a discouraging mess of unfamiliar words instead of the important ideas.

| Exercise **14** | **Your Personal Vocabulary** |
|---|---|

Begin a list of words you would like to add to your vocabulary. Enter these words in a notebook, on a computer list, or individually on 3 × 5" cards, record them in a place where it will be easy for you to check them periodically for a quick review.

1.  Begin by choosing five vocabulary words that you would like to learn from the readings in this chapter or from any other college reading you're currently doing. For example, you might choose the word *authoritatively* from pages 6–7 in the reading by Denis Waitley about positive self-esteem.
2.  Write the sentence where you first saw the word used. For example, the word *authoritatively* is in item 6: "Walk more erectly and *authoritatively* in public with a relaxed but more rapid pace."

3. Look up the word in a college-level dictionary. Write the appropriate definition and its part of speech. For example, you will find this word under "authoritative" in the dictionary. The definition is "Having proper authority (power) (adverb)."
4. Write the other forms of the word listed in the dictionary and the part of speech of each.
5. Then use the word in a sentence of your own. For example, "My boss gives orders authoritatively."

Your final entry will look like this example:

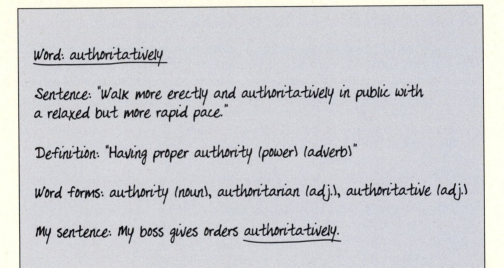

Word: authoritatively

Sentence: "Walk more erectly and authoritatively in public with a relaxed but more rapid pace."

Definition: "Having proper authority (power) (adverb)"

Word forms: authority (noun), authoritarian (adj.), authoritative (adj.)

My sentence: My boss gives orders authoritatively.

## Applying Your Skills

### *Think Big*

Benjamin Carson, M.D.

*As a child Benjamin Carson felt he "really was the most stupid kid in fifth grade." One day, when he brought home a poor report card, his mother, a single mom who worked as a maid in rich people's homes, told him that the only way to get out of poverty was with a good education. She decided that she had to adopt a plan to improve both his and his brother's school-work. Benjamin became a good student, and developed a high sense of self-worth. Today he is a surgeon at the Johns Hopkins Hospital in Baltimore, Maryland. This excerpt is part of a chapter from his autobiography entitled* Think Big. *It begins the day after his mother saw his report card.*

## Preparing to Read

1. What memories do you have of your parents' reactions to your report cards? How do you react to your children's report cards?
2. What experiences did you have in libraries when you were young?
3. Have you ever learned something or learned how to do something that you had previously assumed you would never be able to do?
4. As you read, notice especially how Carson improved his reading and vocabulary skills.

Dr. Benjamin Carson with his wife and children.

The next day was like the previous ones—just another bad day 1
in school, another day of being laughed at because I did not get a
single problem right in arithmetic and couldn't get any words right
on the spelling test. As soon as I came home from school, I
changed into play clothes and ran outside. Most of the boys my age
played softball, or the game I liked best, "Tip the Top."

We played Tip the Top by placing a bottle cap on one of the 2
sidewalk cracks. Then taking a ball—any kind that bounced—we'd
stand on a line and take turns throwing the ball at the bottle top,
trying to flip it over. Whoever succeeded got two points. If anyone
actually moved the cap more than a few inches, he won five points.
Ten points came if he flipped it into the air and it landed on the
other side.

When it grew dark or we got tired, Curtis and I would finally go 3
inside and watch TV. The set stayed on until we went to bed. Because Mother worked long hours, she was never home until just
before we went to bed. Sometimes I would awaken when I heard
her unlocking the door.

Two evenings after the incident with the report card, Mother 4
came home about an hour before our bedtime. Curtis and I were
sprawled out, watching TV. She walked across the room, snapped
off the set, and faced both of us. "Boys," she said, "you're wasting
too much of your time in front of that television. You don't get an
education from staring at television all the time."

Before either of us could make a protest, she told us that she 5
had been praying for wisdom. "The Lord's told me what to do," she
said. "So from now on, you will not watch television, except for two
preselected programs each week."

"Just *two* programs?" I could hardly believe she would say 6
such a terrible thing. "That's not—"

"And *only* after you've done your homework. Furthermore, 7
you don't play outside after school, either, until you've done all
your homework."

"Everybody else plays outside right after school," I said, un- 8
able to think of anything except how bad it would be if I couldn't
play with my friends. "I won't have any friends if I stay in the house
all the time—"

"That may be," Mother said, "but everybody else is not going 9
to be as successful as you are—"

"But, Mother—"                                                    10

"This is what we're going to do. I asked God for wisdom, and 11
this is the answer I got.

I tried to offer several other arguments, but Mother was firm. I 12
glanced at Curtis, expecting him to speak up, but he did not say
anything. He lay on the floor, staring at his feet.

13    "Don't worry about everybody else. The whole world is full of 'everybody else,' you know that? But only a few make a significant achievement."

14    The loss of TV and play time was bad enough. I got up off the floor, feeling as if everything was against me. Mother wasn't going to let me play with my friends, and there would be no more television—almost none, anyway. She was stopping me from having any fun in life.

15    "And that isn't all," she said. "Come back, Bennie."

16    I turned around, wondering what else there could be.

17    "In addition," she said, "to doing your homework, you have to read two books from the library each week. Every single week."

18    "Two books? Two?" Even though I was in fifth grade, I had never read a whole book in my life.

19    "Yes, two. When you finish reading them, you must write me a book report just like you do at school. You're not living up to your potential, so I'm going to see that you do."

20    Usually Curtis, who was two years older, was the more rebellious. But this time he seemed to grasp the wisdom of what Mother said. He did not say one word.

21    She stared at Curtis. "You understand?"

22    He nodded.

23    "Bennie, is it clear?"

24    "Yes, Mother." I agreed to do what Mother told me—it wouldn't have occurred to me not to obey—but I did not like it. Mother was being unfair and demanding more of us than other parents did.

25    The following day was Thursday. After school, Curtis and I walked to the local branch of the library. I did not like it much, but then I had not spent that much time in any library.

26    We both wandered around a little in the children's section, not having any idea about how to select books or which books we wanted to check out.

27    The librarian came over to us and asked if she could help. We explained that both of us wanted to check out two books.

28    "What kind of books would you like to read?" the librarian asked.

29    "Animals," I said after thinking about it. "Something about animals."

30    "I'm sure we have several that you'd like." She led me over to a section of books. She left me and guided Curtis to another section of the room. I flipped through the row of books until I found two that looked easy enough for me to read. One of them, *Chip, the Dam Builder*—about a beaver—was the first one I had ever checked out. As soon as I got home, I started to read it. It was the first book I ever read all the way through even though it took me two nights.

Reluctantly I admitted afterward to Mother that I really had liked reading about Chip.

Within a month I could find my way around the children's sec- 31 tion like someone who had gone there all his life. By then the library staff knew Curtis and me and the kind of books we chose. They often made suggestions. "Here's a delightful book about a squirrel," I remember one of them telling me.

**indifferent** uninterested

As she told me part of the story, I tried to appear indifferent, but 32 as soon as she handed it to me, I opened the book and started to read.

Best of all, we became favorites of the librarians. When new books came in that they thought either of us would enjoy, they held 33 them for us. Soon I realized that the library had so many books— and about so many different subjects.

After the book about the beaver, I chose others about ani- 34 mals—all types of animals. I read every animal story I could get my hands on. I read books about wolves, wild dogs, several about squirrels, and a variety of animals that lived in other countries. Once I had gone through the animal books, I started reading about plants, then minerals, and finally rocks.

**practical** useful

My reading books about rocks was the first time the informa- 35 tion ever became practical to me. We lived near the railroad tracks, and when Curtis and I took the route to school that crossed by the tracks, I began paying attention to the crushed rock that I noticed between the ties.

As I continued to read more about rocks, I would walk along 36 the tracks, searching for different kinds of stones, and then see if I could identify them.

Often I would take a book with me to make sure that I had la- 37 beled each stone correctly.

"Agate," I said as I threw the stone. Curtis got tired of my 38 picking up stones and identifying them, but I did not care because I kept finding new stones all the time. Soon it became my favorite game to walk along the tracks and identify the varieties of stones. Although I did not realize it, within a very short period of time, I was actually becoming an expert on rocks.

Two things happened in the second half of fifth grade that 39 convinced me of the importance of reading books.

First, our teacher, Mrs. Williamson, had a spelling bee every 40 Friday afternoon. We'd go through all the words we'd had so far that year. Sometimes she also called out words that we were supposed to have learned in fourth grade. Without fail, I always went down on the first word.

One Friday, though, Bobby Farmer, whom everyone acknowl- 41 edged as the smartest kid in our class, had to spell "agriculture" as his final word. As soon as the teacher pronounced his word, I thought, *I can spell that word.* Just the day before, I had learned it from reading one of my library books. I spelled it under my breath, and it was just the way Bobby spelled it.

42    *If I can spell "agriculture," I'll bet I can learn to spell any other word in the world. I'll bet I can learn to spell better than Bobby Farmer.*

43    Just that single word, "agriculture," was enough to give me hope.

44    The following week, a second thing happened that forever changed my life. When Mr. Jaeck, the science teacher, was teaching us about volcanoes, he held up an object that looked like a piece of black, glass-like rock. "Does anybody know what this is? What does it have to do with volcanoes?"

45    Immediately, because of my reading, I recognized the stone. I waited, but none of my classmates raised their hands. I thought, *This is strange. Not even the smart kids are raising their hands.* I raised my hand.

46    "Yes, Benjamin," he said.

47    I heard laughter around me. The other kids probably thought it was a joke, or that I was going to say something stupid.

48    "Obsidian," I said.

49    "That's right!" He tried not to look startled, but it was obvious he hadn't expected me to give the correct answer.

50    "That's obsidian," I said, "and it's formed by the supercooling of lava when it hits the water." Once I had their attention and realized I knew information no other student had learned, I began to tell them everything I knew about the subject of obsidian, lava, lava flow, super-cooling, and compacting of the elements.

51    When I finally paused, a voice behind me whispered, "Is that Bennie Carson?"

52    "You're absolutely correct," Mr. Jaeck said and he smiled at me. If he had announced that I'd won a million-dollar lottery, I couldn't have been more pleased and excited.

53    "Benjamin, that's absolutely, absolutely right," he repeated with enthusiasm in his voice. He turned to the others and said, "That is wonderful! Class, this is a tremendous piece of information Benjamin has just given us. I'm very proud to hear him say this."

54    For a few moments, I tasted the thrill of achievement. I recall thinking, *Wow, look at them. They're all looking at me with admiration. Me, the dummy! The one everybody thinks is stupid. They're looking at me to see if this is really me speaking.*

55    Maybe, though, it was I who was the most astonished one in the class. Although I had been reading two books a week because Mother told me to, I had not realized how much knowledge I was accumulating. True, I had learned to enjoy reading, but until then I hadn't realized how it connected with my schoolwork. That day— for the first time—I realized that Mother had been right. Reading is

**accumulating**
gathering, storing up

the way out of ignorance, and the road to achievement. I did not have to be the class dummy anymore.

For the next few days, I felt like a hero at school. The jokes 56 about me stopped. The kids started to listen to me. *I'm starting to have fun with this stuff.*

As my grades improved in every subject, I asked myself, "Ben, 57 is there any reason you can't be the smartest kid in the class? If you can learn about obsidian, you can learn about social studies and geography and math and science and everything."

That single moment of triumph pushed me to want to read 58 more. From then on, it was as though I could not read enough books. Whenever anyone looked for me after school, they could usually find me in my bedroom—curled up, reading a library book— for a long time, the only thing I wanted to do. I had stopped caring about the TV programs I was missing; I no longer cared about play- ing Tip the Top or baseball anymore. I just wanted to read.

In a year and a half—by the middle of sixth grade—I had 59 moved to the top of the class.

## Exercise 15 | Checking Your Understanding

1. According to Benjamin's mother's plan, what did the boys have to do to suc- ceed in school?
2. What did Benjamin think of his mother's plan initially?
3. What kinds of books did Benjamin read?
4. Explain what happened in Benjamin's "moment of triumph."
5. How was Benjamin doing in school a year and a half later?

## Exercise 16 | Working with Words

Find three to five words that you did not know from the article. Add them to you personal vocabulary list in your notebook, computer, or on your 3 × 5" cards. Follow the guidelines given on pages 21–22.

## Exercise 17 | Making Connections

1. Why do you think Benjamin's mother's plan worked so well for him?
2. Can you identify moments of triumph in your schooling like those Benjamin experienced? Explain your answer.
3. What can other students learn about vocabulary building from Benjamin's experience?

**Exercise 18**  |  **Organizing to Learn**

Chart the steps that Benjamin took to reach his goal of becoming a successful student. Also, indicate the successes that he had along the way.

---

**Long Term Goal—Become a Successful Student**

1. His television was limited to two shows per week.
2. He _____ only after he finished his homework.
3. He had to _____ each week.
4. He asked the librarian for help finding books.
5. He learned _____ around the children's library.
6. _____ became friends with _____
7. He became an expert on one subject, _____
8. He got better at spelling and realized that he could spell some words that were given to the smartest kids in the class.
9. He successfully _____ about _____
10. His teacher praised him.
11. He started to enjoy learning and to feel good about himself.
12. By the end of the sixth grade, he _____

---

# *Chapter Review*

- - - - - - - - - - - - - - - - - - - - - - - - - - - - - - - - - - - - - - -

**Exercise 19**  |  **Skills Review**

Alone, or with your classmates, fill in the basic steps you should take to review your time management plan. Briefly explain each step.

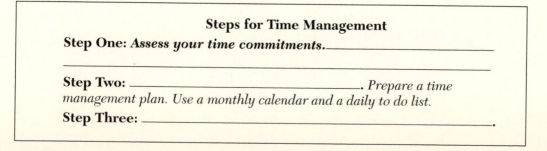

---

**Steps for Time Management**

**Step One: *Assess your time commitments.*** _____

_____

**Step Two:** _____. *Prepare a time management plan. Use a monthly calendar and a daily to do list.*

**Step Three:** _____.

---

**Exercise 20**   **Writing**

1. Using the goals you have identified in Exercise 12 on page 18, write a paragraph or a short essay explaining your goals and how, step-by-step, you plan to accomplish them.
2. Describe yourself ten years from now. What goals have you accomplished? Explain in a paragraph or short essay what steps you took to achieve your goals.

**Exercise 21**   **Collaborative Activity**

Share with your class group your goals for this semester. Discuss in a group what steps can be taken by each of you to achieve your goals.

**Exercise 22**   **Extension Activity**

List some of the campus resources available to you. Investigate two of them and report back to the class. Include in your report:

Hours of operation: _____

Location: _____

Services offered: _____

# CHAPTER 2

# *Joining the Academic Community*

## BECOMING AN ACTIVE READER

As you learned in Chapter 1, joining an *academic community* means learning to take charge of your future by setting your goals and managing your time so success is possible. It also means that you will change your learning habits. The word *learning* itself means "a change in behavior." In college you will discover ways to use all of your learning skills—reading, writing, listening, speaking, computing, and thinking—to become a successful student and to be competent in the career of your choice.

By choosing to enter college, you have joined a community of learners, which includes fellow students, teachers, counselors, librarians, other staff, and administrators. Your learning skills make communication in this community work for you. In this chapter we'll introduce some of those essential skills for sharing ideas: especially **reading** and **listening.**

### *Learning to Read: Maxine Kingston*

MAXINE HONG KINGSTON

*The following reading is from Maxine Hong Kingston's autobiography,* The Woman Warrior. *It tells the story of her struggle to read aloud when she was in the first grade. As you read this piece, think about your own "story" of becoming a reader. Has it always been easy?*

It was when I found out I had to talk that school became a misery, that the silence became a misery. I did not speak and felt bad each time that I did not speak. I read aloud in first grade, though, and heard the barest whisper with little squeaks come out of my throat. "Louder," said the teacher, who scared the voice away again. The other Chinese girls did not talk either, so I knew the silence had to do with being a Chinese girl. 1

Reading out loud was easier than speaking because we did not have to make up what to say, but I stopped often, and the teacher would think I'd gone quiet again. I could not understand "I." The Chinese "I" has seven strokes, intricacies. How could the American "I," assuredly wearing a hat like the Chinese, have only three strokes, the middle so straight? Was it out of politeness that this writer left off strokes the way a Chinese has to write her own name small and crooked? No, it was not politeness; "I" is a capital and "you" is lower-case. I stared at that middle line and waited so long for its black center to resolve into tight strokes and dots that I forgot to pronounce it. The other troublesome word was "here," no strong consonant to hang on to, and so flat, when "here" is two mountainous ideographs. The teacher, who had already told me everyday how to read "I" and "here," put me in the low corner under the stairs again, where the noisy boys usually sat. 2

**ideographs** Chinese writing, also called characters

---

**Exercise 1**    **Discussion Questions**

1. What scared Kingston's voice away when she tried to read aloud in first grade?
2. Which words did Kingston have trouble reading when she was called on to read aloud? Why?

---

**Exercise 2**    **Making Connections**

1. What are your first memories of learning how to read?
2. What was your favorite book as a young reader?
3. Who helped you become a reader, or a better reader. What is that person's name? What did that person do to help you?
4. Have you ever helped someone with their reading?

---

**Exercise 3**    **Writing: Becoming a Reader**

Write a paragraph or two explaining how you have developed as a reader. Use your answers to the questions in Exercise 2 to help you organize your writing. Be prepared to share your writing with your class group or your instructor.

Maxine Hong Kingston is one of the best-known Chinese American writers today.

## READING IS COMMUNICATION

Reading is a way of communicating with others. Through reading you can learn from and think about the ideas of people you have never met, who may live in other countries, or who may have lived hundreds of years ago. Reading makes it possible for you to understand new ideas you've never encountered before, to master skills and concepts you may have thought were beyond your grasp, and to reinforce understandings you have gained in your own life experience.

• • • • • • • • • • • • •

# Reading Is a Process: PRO

• • • • • • • • • • • • • • • • • • • • • • • • • • • • • • • • • •

This communication called reading is easier to understand if you view it as a process. That is, the understandings you acquire by reading don't just happen automatically by looking at a page, or a computer screen, full of print. There are three basic steps that can help you succeed in the reading/studying process. All good readers follow these steps even though they may not be aware that they are doing so. First they *prepare* to read, then they *read actively,* and then they *organize* what they've read. You can remember this process by using the initial letters to form **PRO.**

- P = *Prepare to read*
- R = *Read actively*
- O = *Organize what you've read*

When you've mastered this system, you will be a reading "pro."

## PREPARE TO READ

### Concentrate

The first consideration in preparing to read is a very practical one. Begin by choosing a time when you won't be disturbed and a place where you can concentrate. By establishing regular times and places to work, you can form a habit of reading effectively. Plan to avoid potential distractions. For example, choose to play music only if you know it won't detract from your ability to focus on the reading goals you have set for yourself. Studies have shown that some classical music actually helps the mind to focus, but the beat of heavy rock interferes with that ability.

### Preview

Once you have chosen an appropriate atmosphere for reading, you are ready to begin the process itself. The first step is to preview, or to look quickly at, what you are going to read before you read it. For studying purposes it's best to only preview a section (no more than three or four pages) at a time. The preview of a short piece should not take more than a couple of minutes. In your preview look for the "framework" of the reading. The framework is the basic structure, like the skeleton of a house that is being built. In your preview, "read" only the following things:

- Titles and subtitles
- Introduction
- Headings and subheadings
- Pictures, charts, tables, and other graphics
- Special print: **boldface,** *italics,* and <u>underlined</u>
- Summary or conclusion

# The Essence of Active Reading
## The Four Basic Questions a Reader Asks

Mortimer J. Adler and Charles Van Doren

*For an example of how to preview a reading, examine the following excerpt from* How to Read a Book, *a popular text for college freshmen.*

**essence** main characteristic

1    *Active reading* is better reading, and we have noted that inspectional reading is always active. It is an effortful, not an effortless, undertaking. *Ask questions while you read—questions that you yourself must try to answer in the course of reading.* The art of reading on any level above the elementary consists in the habit of asking the right questions in the right order. There are four main questions you must ask about any book.

1. **What is the book about as a whole?** You must try to discover the leading theme of the book, and how the author develops this theme in an orderly way by subdividing it into its essential subordinate themes or topics.

   **essential** necessary, extremely important

2. **What is being said in detail, and how?** You must try to discover the main ideas, assertions, and arguments that constitute the author's particular message.
3. **Is the book true, in whole or part?** You cannot answer this question until you have answered the first two. You have to know what is being said before you can decide whether it is true or not. When you understand a book, however, you are obligated, if you are reading seriously, to make up your own mind. Knowing the author's mind is not enough.

   **obligated** required

4. **What of it?** If the book has given you information, you must ask about its significance. Why does the author think it is important to know these things? Is it important to you to know them? And if the book has not only informed you, but also enlightened you, it is necessary to seek further enlightenment by asking what else follows, what is further implied or suggested.

2    Knowing what the four questions are is not enough. You must remember to ask them as you read. The *habit* of doing that is the mark of a demanding reader. More than that, you must know how to answer them precisely and accurately. The trained ability to do that is the *art* of reading.

Below is the information you most likely found in your preview (notice that we've included here only part of the introductory paragraph and part of the concluding paragraph).

### The Essence of Active Reading
### The Four Basic Questions a Reader Asks

From the introduction

*Active reading* is better reading. *Ask questions while you read—questions that you yourself must try to answer in the course of reading.* There are four main questions you must ask about any book.

1. What is the book about as a whole?
2. What is being said in detail, and how?
3. Is the book true, in whole or part?
4. What of it?

From the conclusion

The *habit* of doing that is the mark of a demanding reader. The trained ability to do that is the *art* of reading.

---

### Exercise **4**    Previewing

Based on the information you discovered in your preview above, answer the following questions about "The Essence of Active Reading."

1. What is the article about? *(See title)*
2. What must you do to become an active reader? *(See subtitle and introduction)*
3. What are the four main questions you must ask about any book? *(See headings 1–4)*
4. What is the art of reading? *(See conclusion)*

• • • • • • • • • • • •

# Organizing to Learn
## Previewing the Parts of a Textbook
• • • • • • • • • • • • • • • • • • • • • • • • • • • • • • • • • • •

Besides previewing a short section you are about to read, it's helpful to preview an entire text, especially when you first get a new book. College textbooks are usually divided into a number of parts or sections. Each of these sections has its own name, and you can expect to find certain information in each part. Here is a chart of these sections, their usual location, and their use to you as a student.

| Part of a Book | Where to Find It | The Information It Gives |
|---|---|---|
| Title page | The first page of the book | Title of the book, name of the author(s), place of publication |
| Copyright page | On the back of the title page | Number of editions, date of publication, ordering information |
| Table of contents | After the copyright page | A listing of the book's major topics and subtopics in the order they'll be presented, organized in chapters, sections, or units with page numbers |
| Preface | Before the first chapter | Information about the book's purpose, special features, student aids |
| Appendix (appendices) | At the end of the text | Additional useful information, such as maps, lists of presidents, charts and tables |
| Glossary | At the back of the book | A dictionary of important terms for the text |
| Index | At the end of the book, after appendices and glossary | Usually an *alphabetical* listing of all important topics and terms found in the text, with page numbers for each |
| Bibliography | At the end of a chapter or a special section at the end of the book | A listing of additional information on a topic, including books, journals, audiovisual materials, and web sites |
| Answer keys | At the back of a text or in an appendix | Provides answers so students can check their work |

**Exercise 5**  **Using the Parts of a Textbook**

Preview this text, *Joining a Community of Readers*, and answer the following questions about it.

1. Who are the authors of this book?
2. When was this book published?
3. In which chapters do you learn how to identify main ideas?
4. Where do you find out what you will be working on in each chapter?
5. In which chapters will you be studying material about the environment?
6. Where will you find instructions on how to write a summary?
7. Where in this book can you find exercises on vocabulary?
8. Which unit looks most interesting to you?

## Use Previous Knowledge

As you prepare to read, think about what you already know about a topic. In your preview you will often recognize information about which you have previous knowledge—from your experience and prior learning. For example, in "The Essence of Active Reading" on page 35, you should have considered what you already know about reading. If you are reading a chapter in a health text about nutrition, you probably already know many things like fresh vegetables and fruit are healthy parts of a diet, and french fries and candy are not. Recognizing what you already know will make it easier to understand the new material and to see how it relates to the skills and information you already have. When you preview and ask questions in the process of preparing to read, always consider how this new material fits in with what you already know.

## Ask Questions

The last thing you need to do to prepare to read is to ask yourself questions that you think the reading will answer. In this process you are *predicting* what you will learn. You are preparing to be actively involved as you read. There are many sources of questions for reading—your preview is a good one.

As you preview, ask questions about what you are going to read. Use the points in the preview—titles, headings, boldface print, etc.—to predict what you will learn in the reading. Turn these tips into questions so you will be actively engaged when you read the piece. For example, as you previewed "The Essence of Active Reading" on page 35, the first thing you saw was the title. From the title you might form the question: "What is the essence of active reading?" You might use "who? what? when? where? how? and why?" to help you formulate questions from other information in the preview. For example, questions might include, "What are the four main questions you must ask about a book?" "Why should I ask questions?" "When do I ask these questions?" "How can I develop the art of reading?"

| Exercise **6** | Asking Reader's Questions |

Preview the following paragraph. Read the first sentence or two and the *italicized* words. Then write three reading questions you predict the reading will answer.

1. _____

2. _____

3. _____

Since reading of any sort is an activity, all reading must to some degree be active. Completely passive reading is impossible; we cannot read with our eyes immobilized and our minds asleep. Hence when we contrast active with passive reading, our purpose is, first, to call attention to the fact that reading can be *more* or *less* active, and, second, to point out that the *more active* the reading the *better*. One reader is better than another in proportion as he is capable of a greater range of activity in reading and exerts more effort. He is better if he demands more of himself and of the text before him. (Mortimer J. Adler and Charles Van Doren, *How to Read a Book*)

You may have written questions similar to these:

1. What is active reading?
2. How can reading be more or less active?
3. Why is more active reading better?

Among the possible sources for your reader's questions are the following:

- **Preview**—When you do your quick preview of a passage, you will find that you might want to formulate questions based on the titles or the words that are highlighted in some way. (In the above paragraph, important words are italicized.)
- **Your experience and previous knowledge**—Think about your own experience and what you already know about the topics. For example, in the paragraph above, think about how you read and how the information in the paragraph can help you. Put this information in your questions because you are looking for answers.
- **Instructor's directions**—Listen carefully. Very often the instructor will make suggestions for prereading questions.
- **Course objectives**—Keep in mind your purpose for studying this course. Reread your syllabus from time to time to be sure you're focusing on the right things.
- **Study guides**—Often your instructor or the text itself will provide study guides for the material. Keep these in mind when you form your prereading questions.
- **Questions in the book**—Some textbooks now provide prereading questions to help students. Otherwise read the questions at the end of the section *before* you read the section. You can use these questions as your prereading questions also.

Whatever the source, raising prereading questions is an important habit to acquire in mastering the reading process. At first you will need to actually write reader's questions as part of the preparing to read process. Eventually, you will probably be in the habit of forming such questions in your mind every time you begin to read something new.

**Exercise 7**    **Previewing**

Preview the selection "Some Reflections on Reading" by Daniel R. Walther on pages 40–42. List the information you noticed in your preview:

Title: _____

From the introduction: _____

Heading: _____

Subheadings:  1. _____

             2. _____

             3. _____

             4. _____

Italicized quote in the margin: _____

## Exercise 8    Asking Reader's Questions

What reader's questions can you ask yourself that will help you read this passage?
Ask a question for each of the items identified in your preview.
     The first two have been done for you.

| Item from Preview | Reader's Question |
|---|---|
| Title | 1. *What are reflections? What are the author's reflections about reading?* |
| From the introduction | 2. *What does the author mean by reading process?* |
| Heading | 3. _____ |
| Subheadings | 4a. _____ |
| | 4b. _____ |
| | 4c. _____ |
| | 4d. _____ |
| Italicized quote in the margin | 5. _____ |

## Some Reflections on Reading

### Daniel R. Walther

*Below is the entire selection "Some Reflections on Reading."
While you read, think about the questions that you asked in Exercise 8.*

     This chapter does not presume to teach you how to read. You    1
already know how to do that. But most students have never approached the process of reading from the perspective of under-

standing what happens when reading takes place and what practices might be useful to make reading textbook assignments an easier and more fruitful activity. That's what this chapter is all about.

2    In this theory section, our concern is to develop a better grasp of the process of reading. We can begin by focusing on some new perspectives on the reading process.

## Reading Principles

### We Become Better Readers by Reading

3    Many people are under the impression that reading improvement comes from learning "tricks" or mastering some mechanical gimmicks that will magically improve reading speed and comprehension. However, most reading professionals agree that we learn to read better simply as a result of reading widely. So much of reading depends on our "prior knowledge"—that information that we carry inside our head when we open the page and begin reading. Many learning theorists maintain that we remember new information only if we relate it to knowledge we already hold. There is no greater guarantee of a person's reading efficiency than extensive experience with words on the printed page. You can make slow but steady progress as a reader simply by reading more extensively to increase your base of knowledge.

**extensive** a lot

### More Than Anything Else, Reading Is a Process of Predicting

4    If you were to pick up a book, turn to the first page, and read the line, "Once upon a time, in a magical land and a magical time . . ." your mind automatically begins to make predictions: "This is a fairy tale or fable of some kind . . . some of the characters will be 'bad' and others will be 'good.' There will probably be a happy ending, and the story will teach a simple little lesson. . . ." and so on. As we actively read, our mind is always racing ahead of where our eyes are on the page, wondering, speculating, predicting, and then eventually either confirming those predictions or correcting those predictions that were not accurate. (In understanding that reading is largely a process of predicting, you are well under way to learning how to improve your comprehension and reading rate in text reading assignments. . . .)

**confirming** agreeing with

*Reading is a means of thinking with another person's mind: it forces you to stretch your own.* CHARLES SCRIBNER JR.

### Reading Is an Interactive Process, Not a Passive One

5    Many students are under the impression that reading is a "laidback" activity—that the mind is some sort of sponge that soaks up meaning as the eyes move across the page. Effective readers are mentally involved—questioning, probing, analyzing, disagreeing, doubting, criticizing, or in some other way *reacting* to the words on the page.

**interactive** involving two-way communication

Because textbook reading is an interactive process, we must 6 treat it differently from the reading we do for leisure or entertainment. You may be able to take a spellbinding novel to your bed, tuck a comfortable pillow under your head, and spend an hour or more reading. You may even have a radio going in the background and still stay focused on your book. Using the same strategy with your chemistry textbook, however, can lead to disaster. You may find that you can read your textbooks much more successfully if you put yourself in a different environment. Go to the library, the kitchen table, or your desk. Read sitting straight up and in a well-lighted area. Choose an environment with a minimum of distractions. You may see a marked improvement in your reading efficiency if you treat reading as the challenging mental activity it is and put yourself in an environment and a posture that will better support it.

### Comprehension Improves at a Rate Slightly Above Our Habitual, Comfortable Rate

As we fail to do with so many other mental activities, we typically 7 do not work up to our mental potential when we read. More often than not, we lapse into a nice comfortable rate—one that barely keeps the mind busy and that allows us to be distracted by our surroundings or other pressing thoughts unrelated to the task of reading. Many students have been led to believe that they will read better if they just slow down, but that advice is as valid as saying that they will "drive better" if they slow down to forty-five miles per hour on an interstate highway. The slow driver is prone to being distracted by the scenery, may become drowsy from the slower pace, or perhaps will attend to other, more interesting, pursuits, such as adjusting the graphics equalizer on the car stereo system. Driving thus becomes only one of the activities competing for the driver's attention.

You will probably do a better job of reading if you press yourself to read 10 percent or so above your typical rate, just enough to require your mind to stay alert and focused. (You are probably capable of reading 30 or 40 percent faster with some effort, but the point is not to make reading a frenzied activity—just a focused one.)

**Exercise 9**    **Reader's Questions: Collaborative Activity**

1. Compare your reader's questions with the questions that other members of class (or your class group) wrote. Of all the questions, pick the ones that you think were the best predictors of what the article covered.
2. Answer the reader's questions that your group chose.

| Exercise **10** | Checking Your Understanding |

1. List the four principles we should focus on in the reading process.
2. What is "prior knowledge"?
3. How can more reading make us better readers?
4. What is "predicting"?
5. What is meant when the author says that reading is an "interactive process?"
6. How can we improve our reading efficiency?

| Exercise **11** | Checking Your Reader's Questions |

1. Did answering your own reader's questions help you answer the questions in Exercise 10? Why or why not?
2. How much of the content of the article did you "predict" with your reader's questions? Which of your questions were answered? Which were not?
3. How did your focus on preview items help you understand the framework of the article?

## Choose a Reading Strategy

Once you have previewed and asked reader's questions, you are ready to choose a strategy for reading.

**Purpose.**    Ask yourself, what is your *purpose* for reading this material? Do you just need a general understanding of the information? For example, you might read the morning newspaper or a magazine article for a general understanding of current events; however, for college course work your purpose is often much more demanding. For example, if you are assigned a chapter in a health text, you may need to be prepared for a quiz on the content at the next class meeting. Or perhaps you are planning to use this information for a job in the future, such as working as a personal trainer in a gym. In both cases, your purpose for reading is much more serious and your reading strategy should reflect this. Plan to devote plenty of time to the reading assignment and be sure you can concentrate on completing the task.

**Difficulty.**    A second consideration in determining your reading strategy is to ask yourself: How difficult does the material seem to be? Will it take a lot of time and effort to understand? Plan more time than you think you will need. How much do you already know about this topic? If the material is familiar to you or looks fairly easy, you can plan to read it faster and a little less carefully. The amount of time it takes you to complete a reading task will vary from assignment to assignment, and it certainly varies from student to student. Schedule your time carefully (see Chapter

1 for more details). Monitor the time it takes to complete assignments and as your reading and study skills improve, your use of time should become more efficient.

## READ ACTIVELY

Active reading is involved reading. As you've no doubt noticed in the various excerpts you've been reading in this chapter, to succeed as a reader you must be alert and actively involved in every part of the reading process. You

1. must prepare to read,
2. check yourself as you read to be sure you are understanding, and then
3. think about all the ideas you read and
4. make connections.

As Charles Scribner Jr. says, "Reading is a means of thinking with another person's mind: it forces you to stretch your own." This openness to new ideas, "stretching your mind," is part of what makes active reading happen.

### Making Connections

Reading is a way to receive the ideas of others, to learn what other people want us to learn. However, you must also be a **critical reader.** Think about what you read and

1. *connect* what you already know to the new information you are acquiring and
2. *question* whether to accept all of the new information you read.

In other words, do you agree with everything the writer says? Part of what she says? Do you think the opposite is true? Do you question her facts? Are some facts missing? Are her points reasonable?

For example, if you are reading an article in which a smoker argues that he smokes because he enjoys it and he doesn't care about the future consequences, you already know what the consequences of smoking are (lung cancer, emphysema, constant cough, etc.). As an active reader, you make connections between what he is saying and what you know. You think about what he wrote and come to your own conclusions about the topic.

**Exercise 12**    **Making Connections**

Read the following passage about active reading and answer the questions that follow.

Reading and listening are thought of as *receiving* communication from someone who is actively engaged in *giving* or *sending* it. The mistake here is to suppose that receiving communication is like receiving a blow or a legacy or a judgment from the court. On the contrary, the reader or listener is much more like the catcher in a game of baseball.

Catching the ball is just as much an activity as pitching or hitting it. The pitcher or batter is the *sender* in the sense that his activity initiates the motion of the ball. The catcher or fielder is the *receiver* in the sense that his activity terminates it. Both are active, though the activities are different. If anything is passive, it is the ball. It is the inert thing that is put in motion or stopped, whereas the players are active, moving to pitch, hit, or catch. . . . The art of catching is the skill of catching every kind of pitch—fast balls and curves, changeups and knucklers. Similarly, the art of reading is the skill of catching every sort of communication as well as possible. (Mortimer J. Adler and Charles Van Doren, *How to Read a Book*)

1. Have you ever played catcher on a softball team? Or simply played catch? Explain your experience.
2. When you read, do you feel that you are actively receiving the message that the writer is sending? Explain.
3. Do you agree with the writer that reading is very much like catching a ball? Why or why not?
4. To what other actions do you think active reading could be compared?

## What Do Active Readers Do?

They ask themselves questions and they answer their questions continuously.

- Preparing to read questions
    Using previous knowledge
    Previewing
    Asking questions
- Checking comprehension questions
    Do I understand?
    Were my reader's questions answered?
- Making connections questions
    How does this fit in with what I already know?
    What do I know that I could add this information to?
- Critical thinking questions
    Do I agree? Or, what part do I agree with? What part don't I agree with?

## *Learning to Read: Malcolm X*

### MALCOLM X

*Malcolm X was born Malcolm Little in Omaha, Nebraska. As an adult, he changed his name to Malcolm X because Little was the name his family had gotten from the slave master. When he was a young boy, his father died in an "accident," but his family believed he was murdered by white racists. When he was 20, Malcolm was arrested for burglary and sentenced to ten years in prison. While in prison he began to learn about the Nation of Islam, a black Muslim organization led by Elijah Muhammad. In this passage from his autobiography, he explains his struggle to become an educated person while he was in prison.*

What kind of *connections* can you make to the information in this introduction?

- Did you know that slaves took the names of their masters?
- Have you ever been in Nebraska?
- What do you know about the Nation of Islam?
- What do you already know about Malcolm X?
- Have you heard about other people studying while they were in prison?

**Exercise 13** | **Preparing to Read**

This excerpt, which is not from a textbook, does not have subheads, boldfaced and italicized words, or pictures. To preview a passage like this, look at the first and last paragraphs and glance at the first sentences of the other paragraphs. Preview this passage and write two reader's questions that you think will be answered in the reading.

You can study the questions and answers in the margins as examples of the kinds of thinking you should be doing while you read. Some of the questions are checking understanding, while others are making connections.

*Why did Malcolm want to learn to read and write?*

*He wanted to write letters*

It was because of my letters that I happened to stumble upon starting to acquire some kind of a homemade education. 1

I became increasingly frustrated at not being able to express what I wanted to convey in letters that I wrote, especially those to Mr. Elijah Muhammad. In the street, I had been the most articulate hustler out there—I had commanded attention when I said something. But now, trying to write simple English, I not only wasn't articulate, I wasn't even functional. How would I sound writing in slang, the way I would *say* it, something such as, "Look, daddy, let me pull your coat about a cat, Elijah Muhammad—" 2

Many who today hear me somewhere in person, or on television, or those who read something I've said, will think I went to school far beyond the eighth grade. This impression is due entirely to my prison studies. 3

4     It had really begun back in the Charlestown Prison, when Bimbi first made me feel envy of his stock of knowledge. Bimbi had always taken charge of any conversation he was in, and I had tried to emulate him. But every book I picked up had few sentences which didn't contain anywhere from one to nearly all of the words that might as well have been in Chinese. When I just skipped those words, of course, I really ended up with little idea of what the book said. So I had come to the Norfolk Prison Colony still going through only book-reading motions. Pretty soon, I would have quit even these motions, unless I had received the motivation that I did.

*"emulate" act like him*

5     I saw that the best thing I could do was get hold of a dictionary—to study, to learn some words. I was lucky enough to reason also that I should try to improve my penmanship. It was sad. I couldn't even write in a straight line. It was both ideas together that moved me to request a dictionary along with some tablets and pencils from the Norfolk Prison Colony school.

*How did he teach himself?*

6     I spent two days just riffling uncertainly through the dictionary's pages. I'd never realized so many words existed! I didn't know *which* words I needed to learn. Finally, just to start some kind of action, I began copying.

7     In my slow, painstaking, ragged handwriting, I copied into my tablet everything printed on that first page, down to the punctuation marks.

8     I believe it took me a day. Then, aloud, I read back, to myself, everything I'd written on the tablet. Over and over, aloud, to myself, I read my own handwriting.

9     I woke up the next morning thinking about those words—immensely proud to realize that not only had I written so much at one time, but I'd written words that I never knew were in the world. Moreover, with a little effort, I also could remember what many of these words meant. I reviewed the words whose meanings I didn't remember. Funny thing, from the dictionary first page right now, that "aardvark" springs to my mind. The dictionary had a picture of it, a long-tailed, long-eared, burrowing African mammal, which lives off termites caught by sticking out its tongue as an anteater does for ants.

10     I was so fascinated that I went on—I copied the dictionary's next page. And the same experience came when I studied that. With every succeeding page, I also learned of people and places and events from history. Actually the dictionary is like a miniature encyclopedia. Finally the dictionary's A section had filled a whole tablet—and I went on into the B's. That was the way I started copying what eventually became the entire dictionary. It went a lot faster after so much practice helped me to pick up handwriting speed. Between what I wrote in my tablet, and writing letters, during the rest of my time in prison I would guess I wrote a million words.

*He copied the dictionary*

*Is that a good idea for me?*

*I don't have that much time!*

"My word-base broadened" (does that mean he knew more words?)

I suppose it was inevitable that as my word-base broadened, I could for the first time pick up a book and read and now begin to understand what the book was saying. Anyone who has read a great deal can imagine the new world that opened. Let me tell you something: From then until I left that prison, in every free moment I had, if I was not reading in the library, I was reading on my bunk. You couldn't have gotten me out of books with a wedge. Between Mr. Muhammad's teachings, my correspondence, my visitors—usually Ella and Reginald—and my reading of books, months passed without my even thinking about being imprisoned. In fact, up to then, I never had been so truly free in my life. 11

Why does he say he was "free" when he was in prison?

The Norfolk Prison Colony's library was in the school building. A variety of classes was taught there by instructors who came from such places as Harvard and Boston universities. The weekly debates between inmate teams were also held in the school building. You would be astonished to know how worked up convict debaters and audiences would get over subjects like "Should Babies Be Fed Milk?" 12

Available on the prison library's shelves were books on just about every general subject. Much of the big private collection that Parkhurst had willed to the prison was still in crates and boxes in the back of the library—thousands of old books. Some of them looked ancient: covers faded, old-time parchment-looking binding. Parkhurst, I've mentioned, seemed to have been principally interested in history and religion. He had the money and the special interest to have a lot of books that you wouldn't have in general circulation. Any college library would have been lucky to get that collection. 13

As you can imagine, especially in a prison where there was heavy emphasis on rehabilitation, an inmate was smiled upon if he demonstrated an unusually intense interest in books. There was a sizable number of well-read inmates, especially the popular debaters. Some were said by many to be practically walking encyclopedias. They were almost celebrities. No university would ask any student to devour literature as I did when this new world opened to me, of being able to read and *understand*. 14

I read more in my room than in the library itself. An inmate who was known to read a lot could check out more than the permitted maximum number of books. I preferred reading in the total isolation of my own room. 15

When I had progressed to really serious reading, every night at about ten P.M. I would be outraged with the "lights out." It always seemed to catch me right in the middle of something engrossing. 16

Fortunately, right outside my door was a corridor light that cast a glow into my room. The glow was enough to read by, once 17 my eyes adjusted to it. So when "lights out" came, I would sit on the floor where I could continue reading in that glow.

18     At one-hour intervals the night guards paced past every room. Each time I heard the approaching footsteps, I jumped into bed and feigned sleep. And as soon as the guard passed, I got back out of bed onto the floor area of that light-glow, where I would read for another fifty-eight minutes—until the guard approached again. That went on until three or four every morning. Three or four hours of sleep a night was enough for me. Often in the years in the streets I had slept less than that.

*Why did he stay up so late?*

*What does this reading about Malcolm X have to do with me?*

| Exercise **14** | **Checking Your Reading** |

Did the notes in the margins help keep you reading actively? Why or why not?

| Exercise **15** | **Checking Your Understanding** |

1. How many years did Malcolm X attend school?
2. Why did he decide to start copying down the words in the dictionary?
3. What did he do to be able to read until late at night?
4. What did the prison authorities think about prisoners who read a lot?

| Exercise **16** | **Making Connections** |

1. Many prisoners begin to read and to exercise a lot. Why do you think this is so?
2. Malcolm X had a lot of time, so studying the whole dictionary was not a problem for him. Do you think that it would be a good idea for you to study the whole dictionary to improve your vocabulary?
3. What are some other ways that you might go about learning new vocabulary?

## ORGANIZE WHAT YOU'VE READ

After you have completed the first two steps in the PRO reading process—preparing to read and reading actively—you are ready to organize what you've read. Organizing what you've read accomplishes two things: it helps you to *understand* better what you've read, and it helps you to *remember* what you've read for future tests or job requirements. There are a number of ways to select and use—that is, to organize—reading material. They include answering questions, marking the text, charting, outlining, mapping, summarizing, and others. Then, recite, or test yourself on what you have learned. Review periodically to make sure you are prepared for the test. You will practice a number of these strategies as you proceed through the chapters of this book.

In organizing to learn you should consider which ways you learn best. What is your preferred learning style? Do you learn best when you hear information? You might try recording the key points you need to memorize and listening to them. Are you a very social person? Take time to learn and review in study groups. Are you primarily a visual learner? Making a chart, map, or some kind of visual aid may be very useful to you. Does motion help your learning process? Try reviewing math formulas as you jog around the track.

## THE PRO READING PROCESS

### P = Prepare to Read

- Concentrate
- Preview
- Use previous knowledge
- Ask questions
- Choose a strategy

### R = Read Actively

- Check on your prereading questions
- Check your understanding
- Make connections to what you already know
- Think critically about the new information

### O = Organize What You've Read

- Answer questions
- Mark the text
- Make charts
- Outline
- Map
- Summarize

# Applying Your Skills

## Effective Speaking and Listening

CURTIS O. BYER AND LOUIS SHAINBERG

*The following excerpt from a college health textbook presents some important pointers for learning how to speak and listen effectively—important skills for life and for success in college. As you read, think about which of the suggestions you are already good at as a speaker and listener. Which ones do you need to work on?*

---

## Preparing to Read

In this reading you will notice that every effort has been made to make it easy for you to understand this textbook. In addition to using titles, lists, and italics, the authors even ask questions in the middle of the chapters. Don't skip over these questions. Use them to test yourself on how well you are understanding and remembering what you are reading.

1. Preview the following excerpt from a college text. List three things you notice that help you to understand the overall ideas of the article.
2. While you are previewing, consider the level of difficulty of this excerpt. Is the information familiar to you or unfamiliar?
3. Write two reader's questions that you think will be answered in the excerpt.

## Effective Speaking

1   Do you ever feel that people don't seem to understand what you are saying or, worse still, just aren't interested in what you have to say? Being an interesting, effective speaker is a characteristic that anyone can develop and one that contributes greatly to the quality of your relationships.

2   For starters, you need to *have something interesting to say.* This means having familiarity with a broad range of topics and being sensitive to the interests of the listener.

3   Even though the pressures of school or work may dictate where much of your attention is directed, you need to reserve time to broaden your interests and expand your awareness of a variety of subjects. If you are highly knowledgeable about your major field, but have little awareness of other subjects, there will be relatively few people who find you a stimulating conversational partner.

4   If you find yourself being misunderstood, you may need to *improve the exactness of your communication.* Vocabulary building may be necessary. Communication is often handicapped by a lack of the precise word to express a particular idea or feeling. It can be very frustrating to know what you want to say, but to lack the words that would convey that thought. Many colleges offer vocabulary-building courses. Books, tapes, computer programs, and other media are also available to help expand your vocabulary.

**convey** to express

When communicating with someone from another ethnic 5
group, remember that you may use a word or phrase to convey a
particular meaning but it may only have that meaning to someone
with your own background. Even people from different regions of
the United States may interpret the same phrase differently.

In health-related communication, vocabulary is especially im- 6
portant. Many problems arise in communication between health
care providers and their clients when the clients are unable to describe symptoms or concerns adequately or the providers speak
above or below the ability of the client to comprehend.

Example: "Some people describe any pain between their neck and
their crotch as a "stomachache."

**terminology** spe-
cialized vocabu-
lary

If this book seems to use a lot of terminology, it's because 7
precise communication does require using the proper term. Too often, health-related communication suffers from inadequate vocabulary. One unfortunate result of inadequate vocabulary is that
sometimes, not knowing which word to use, we simply fail to communicate at all.

To ensure the clarity of your communication, *think through* 8
*what you intend to say before you say it.* Even though this may
cause a slight pause in the flow of the conversation, it reduces the
risk of your being misinterpreted. To further reduce this risk, when
you have something important to say, repeat it several times,
phrasing it in different ways. Of course, don't go overboard with
repetition. It can get annoying!

**feedback** re-
sponse

*Be very alert to the verbal and nonverbal feedback* you get 9
from your listener and use this feedback to guide your communication. For example, you may sense the need to speak more slowly or
to rephrase your message.

### Checkpoint
1. What are four guidelines for effective speaking?
2. Do you feel that you have an adequate vocabulary for most
   communication situations?
3. What do you usually do when someone seems not to understand what you are saying?

## Effective Listening

An effective listener is just as actively involved in communication 10
as the speaker. In fact, effective listening requires greater effort and
concentration than speaking. Your attention must remain focused
on the speaker and not wander. Any momentary inattention can
cause you to miss the meaning of what is being said.

11    In any important discussion, it is essential to minimize distractions so that your full attention can be focused on the speaker. Turn off the TV or stereo; close the door; suggest moving to a less distracting location; ask the other person to speak louder. If you can't eliminate distractions, at least make every effort to concentrate on the discussion.

12    Often the speaker's nonverbal communication reveals more than his or her actual words. Be very alert to posture, gestures, facial expressions, eye movements, and the tone and inflection in the speaker's voice.

13    Listeners often misinterpret what they hear. For instance, people sometimes interpret messages as being hostile or critical when they were not intended that way. Major misunderstandings can develop when you fail to ask for clarification of some vague or seemingly hurtful statement. If you have any doubt about the meaning of what you have just been told, immediately ask for clarification.

**hostile** angry

14    When someone makes a statement that causes you to feel hurt, angry, or defensive, it is often productive to reveal your feelings, allowing the misunderstanding or conflict to be worked out *at that time.* Otherwise, hostility builds up and will be expressed eventually, often in a nonproductive manner, which can severely damage or even destroy a relationship.

15    In summary, Eugene Raudsepp has identified seven ways to improve your listening abilities.

16    1. *Take time to listen.* Sometimes people aren't sure just what they need to say or how best to express their message. They think as they speak and may modify their message as they go. Though you may wish they would hurry up and get to the point, effective listening requires you patiently to allow the speaker to finish his or her message, and reassure him or her on that point.

Example: "Take your time. I'm listening to you. There's no rush."

17    2. *Don't interrupt.* Even though you think you know what the speaker is leading up to and you are impatient for him or her to make a point, resist the temptation to interrupt and finish sentences. Doing so implies a sense of superiority and may break down communication. Interruptions often confuse the speaker and there is a possibility that your assumptions may be wrong.

Example: "I know what you are going to say and I think you're wrong. You think that. . . ."

18    If you have the habit of interrupting, as many of us do, Raudsepp suggests breaking that habit by making yourself apologize

every time you interrupt. After a few apologies, you'll think twice before interrupting someone.

> Example: "Excuse me for interrupting you. It's a habit I'm trying to break, so let me know whenever I do it."

3. *Teach yourself to concentrate.* One reason we sometimes 19 have trouble concentrating on a speaker is that we can think much faster than a person can speak. We get bored and begin to think about something else. To remain focused on the speaker, keep analyzing what he or she is saying.

4. *Disregard speech mannerisms.* Don't focus on a person's 20 accent, speech impediment, or delivery style; you will lose track of his or her message.

5. *Suspend judgment.* We tend to listen to the ideas we want 21 to hear and to shut out others. We unconsciously do this because ideas that conflict with our own are threatening. But by listening to what others have to say, we can come to understand our own line of reasoning better and may even change our mind.

6. *Listen between the lines.* Much of the important content in 22 the messages we receive is unstated or only indirectly implied. Focusing only on the message actually verbalized leads us to miss

Listen with your eyes. Watch closely for nonverbal signals; they may reveal far more than a speaker's words.

most, if not all, of the true message. Be sensitive to what the speaker is feeling and the true message may become evident.

Example: Lori says, "I've heard that that's a good place to get a sandwich." Lori means, "I'm hungry!"

23      7. *Listen with your eyes.* Pay attention to the speaker's nonverbal signals. Rarely can the full message be gained from words alone.

Example: "How are you feeling today?" "I'm fine." "Well, the sad look on your face and the way you're wringing your hands tells me that something is bothering you. Would you like to talk about it?"

### Checkpoint
1. List seven suggestions for improving listening abilities.
2. In addition to being rude, what implications does interrupting a speaker carry?

**Exercise 17    Checking Your Preparing to Read**

1. Were your reader's questions answered?
2. Was the passage as easy, or as difficult, as you predicted?

**Exercise 18    Checking Your Understanding**

1. What two things does the author suggest speakers should do so they have something interesting to say?
2. How can speakers increase the exactness of their communication?
3. What can people do to increase the clarity of what they say?
4. Why does effective listening require so much effort?
5. What should a listener notice about nonverbal communication?
6. What should a listener do if the speaker says something that hurts his feelings?

**Exercise 19    Your Personal Vocabulary**

Choose five words from the article that you would like to be able to use in your own vocabulary. Write the word, its definition, and its part of speech in your reading notebook or on 3 × 5" cards. Then write your word in a sentence.

**Exercise 20** | **Making Connections**

Share your answers with your class group.

1. Do you have any friends that you really like to talk to? What kind of listeners are they? List words that describe how they listen to you.
2. How much time a day do you spend listening? How much time a day do you spend speaking?
3. What kind of a listener are you? List what you do well and what you do that may not be good for listening.

**What I Do Well as a Listener**

1. _____
   _____
2. _____
   _____
3. _____
   _____
4. _____
   _____
5. _____
   _____

**What I Do Poorly as a Listener**

1. _____
   _____
2. _____
   _____
3. _____
   _____
4. _____
   _____
5. _____
   _____

**Exercise 21** | **Organizing to Learn**

Use information from the article to finish filling in the following graphic organizer.

| Tips for Effective Speaking | Tips for Effective Listening |
| --- | --- |
| 1. Have something interesting to say | 1. Take time to listen |
| 2. _____ | 2. Don't interrupt |
| _____ | 3. _____ |
| 3. _____ | 4. _____ |
| _____ | 5. _____ |
| 4. Be alert to verbal and nonverbal feedback | 6. _____ |
| | 7. _____ |

# Chapter Review

• • • • • • • • • • • • • • • • • • • • • • • • • • • • • • • • • • • • • • • • • • • • •

**Exercise 22**   **Skills Review**

Complete the following exercises individually or in your group. Fill in the chart which shows the basic steps of the reading process and what is involved in each one.

| Preparing to read | Reading Actively | Organizing |
|---|---|---|
| • Concentrate<br>• Preview<br>• _____<br>• _____<br>• _____ | • Check your prereading questions<br>• Check understanding<br>• _____<br>• _____ | • Answer questions<br>• _____<br>• Make charts<br>• _____<br>• Map<br>• Summarize |

**Exercise 23**   **Writing**

In the box above, circle all the steps in the reading process that you already use. Which steps do you need to add to improve your reading process? Explain in a paragraph how you will use the steps of the reading process to complete your reading assignments.

**Exercise 24**   **Collaborative Activity**

In your group, compare how you are using the PRO system. Discuss what you can do to improve your reading processes. Take notes about how each student plans to use PRO.

**Exercise 25**   **Extension Activity**

Choose a textbook from any of your other college courses and preview it. Identify the various features of the book. Does it have any unique parts? What parts, as a student, will you find most helpful in this text?

# Unit Review

## Latinas: Journeys of Achievement and Vision

### NICHOLASA MOHR

*Nicholasa Mohr grew up in the barrio, in Spanish Harlem, where she struggled to find role models to foster her self-esteem and pride in her Latino heritage. She writes about her own life as a "female and Puerto Rican in New York City," and goes on to praise the many "talented Latinas" whose stories are available today to inspire us. Mohr is now herself an award-winning writer and artist; she had published a number of outstanding works for children and adults including* Nilda, El Bronx Remembered, In Nueva York, *and* Rituals of Survival: A Woman's Portfolio.

### Preparing to Read

1. Who were your role models as a young child?
2. Are you aware of people who faced challenges similar to yours in life and have succeeded? Who are they and what did they do?
3. What challenges do you still have as a college student?
4. Preview the article, and from your preview, ask two reader's questions that you think will be answered.

### Searching for Role Models

There were no positive role models for me—out there in the dominant society—when I was growing up. When I looked and searched for successful Latinas to emulate, my efforts were futile. As a Puerto Rican and a female of color, my legacy was one of either a negative image or was invisible. . . . 1

**emulate** model after, imitate

Yet I knew even at an early age that this typecasting was not the truth: Where were the valiant women I knew? Where were my mother, my aunts, and all the courageous females who had been forced to leave Puerto Rico out of necessity, arriving in the United States by themselves for the most part, bringing children to a cold and hostile environment? They had come ill-equipped, with limited 2 education and few survival skills, and no knowledge of English. But they all were determined to give their children a better life—a future. This is where I came from and it was these women who became my heroes.

3    Many . . . Latinas . . . are the daughters of these undaunted women, descendants of strong females who passed on the survival techniques they learned and bestowed upon us the strength and determination that pressed the next generation to continue to succeed. . . .

## Defying Stereotypes

4    [Latina] women have excelled—in the disciplines of science, law, government, education, social activism, visual arts, music, fashion, literature, sports, media, and entertainment. Their backgrounds vary: some have come from privileged families while many have had to surmount modest beginnings and sometimes, extreme poverty. But these talented individuals share a common bond. They have triumphed over society's bias to exclude them by succeeding brilliantly in their professions and thus, have defied the stereotypes.

**surmount** overcome

**exclude** leave out

## Women of Achievement

5    Carmen Zapata, actress, producer, and community activist, born in New York City to a Mexican father and an Argentine mother, first used the name Marge Cameron in a singing and comedy act she created. "At one time it was not 'in' to be Hispanic. I had a hard time getting club owners to hire me unless I shook my fanny and played the maracas." Eventually her film roles caused the producers to claim that Marge Cameron did not look 'All-American.' Zapata began using her real name. However, she was then stereotyped in roles of either a maid or a mother. Despite a successful career that earned her money, Zapata decided to delve further into her Latino roots. Today she is the president and managing producer of the Bilingual Foundation of the Arts, a successful, Los Angeles-based theatrical organization, which she co-founded. She states that the Foundation's goal is to "have everyone learn about, share and become part of our literature and tradition."

6    Astronaut Ellen Ochoa, born in California and of Mexican descent, understands her success may encourage young girls to achieve their goals because she is similar to them.

7    Antonia Novello, born in Puerto Rico, was both the first woman and first Hispanic to hold the position of Surgeon General of the United States. Novello claims she is for the people who deserve help, "I think that as a woman, as a Hispanic, as a member of a minority . . . I bring a lot of sensitivity to the job." . . .

In 1992 three Latinas were elected to the U.S. Congress: Lucille   8
Roybal-Allard, democrat, is the first woman of Mexican-American
ancestry; Ileana Ros-Lehtinen, republican, is the first Cuban-born
woman; and Nydia Margarita Velazquez, democrat, is the first
Puerto Rican woman. Velazquez is dedicated to showing that Hispanic women can serve proudly in the political arena, fighting the
notion that, "we are the ones who go out and collect signatures but
when it comes to the final process, we were not good enough to
run for office."

Rosie Perez, actress, dancer, and choreographer, was born in   9
Brooklyn and grew up watching her Puerto Rican parents dance
*salsa* on the weekends and holidays. Singer Linda Ronstadt reveals
that "when we were little, we spoke Spanish at home, but the
schools pounded it out of us pretty early." Ronstadt celebrated her
paternal Mexican heritage with a successful album of *mariachi*
songs that her father used to sing.

Nely Galán, television anchor and producer, born in Cuba,   10
came here when she was an infant. As a popular television personality, Galán is determined to help shape the future of television produced for the U.S.-born Hispanics and warns that, "You damage a
whole group of people because they're not seen anywhere, and
that reflects badly on their self-esteem."

Pat Mora, poet and educator, born in El Paso, Texas, is well   11
aware of the influence she has on minority youths and minority issues, "I write to try to correct these images of worth." Mora states
her pride in being a Hispanic writer.

| Exercise **1** | Checking Your Prereading |
|---|---|

1. Did you think about experiences with role models in your life as you read Mohr's article? Did doing so help you read and think about her story? Explain.
2. Were your reader's questions answered?

| Exercise **2** | Checking Your Understanding |
|---|---|

State whether the following statements are true or false.

1. _____ When Mohr was growing up, she felt there were no positive role models for her to follow.
2. _____ Latina women have succeeded brilliantly in careers from science to law to entertainment.
3. _____ Astronaut Ellen Ochoa believes her success may encourage young girls to achieve their goals because she is similar to them.

4. _____ Antonia Novello was the tenth Hispanic woman to hold the position of surgeon general of the United States.
5. _____ No women of Hispanic descent have ever been elected to the U.S. Congress.
6. _____ Pat Mora, poet and educator, takes pride in being a Hispanic writer.

Write short answers for the following questions.

1. Who were the courageous females that Mohr recognized as role models in her youth?
2. What are some of the disciplines that Latinas have excelled in today?
3. Who are two of the Latina women who have been very successful? What did they do?
4. What do you think were some of the personal characteristics that helped Mohr to be successful? What helped some of the other women mentioned to achieve their goals?

| Exercise **3** | **Working with Words** |

Find three to five words that you did not know in this reading. Add them to your personal vocabulary list in your notebook, computer, or on your 3 × 5" cards. Follow the guidelines given on pages 21–22.

| Exercise **4** | **Making Connections** |

1. What challenges do you have to face while you are a student?
2. What can you do to meet these challenges? Which of your own personal qualities do you want to work on to help you do it?
3. Who are the role models that you might follow in achieving your goals?

| Exercise **5** | **Organizing to Learn** |

Write the part of the textbook that best matches each description below. You may choose from the following:

Answer key        Index
Appendix          Preface
Bibliography      Table of contents
Copyright page    Title page
Glossary

1. _____ information about the book's purpose, special features, student aids
2. _____ a listing of additional information on a topic, including books, journals, and audiovisual materials
3. _____ provides answers so students can check their work
4. _____ usually an *alphabetical* listing of all important topics and terms found in the text, with page numbers for each
5. _____ contains additional useful information, such as maps, charts, and tables
6. _____ a dictionary of important terms for the text and their definitions
7. _____ list of the book's major topics and subtopics in the order they'll be presented
8. _____ gives number of editions and date of publication

# UNIT
# 2

# Learning and Education

## *Main Ideas*

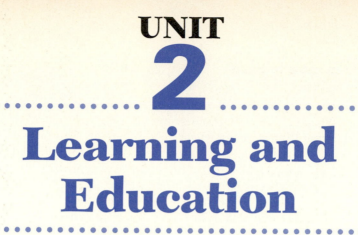

Both Albert Einstein (left) and Winston Churchill (right) enjoyed creative arts that didn't have anything to do with the work for which they were famous. In the above pictures, Einstein is playing a violin on a ship headed for California in 1931. Churchill is painting a landscape in southern France in 1948.

*Education is the process through which we discover that learning adds quality to our lives.*

**William Glasser**

### Preparing to Read

1. The pictures on the opposite page show Albert Einstein playing the violin and Winston Churchill painting a picture. They are engaged in activities very different from those for which they are famous. Einstein was a brilliant physicist and Churchill was one of the most important prime ministers of England, yet both enjoyed the arts. Do you enjoy playing music, drawing, or creative writing? In what ways do you think doing creative activities is different from studying for a subject in college?

2. Read the quotation. Why do you think that education is a "process?" In what ways do you think that education adds to the quality of your life?

## UNIT OBJECTIVES/SKILLS TO LEARN

In this unit you will learn how to

- Identify topics
- Identify stated and unstated main ideas

In the process of acquiring these skills, you will read and use information about

- Thinking and learning
- What some of the best teachers do
- Learning and expectations in American schools
- Challenges in education and how some people meet them

### Key Terms and Concepts

**topic**  "What is this reading about?"
**main idea**  "What did the reading say about the topic?"
**"brain power"**  You can strengthen your brain like a muscle by exercising it.
**expectations**  how you and others expect you to perform
**self-fulfilling prophecy**  what you expect can limit what you achieve
**bilingual education**  conducting classes in two languages

• • • • • • • • • • • • •

# Raising Issues

## Learning to Learn

• • • • • • • • • • • • • • • • • • • • • • • • • • • • • • • • • • • • • • • •

What is learning? According to Webster's dictionary, *to learn* means "to acquire new knowledge and skills." Students come to college, or any school, to learn, to be educated. Over two thousand years ago the Greek thinker Epictetus observed, "Only the educated are free." You, and many generations of students before you, have come to schools to learn all that you can to improve your life—to make more money, to learn skills for a career, to make friends, to broaden your thinking, and to enrich your understanding of the world around you. But, how do you actually learn all that you want and need to know? How can you get this knowledge and skill as quickly and as easily as possible? What conditions, attitudes, surroundings, multimedia computer tools, etc., encourage learning? How can you continue a lifetime of learning for the ever-changing world of the future?

In Chapters 3 and 4, you will read about some factors that affect learning and education in schools today. At the same time you will be focusing on some important reading comprehension skills: identifying topics and main ideas in sentences, paragraphs, and longer passages.

## *Building a Better Brain*

### Daniel Golden

*The following reading is an excerpt from a Life magazine report on how to increase the power of our brains, the physical storehouse of all we know and learn. Recent research suggests that we can control the remarkable power of the brain more easily than we ever expected, and that its strength stays with us "well into old age."*

1    Evidence is accumulating that the brain works a lot like a muscle—the harder you use it, the more it grows. Although scientists had long believed the brain's circuitry was hard-wired by adolescence and inflexible in adulthood, its newly discovered ability to change and adapt is apparently with us well into old age. Best of all, this research has opened up an exciting world of possibilities for treating strokes and head injuries—and warding off Alzheimer's disease.

## How to Make Your Dendrites Grow and Grow

2   What can the average person do to strengthen his or her mind? "The important thing is to be actively involved in areas unfamiliar to you," says Arnold Scheibel, head of UCLA's Brain Research Institute. "Anything that's intellectually challenging can probably serve as a kind of stimulus for dendritic growth, which means it adds to the computational reserves in your brain."

3    So pick something that's diverting and, most important, unfamiliar. A computer programmer might try sculpture; a ballerina

**dendritic growth**
growth of nerve cells (dendrites) in the brain

might try marine navigation. Here are some other stimulating suggestions from brain researchers:

- Do puzzles. "I can't stand crosswords," says neuroscientist Antonio Damasio of the University of Iowa, "but they're a good idea." Psychologist Sherry Willis of Pennsylvania State University says, "People who do jigsaw puzzles show greater spatial ability, which you use when you look at a map." 4

- Try a musical instrument. "As soon as you decide to take up the violin, your brain has a whole new group of muscle-control problems to solve. But that's nothing compared with what the brain has to do before the violinist can begin to read notes on a page and correlate them with his or her fingers to create tones. This is a remarkable, high-level type of activity," says Scheibel. 5

- Fix something. Learn to reline your car's brakes or repair a shaver, suggests Zaven Khachaturian, a brain expert at the National Institute of Aging. "My basement is full of electronic gadgets, waiting to be repaired. The solution is not the important thing. It's the challenge." 6

- Try the arts. If your verbal skills are good, buy a set of watercolors and take a course. If your drawing skills are good, start a journal or write poetry. 7

- Dance. "We keep seeing a relationship between physical activity and cognitive maintenance," says Harvard brain researcher Marilyn Albert. "We suspect that moderately strenuous exercise leads to the development of small blood vessels. Blood carries oxygen, and oxygen nourishes the brain." But be sure the activity is new and requires thinking. Square dancing, ballet or tap is preferable to twisting the night away. 8

- Date provocative people. Better yet, marry one of them. Willis suggests that the most pleasant and rewarding way to increase your dendrites is to "meet and interact with intelligent, interesting people." Try tournament bridge, chess, even sailboat racing. 9

**cognitive** having to do with understanding and thinking

And remember, researchers agree that it's never too late. Says Scheibel: "All of life should be a learning experience, not just for the trivial reasons but because by continuing the learning process, we are challenging our brain and therefore building brain circuitry. Literally. This is the way the brain operates." 10

**Exercise 1**   **Discussion Questions**

1. What does the statement "the brain works a lot like a muscle" mean?
2. What can the average person do to strengthen his or her mind?

3. What types of things do brain researchers suggest we can do to make our brains grow?

**Exercise 2**    **Making Connections**

1. Which of the activities suggested in this article do you already do? Which would you like to start doing to keep your mind growing?
2. Are there any other activities that you think could be added to the list to "strengthen our minds"? What are they?

# CHAPTER
# 3

# *Learning and Expectations*

## TOPICS AND MAIN IDEAS

If you understand what you read, you should always be able to answer two basic questions about the material. The first of these questions is:

1. What is this reading about?

When you answer this question, you are identifying the *topic* of the reading. You should be able to name the topic in just a few words. For example, if you were asked to identify the topic of the excerpt you read on pages 65–66, you might say it was "the human brain." A more specific answer might be "how to strengthen your brain." The topic is a key word or phrase that describes the focus of the article and is often repeated throughout the reading. For example, you probably noticed that the word *brain* and phrases such as *strengthening the brain* appeared several times in the previous reading.

The second question you should be able to answer is:

2. What did the reading say about the topic?

When you answer this question, you are identifying the *main idea* of the reading. The main idea should be stated as a *complete sentence.* For example, if someone asked you for the main idea of the reading on pages 65–66, you might say it was the first sentence: "Evidence is accumulating that the brain works a lot like a muscle—the harder you use it, the more it grows." Or, to state it in your own words, "Scientists now believe that you can strengthen your brain by exercising it." The topic sentence is a broad, or general, statement of the main point of the reading. In a main idea you do not try to include all the important supporting details. For example, for this article, you would not list any of the six specific suggestions that the authors gave for ways to improve your mind.

## TOPICS VERSUS MAIN IDEAS

To understand the difference between topics and main ideas, it's helpful to first see how they work in paragraphs. Remember, the topic is what the paragraph is about and it can be named in a few words. The main idea is the overall point the author is making about the topic, and it should be stated as a complete sentence. See if you can tell the difference between the topic and the main idea in the following paragraph from the reading on page 66.

> Dance. "We keep seeing a relationship between physical activity and cognitive maintenance," says Harvard brain researcher Marilyn Albert. "We suspect that moderately strenuous exercise leads to the development of small blood vessels. Blood carries oxygen, and oxygen nourishes the brain." But be sure the activity is new and requires thinking. Square dancing, ballet or tap is preferable to twisting the night away.

What is the topic?
The topic is "the effect of exercise" on the brain, a very brief answer to the question "What is the paragraph about?" Note that the terms *physical activity* and *exercise* are mentioned three times and that dancing is the specific physical activity used as an example in this paragraph.
What is the main idea?
The main idea statement, "we keep seeing a relationship between physical activity and cognitive maintenance," answers the question, "What is the author saying about the topic 'dance'?" Notice that the main idea sentence tells us how dance and other physical activities seem to benefit the brain.

**Exercise 3** | **Topics versus Main Ideas**

Read the following paragraphs. Then write "T" for the topic and "MI" for the main idea.

1. Try a musical instrument. "As soon as you decide to take up the violin, your brain has a whole new group of muscle-control problems to solve. But that's nothing compared with what the brain has to do before the violinist can begin to read notes on a page and correlate them with his or her fingers to create tones. This is a remarkable, high-level type of activity," says Scheibel.

_____ a.  The effects of playing musical instruments

_____ b.  Creating tones

_____ c.  Playing a musical instrument is a good activity for your brain

2.  Date provocative people. Better yet, marry one of them. Willis suggests that the most pleasant and rewarding way to increase your dendrites is to "meet and interact with intelligent, interesting people." Try tournament bridge, chess, even sailboat racing.

_____ a.  Tournament bridge

_____ b.  Dating interesting, provocative people is a great way to improve your brain.

_____ c.  Dating interesting people

3.  Fix something. Learn to reline your car's brakes or repair a shaver, suggests Zaven Khachaturian, a brain expert at the National Institute of Aging. "My basement is full of electronic gadgets, waiting to be repaired. The solution is not the important thing. It's the challenge."

_____ a.  Fixing things

_____ b.  Zaven Khachaturian

_____ c.  Fixing things is a good challenge for the brain.

## STATED MAIN IDEAS

### Main Ideas at the Beginning

The main idea of a paragraph is often stated at the beginning, in the first or second sentence. Authors put main ideas at the beginning because that makes it easier for readers to understand—readers know what to expect and it gives them a framework for what's to come. Textbook writers often state their topic and main idea at the beginning of a paragraph or longer passage and then go on to explain the main idea in more detail. Read the following two examples of paragraphs that have a stated main idea at the beginning.

> *There is widespread concern over the condition of education in this country today.* Over one-fourth of students drop out of school before graduation. Some 13 percent of the nation's 17-year-olds are functionally illiterate. Achievement tests given to students in 13 industrialized countries show American students rank 11th in chemistry, 9th in physics (for students who have taken two years of physics), and last in biology. Average Japanese 12th graders have a better command of mathematics than the top 5 percent of their American counterparts generally do. (From Turley Mings, *The Study of Economics: Principles, Concepts, and Applications*)

What is the topic?

*The topic of this paragraph is "American education" or the "condition of American education."*

What is the main idea?

*The main idea is stated in the first sentence: "There is widespread concern over the condition of education in this country today." The rest of the sentences in the paragraph explain in detail why we should be concerned: high school dropouts, illiteracy, and low achievement scores in sciences and math.*

The following paragraph develops the main idea by explaining it again in other words. Read the following example and see if you can identify the topic and the main idea.

*Your biggest thinking problem, and mine, and everybody's, is that our thinking becomes rigid.* We respond to new situations and new problems with the same old ideas. Our thinking falls into a well-worn pattern—a rut. We tend to think in clichés.

What is the topic of this paragraph?
*The topic of this paragraph is "thinking" or "problems with thinking."*
What is the main idea of this paragraph?
*The main idea is stated in the first sentence: "Your biggest thinking problem, and mine, and everybody's, is that our thinking becomes rigid." The idea that our thinking becomes rigid is repeated three different ways in the rest of the sentences in the paragraph: "same old ideas," "a rut," and we "think in clichés."*

## Main Ideas in the Middle

Sometimes writers place the main idea statement closer to the middle of a paragraph. For an example, read the following paragraph:

Luisa Hernandez is like a lot of other college students. Every morning she searches for a decent parking place at her local community college. She commutes to school, holds down a full-time job, and is raising her two daughters while trying to study. She is only one example of a current trend in American education: *More students who are attending college have adult responsibilities than ever before, and their concerns are somewhat different from the 18-year-old typical college freshman of earlier decades.* Very often these older students aren't as interested in sports or extra-curricular activities that most campuses offer. They are more concerned with having classes available to them both day and night, and with achieving their goal of getting from school to a good job as quickly as possible. In addition, since these students are usually not receiving aid from their parents, the cost of their education is an even more important factor for them.

What is the topic?
*The topic of this paragraph is "college students."*
What is the main idea?
*The main idea is stated in the middle: "More students who are attending college have adult responsibilities than ever before, and their concerns are somewhat different from the 18-year-old typical college freshman of earlier decades."*

The rest of the paragraph goes on to explain in examples how their concerns are different: less interest in sports and extracurricular activities and more concern with flexible class schedules, getting to work, and the cost of their education.

## Main Ideas at the End

Sometimes writers wait until the end of a paragraph to state their main idea. Often they do this when they are trying to argue a point, because you may be more convinced if you hear the facts first and then hear their conclusions or suggestions. For example, read the following paragraph.

When it comes to homework, Japanese children study an average of 16 hours a week in junior high school and 19 hours a week in high school. U.S. students, in contrast, spend 3 hours a week on homework in junior high and 4 hours a week in high school. Taking into account the relative numbers of school days per year, some simple math brings us to the conclusion that *U.S. high school students spend less than half the time studying in a year, whether in or out of school, than their Japanese peers!*

What is the topic?
*The topic of this paragraph is "homework" or "hours spent on homework."*
What is the main idea?
*The main idea is "U.S. high school students spend less than half the time studying in a year, whether in or out of school, than their Japanese peers." In this case the writers give their readers the facts and then lead them to the conclusion and main idea they are attempting to make.*

| Exercise **4** | Identifying Topics and Stated Main Ideas |
|---|---|

Read each of the following paragraphs. Then write "T" for the topic and "MI" for the main idea. The first one has been done for you.

1. Another major . . . function of schooling is to offer custodial care of children—providing a place to put them and having someone to watch them. Schools keep children off the streets, presumably out of trouble. The importance of this function has increased, as there have been many more two-career and single-parent households. Schools have traditionally been effective in performing their custodial role. In the past many schools were run under strict discipline, with teachers diligently enforcing rules and regulations and students obeying without question. But since the middle of this century a growing number of schools fit the description of "blackboard jungle," where violence and drugs are rampant. Nevertheless, an orderly routine still prevails in most schools. (Alex Thio, *Sociology*)
   What is the topic?
   _____ a. Two-career families

_____ b.  Violence and drugs

__7__ c.  Custodial care of children in schools

*The best choice of topic for this paragraph is "c," the "custodial care of children in schools." This paragraph is about children and schools, but is primarily about the custodial care of children in schools. The increase in two-career families is one of the reasons why more custodial care is needed from schools, but it's not the major topic of this paragraph. Custodial care is mentioned and defined in the first sentence. Sentences 2 and 3 explain this function more completely. The rest of the paragraph gives some history about the role of schools providing custodial care for children.*

What is the main idea?

__MI__ a.  Another major . . . function of schooling is to offer custodial care of children—providing a place to put them and having someone to watch them.

_____ b.  Schools have traditionally been effective in performing their custodial role.

_____ c.  But since the middle of this century a growing number of schools fit the description of blackboard jungle, where violence and drugs are rampant.

*The main idea is expressed in "a," the first sentence of the paragraph. "Another major . . . function of schooling is to offer custodial care of children— providing a place to put them and having someone to watch them." The rest of the paragraph explains this function of schools in more detail and provides some history of it as a school function. Choices two and three above are part of this detail about the history of the school's role in custodial care.*

2.  Learning how to think is a two-step process. First you have to understand how your mind works, its strong points and its limitations. Then you need concrete and immediate advice and exercises that will help you improve your thinking skills. Without the basic understanding, the concrete steps are of limited value. You may find how to do something, but you don't know why, and therefore it will be hard for you to apply the techniques in a variety of situations. But the theory without the practical applications is equally limited. Thinking does not flow from the mere accumulation of facts; it's a skill that takes practice. (Daniel Cohen, *Re: Thinking, How to Succeed by Learning How to Think*)

What is the topic?

_____ a.  Accumulating facts

_____ b.  Strong points and limitations

_____ c.  Learning how to think

What is the main idea?

_____ a.  First you have to understand how your mind works, its strong points and its limitations.

_____ b.  Learning how to think is a two-step process.

_____ c.  Then you need concrete and immediate advice and exercises that will help you improve your thinking skills.

3. Students are also expected to compete with other students in school. They are taught that they must do better than others to receive attention, good grades, and privileges. Those who do not compete, who pursue the activities they enjoy, may fail, be separated from their peer group, and be labeled as slow, hyperactive, disabled, or otherwise deviant. (J. Ross Eshleman, Barbara G. Cashion, and Lawrence A. Basirico, *Sociology*)

    What is the topic?

    _____ a. Students and competition

    _____ b. Separation from the peer group

    _____ c. Deviant behavior in schools

    What is the main idea?

    _____ a. Those who do not compete well are slow thinkers.

    _____ b. Students are also expected to compete with other students in school.

    _____ c. Competing for attention, good grades, and privileges.

4. I am suggesting that we must reach for a higher standard to prepare kids to think for themselves and to think globally. And we must do this at a time when many parents and educators are seeking to lower standards because they have lost faith in our schools and our children. The key does not lie in setting up minimum standards or moderate standards or even stringently high standards. Instead, the key obviously lies in setting up proper incentives, where the principals and the teachers are told the higher the performance of your students, the higher your own rewards will be. Thus, they are always striving to meet a higher, not a minimum standard. And then, when they attain the standard, they will want to strive to achieve still higher goals. (Louis Harris, "2001: The World Our Students Will Enter")

    What is the topic?

    _____ a. Global thinking

    _____ b. Parents and educators

    _____ c. Incentives and higher standards

    What is the main idea?

    _____ a. And we must do this at a time when many parents and educators are seeking to lower standards because they have lost faith in our schools and our children.

    _____ b. The key does not lie in setting up minimum standards or moderate standards or even stringently high standards.

    _____ c. Instead, the key obviously lies in setting up proper incentives, where the principals and the teachers are told the higher the performance of your students, the higher your own rewards will be.

5. The dropout rate in American high schools is still more than 25 percent, even though the relationship between education and future earnings is widely publicized. Industries predict a lack of well-prepared workers for technical jobs in the future. American students perform poorly in math and science achievement tests compared to students in other industrialized nations. All of

these factors cause many people to be concerned about education and the strength of the American economy in the years to come.

What is the topic?

_____ a. Concerns about American education

_____ b. High school dropouts

_____ c. Technical knowledge

What is the main idea?

_____ a. The dropout rate in American high schools is still more than 25 percent, even though the relationship between education and future earnings is widely publicized.

_____ b. Industries predict a lack of well-prepared workers for technical jobs in the future.

_____ c. All of these factors cause many people to be concerned about education and the strength of the American economy in the years to come.

6. There is a saying in the American culture that "you are never too old to learn." Increasingly, one sees older and younger people studying together in American institutions of higher learning. Women are encouraged to gain new skills to be able to enter the job market after their children are grown. Other people change careers, which often requires additional education. Institutions are attempting to meet the diverse needs and goals of these students. (Deena R. Levine and Mara B. Adelman, *Beyond Language*)

What is the topic?

_____ a. Sayings in American culture

_____ b. Diverse ages among college students

_____ c. Women and the job market

What is the main idea?

_____ a. There is a saying in the American culture that "you are never too old to learn."

_____ b. Increasingly, one sees older and younger people studying together in American institutions of higher learning.

_____ c. Women are encouraged to gain new skills to be able to enter the job market after their children are grown.

• • • • • • • • • • • • •

# Organizing to Learn

## Marking Main Ideas in Your Text

• • • • • • • • • • • • • • • • • • • • • • • • • • • • • • • • • • • • •

In Chapter 2 you learned that effective readers *organize* (O in the PRO system) what they have learned after they read. One popular way students do this is simply to *mark* the important points in the text itself. Now that you know how to identify main ideas, you can begin to mark them in the material you read. There are different ways to mark texts; many students use a highlighter. Be careful not to mark too much because then everything will look important when you come back to review. Begin by underlining the main idea. This will reinforce the main points you have learned and make it easier to review for tests. In Chapters 5 and 6 you will learn how to select important supporting details to mark as well.

Read the following paragraph. Notice that the main idea has been underlined for you.

> <u>International students and immigrants attending schools in the United States can experience multiple "culture shocks."</u> Students from abroad, accustomed to their countries' educational expectations, must adapt to new classroom norms in a foreign educational institution. In some countries, students must humbly obey their teachers' directions and remain absolutely silent during a class. Yet in other cultures, students are allowed to criticize or even contradict their teachers. In one country, a prayer in the classroom may be acceptable, while in another it may be forbidden. Cultural differences as well as the experience of being a newcomer account for some of the adjustment problems that non-native-born students experience. At the same time, a diverse student population on campuses helps some Americans appreciate that there are different habits, customs, and attitudes, and that the "American way" is not the only way. (Deena R. Levine and Mara B. Adelman, *Beyond Language*)

The topic of this paragraph is the culture shock that students face when they attend school in another country. The paragraph provides a number of examples of the kind of differences students encounter. The main idea is best stated in the first sentence which provides an overview of what the paragraph will cover.

## Exercise 5 — Marking Stated Main Ideas

Read each of the following paragraphs and then underline the main idea. The first one has been done for you.

1. <u>The American education system is based on the idea that as many people as possible should have access to as much education as possible.</u> This fact alone distinguishes the U.S. system from most others, since in most others the objective is as much to screen people out as it is to keep them in. The U.S. system has no standardized examinations whose results systematically prevent students from going on to higher levels of study, as the British and many other systems, do. Through secondary and sometimes in post-secondary institutions as well, the American system tries to accommodate students even if their academic aspirations and aptitudes are not high, even if they are physi-

cally (and in some cases mentally) handicapped, and even if their native language is not English. (Gary Althen, *American Ways: A Guide for Foreigners in the United States*)

2. Before the 1960s education in Portugal had long been largely reserved for the rich and, as a consequence, illiteracy was widespread. Since then schools have been made accessible to large masses of children triggering an explosion in enrollment. But school financing remains low. Today, schools are overcrowded, money for books and equipment is scarce, and there is a shortage of teachers. As a result, the levels of student achievement [in Portugal] are among the lowest in Europe. (Alex Thio, *Sociology*)

3. Resistance to change has been the recurrent reaction to creativity throughout the ages. Galileo came close to losing his life when he suggested the sun, not the earth, was the center of the solar system. The inventors of the plow, the umbrella, the automobile, and the airplane were scoffed at, as were the individuals who first advocated using anesthetics during surgery, performing autopsies to determine the cause of death, and extending voting rights to women. Even the ending of child labor, which we now regard as eminently reasonable, was initially scorned: critics called it a Bolshevik attempt to nationalize children. (Vincent Ryan Ruggiero, *The Art of Thinking*)

4. Bilingual and bicultural education at its best does a number of very positive things for our children and for our society. It teaches the children to be proud of themselves and of who they are. It teaches them to be proud of speaking two languages, and that there are advantages to being able to speak two languages. At the same time, these programs must teach children to be completely prepared to succeed in an English-speaking environment. They must not only be able to speak English well, they must be able to read, write, and learn English as they advance through their years of education. Our society benefits because we need citizens who can speak more than one language as we enter the global economy of the twenty-first century. Our children benefit because they will be prepared to be contributing citizens of this country.

5. In Japan, the average class size is 37 while ours is 24. One reason the Japanese can teach 37 students and attain a higher level of performance than here is because there is more respect for the school and the teacher in Japan than is true in this country. Neither the home nor the school would be willing to tolerate or accommodate the disruptions and disciplinary problems that disproportionately occupy the time and attention of our teachers and hinder the average student's opportunity to learn. (David Pierpont Gardner, "If We Stand, They Will Deliver")

6. The expectations we have of our students is also a crucial factor. What message have we been giving our students over the years as their grades have risen and their performance has fallen? As with our children, we do our students no favor by expecting less of them than they are able to give. If we expect much of them, they will give us much in return. If we stand, they will deliver. If we expect little

of them they will have contempt both for what we are asking them to do and, in the end, for us. (David Pierpont Gardner, "If We Stand, They Will Deliver")

# STATED MAIN IDEAS IN LONGER PARAGRAPHS

## Longer Paragraphs

Identifying topics and main ideas in longer paragraphs and passages requires the same skills as finding them in shorter pieces. Don't be intimidated by a paragraph simply because it is long. For example, read the following paragraph and determine the topic and the main idea.

The history of American education after about 1870 reflects the impact of social and economic change. Although Horace Mann, Henry Barnard, and others had laid the foundations for state-supported school systems, most of these systems became compulsory only after the Civil War, when the growth of cities provided the concentration of population and financial resources necessary for economical mass education. In the 1860s about half the children in the country were getting some formal education, but this did not mean that half the children were attending school at any one time. Sessions were short, especially in rural areas, and many teachers were poorly trained. President Calvin Coolidge noted in his autobiography that the one-room school he attended in rural Vermont in the 1880s was open only in slack seasons when the twenty-odd students were not needed in the fields. "Few, if any, of my teachers reached the standard now required," he wrote, adding that his own younger sister had obtained a teaching certificate and actually taught a class when she was only 12. (John Garraty, *The American Nation,* 8th ed.)

What is the topic?
*The topic is "American education" or "the history of American education." The topic was introduced in the very first sentence and was repeated in many ways—school systems, mass education, formal education—throughout the rest of the paragraph. Various dates are included—about 1870, in the 1860s, in the 1880s—to emphasize the focus on the history of education.*
What is the main idea?
*The main idea is stated in the very first sentence: "The history of American education after about 1870 reflects the impact of social and economic change." The rest of the paragraph continues with examples and explanations of the social and economic changes at this time and discusses their impact.*

**Exercise 6    Identifying Topics and Main Ideas**

Read the following longer paragraph and then identify the topic and the main idea. Remember the topic can be identified in just a few words, but the main idea needs to be stated as a complete sentence.

Aside from the differences in the quality of the schools, achievement is also affected by the expectations the teachers have for their students. There is considerable evidence that if teachers expect less from . . . students both in terms of academic achievement and behavior, for some students those expectations become a self-fulfilling prophecy. Robert Rosenthal and Lenore Jacobson performed an interesting experiment to demonstrate this. Experimenters gave a standard IQ test to pupils in 18 classrooms in a neighborhood elementary school. However, teachers were told that the instrument was the "Harvard Test of Inflected Acquisition" (which does not exist). Next, the experimenters arbitrarily selected 20 percent of the students' names and told their teachers that the test showed that these students would make remarkable progress in the coming year. When the students were retested eight months later, those who had been singled out as intellectual bloomers showed a significantly greater increase in IQ than the others. As you might expect, these findings created quite a controversy when they were first published, and many similar studies have since been made. Most of them supported Rosenthal and Jacobson's findings, but some did not, and it is not yet clear under exactly what conditions teachers' expectations are most likely to become a self-fulfilling prophecy. (J. W. Coleman and D. R. Cressey, *Social Problems*)

What is the topic? _____

What is the main idea? _____

_____

_____

## STATED MAIN IDEAS IN SHORT ESSAYS

Short essays are generally organized around a single main idea. You'll usually find that main idea close to the beginning of the essay, but it could be at the end. The main idea of an essay is also called the *thesis statement*. Sections of textbooks often have a few paragraphs grouped together explaining a concept, and sometimes each paragraph does not have a main idea, but the ideas are joined by a main idea at the beginning, or even the end, of the section. For example, read the following excerpt from a textbook; it tells you about the different ways students may be asked to participate actively in their learning in college classrooms. Notice how the separate paragraphs are unified by an overall main idea.

### *Active Participation*

DEENA R. LEVINE AND MARA B. ADELMAN

1        Student participation in the classroom is not only accepted but also expected in most subjects. Some instructors and professors base part of the student's grade on oral participation. Courses are

often organized around classroom discussions, student questions, and informal lectures, although large classes can involve formal lectures during which the student has a passive role.

In a small percentage of the more informal classes, students may even decide the topics for study and choose appropriate books and articles. . . . In some courses (mainly graduate seminars), the teacher has only a managerial role and the students do the actual teaching through discussions and presentations. It is common for instructors to guide students to take the initiative and to be responsible for their learning. Especially students pursuing advanced degrees are expected to be actively involved in their own education. They must be ready to critique theories, formulate models, and interact with the professor. Students who do not ask questions and do not bring up their own ideas may appear to be uninterested in the course. `2`

**dominating** controlling

**contradict** disagree with, openly deny

A professor's teaching style is another factor that determines the degree and type of student participation. Some instructors and professors prefer to guide the class without dominating it. Many encourage students to question and challenge their ideas. Students who contradict teachers must be prepared to defend their positions. In general, confident and experienced instructors do not object to students who disagree with them. `3`

Instruction in science and mathematics is usually more traditional, with teachers presenting formal lectures and students taking notes. However, the educational trends that have influenced the teaching of the humanities and social sciences have also affected mathematics and the "hard sciences." Students may be asked to solve problems in groups or to design projects. Classes that are considered applied rather than theoretical stress such "hands-on" involvement. `4`

*The topic of this excerpt is student participation or student participation in the classroom. The first sentence seems to state the main idea, or thesis, for the entire article: "Student participation in the classroom is not only accepted but also expected in most subjects." The paragraphs that follow explain how a college student might be expected to participate in small class discussions and later in graduate seminars. The last two paragraphs give more information about how two other factors—professor's teaching style and the approaches of different disciplines, such as science and mathematics—affect the amount of student participation that is expected.*

## Exercise **7** Identifying Topics and Main Ideas

Read the following longer excerpts and then answer the questions that follow. Look for the topic and the overall main idea that unifies the whole piece.

Write the topic and main idea on the lines provided. Remember, the topic is usually stated in just a few words and the main idea is written as a complete sentence.

1. For quite a while now educators have simply assumed that all you had to do was go to school, and if you absorbed a lot of information, somehow you would automatically learn to think. That assumption has turned out to be quite wrong, and the problems spawned by that false assumption are now being felt.

   In New York City, for example, there was great concern over a decline in reading test scores. The decline was considered a scandal and became a political issue, so a massive effort was made to improve reading scores. And the effort paid off, for test scores did improve. But while reading scores were going up, the ability to reason—to think—was going down. Learning to read and learning to think are not the same thing.

   A recent Rockefeller Foundation report recommends that training in thinking be among the basic skills taught by all schools. The report recognizes the fact that thinking is a skill that can be learned. It is not something that grows inevitably out of the accumulation of facts. And anyone can learn to be a better thinker.

   Thinking is not just an activity for the classroom or for the hours you put in at work. It is something that you must do all the time. The only question is whether you will do it well or poorly. If you can improve your thinking skills—and *anybody* can—it will help you improve in every part of your life.

   Start learning How to Think right now. (Daniel Cohen, *Re: Thinking, How to Succeed by Learning How to Think*)

   What is the topic? _____

   What is the overall main idea? _____

   _____

2. In classrooms across the country, there are children who come to school each morning after spending the night in barracks-type shelters. All too often, instead of spending their evenings doing homework, they've had to keep a watchful eye on drug abusers, street criminals, or former mental patients living alongside them. Frequently separated from other family members, wearing clothing that may make them targets of ridicule, and denied a decent breakfast—thanks to shelter policies that rigidly schedule meals without regard to school opening times—these youngsters may be too busy keeping body and soul together to learn the lessons, the sports, and the social skills that we are trying to teach.

   According to the Children's Defense Fund, these youngsters are among the estimated 50,000 to 500,000 homeless children, many of whom are of school age. The National Conference of Mayors estimated that in 1988 the demand for shelter by families increased by 22 percent after increasing 32 percent in 1987.

   The increasing number of homeless children means schools will have to become more responsive to their special needs. This will mean rethinking certain bureaucratic rules—for example, homeless children often have been denied admission to school because their parents were unable to produce the coin of the realm: the necessary birth certificates, guardianship papers, and immunization records. School attendance may also be foreclosed by lack of money for transportation to a school no longer nearby, for school supplies, and for adequate clothing. Schools may also have to get involved in providing or coordinating such special services as health care, counseling services, and before- and after-school care, and special tutoring programs—services that benefit the non-homeless as well. (Karen Chenoweth and Cathy Free, "Homeless Children Come to School")

What is the topic? _____

What is the main idea? (It is not at the beginning.) _____

_____

_____

## *Broaden Your Perspective*

### Vincent Ryan Ruggiero

*The following excerpt is taken from a college critical thinking textbook. In it, the author explains how it is important for you to be able to understand the world and yourself in many different ways. He explains that you should not be limited by others' expectations of you; your individual potential is "undoubtedly much greater than you have ever realized."*

Do you know the story of the six blind men and the elephant? 1
Able to rely only on their sense of touch, they reached out and touched an elephant to learn about it. One touched its side and decided that an elephant was like a wall. The second touched its trunk and decided—a snake. The third, its tail—a rope; the fourth, its ear—a fan; the fifth, its leg—a tree; the last, its tusk—a spear. Now each had a clear picture of the elephant in mind. But because all the pictures were based on a limited perspective, all were wrong.

All too often we are like the six blind men in our perspective 2
on the world. We see narrowly, and our thinking suffers as a result. The first and perhaps saddest way we are victimized by narrow perspectives is in our view of our own potential. Most of us never come to know ourselves fully. We see only what we are and never realize the larger part of us: *what we have the capacity to be.* We never appreciate just how much of what we are is the result of accident.

Our development, for example, and our degree of success are 3
strongly influenced by the way others regard us. In one experiment,

**regard** look at

researchers administered an intelligence test to an entire elementary school. The researchers told the faculty that the test would identify students who were ready to undergo a "learning spurt." Actually, the test did no such thing: The testers merely selected some students at random and identified them as the ones whose learning would enjoy a spurt. Teachers were subsequently observed using the same materials and methods for these students as for others. Nevertheless, at the end of the year, when the researchers again tested the student body, they found that the students that had been singled out had gained twice as many IQ points as the other students.

**at random** without order or reason

4    What was responsible for this gain? Obviously the teachers had formed favorable attitudes toward these students and unconsciously transmitted their attitudes to the students. The students' self-images, in turn, were ultimately changed.

**transmitted** communicated

5    If that experiment seems surprising, the following one, similar in its design will seem astounding. Laboratory assistants were assigned the task of teaching rats to run a maze. They were told the rats were in two groups, fast learners and slow learners. Actually, all the rats were identical. After the test period, the rats that had been designated fast learners were found to have learned the maze better than the other rats. Like the schoolteachers, the lab assistants had formed preconceived notions about the rats, and those notions had not only affected the degree of patience and the amount of attention and encouragement the assistants displayed with the rats but also actually influenced the rats' performance.

6    Studies show that confused, defeatist, helpless reactions are not inborn in us. They are *learned.* In one study people were given problems they were told could be solved but which in fact could not be. As their efforts to solve the problems failed, the subjects experienced increasing frustration, until they finally accepted their helplessness and gave up. The real point of the study, though, came later. When the same people were given solvable problems, they continued to act helpless and to give up without really trying.

7    What do these studies suggest about everyday life? That parents who are inconsistent in their demands and unpredictable in their rections, teachers who focus on the negative rather than the positive, and coaches and activity leaders who ignore actual performance or contribution can rob us of our confidence, lead us into the habit of failure, and blind us to our real potential.

8    One of the distinguishing marks of many successful people is their refusal to define themselves by other people's assessments. Winston Churchill was branded a slow learner. Martha Graham was told that she did not have the right kind of body to become a dancer. Thomas Edison was urged to quit school because he was considered hopelessly stupid. Later, on his first job, working for the

railroad, he set a train on fire with one of his experiments and was dismissed. And Albert Einstein's early record was even worse. Here are some of the details:

- He was not only an unimpressive student; he was told flatly by one teacher, "You will never amount to anything."
- At age 15 he was asked to leave school.
- When he took his first entrance exam to Zurich Polytechnic School, he failed it and was required to spend a year in a Swiss high school before he could be admitted.
- At Zurich he did mediocre work and was so unimpressive to his professors that he was rejected as a postgraduate assistant and denied a recommendation for employment.
- He eventually obtained a job as tutor at a boarding school but was soon fired.
- He submitted a thesis on thermodynamics for a doctoral degree at Zurich. The thesis was rejected.

"Wait," you may be saying, "Churchill, Graham, Edison, and 9 Einstein were very special people. The question is whether the average person can overcome negative assessments." The answer is yes. To cite just one example, a teacher noticed that when students saw themselves as stupid in a particular subject, they unconsciously conformed to that image. They believed they were stupid, so they behaved stupidly. He set about to change their self-image. And when that change occurred, they no longer behaved stupidly.

The lesson here is not that legitimate criticism or advice 10 should be ignored, nor that one can achieve competency in any field merely by belief. It is that you should not sell yourself short; your potential is undoubtedly much greater than you have ever realized. So when you catch yourself saying, "I'll never be able to do this" or "I don't have the talent to do that," remember that the past does not dictate the future. What people call talent is often nothing more than knowing the knack. And *that* can be learned.

**dictate** deter-
mine, decide

**Exercise 8**    **Checking Your Understanding**

1. Why does the author begin the selection with the story of the six blind men and the elephant? What is the point that he wants the story to make? *(Para. 1 and 2)*
2. What happened when researchers at an elementary school identified some students as "spurters"? *(Para. 3)*
3. What does the author think was the reason for the students' gains in the elementary school experiment? *(Para. 4)*
4. What does the author mean when he says: "confused, defeatist, helpless reactions are not inborn in us. They are *learned.*" *(Para. 6)*

5. Who are four people that refused to "define themselves by other people's assessments"? *(Para. 8)*

| Exercise **9** | **Identifying Main Ideas** |

1. Which of the following statements do you think best identifies the main idea, or thesis statement, of this entire passage?
   _____ a.  Do you know the story of the six blind men and the elephant?
   _____ b.  You should not sell yourself short; your potential is undoubtedly much greater than you have ever realized.
   _____ c.  Churchill, Graham, Edison, and Einstein were very special people.
2. Which of the following statements is the main idea of paragraph 3?
   _____ a.  The testers merely selected some students at random and identified them as the ones whose learning would enjoy a spurt.
   _____ b.  Our development . . . and our degree of success are strongly influenced by the way others regard us.
   _____ c.  In one experiment, researchers administered an intelligence test to an entire elementary school.
3. Which of the following statements is the main idea of paragraph 8?
   _____ a.  One of the distinguishing marks of many successful people is their refusal to define themselves by other people's assessments.
   _____ b.  Winston Churchill was branded a slow learner.
   _____ c.  Albert Einstein's early record was even worse.

| Exercise **10** | **Making Connections** |

1. Why do you think that the author of this excerpt gave so much information about Einstein's failure as a child and young man?
2. Have you ever had a teacher who really believed in you? How did you respond to his or her expectations?
3. Did you ever have a teacher you think may have underestimated your potential? How did you respond to his or her expectations?

# Working with Words
## Understanding Words in Context

When you first encounter a word that you don't understand, don't immediately go to the dictionary because very often the meaning of the word is explained in the reading itself. Sometimes the actual definition will be given in the reading. Other times explanations in the reading itself will tell you enough information to give you a pretty good idea of what the word means. Look at the following examples and see if you can figure out what the underlined words mean by reading what comes before and after the word.

In some cases the definition is provided:

- Between commas
- After the words *is* or *means*
- In parentheses
- Between dashes

> *Example:* Another major but latent function of schooling is to offer *custodial* care of children—providing a place to put them and having someone to watch them.

The definition of *custodial care* is provided after the dash (—): "providing a place to put them and having someone to watch them."

> *Example:* [A] growing number of schools fit the description of *"blackboard jungle,"* where violence and drugs are rampant.

In this sentence, the explanation for *blackboard jungle* was provided after the comma (,): schools "where violence and drugs are rampant."

In some cases, you can understand the new word because an example or further explanation is given:

> *Example:* Your biggest thinking problem, and mine, and everybody's, is that our thinking becomes *rigid*. We respond to new situations and new problems with the same old ideas. Our thinking falls into a well-worn pattern—a rut.

What does being *rigid* mean? It means staying with "old ideas" and "well-worn pattern[s]," in other words staying in a "rut."

Exercise **11**    **Understanding Words in Context**

Read the sentences below and guess the meaning of the *italicized* words by looking to see if the definition itself is in the reading or if you can find explanations or examples that give you enough clues to guess the meaning. Write what you think the meaning is and the clues you used for your guess on the lines provided.

1. To some critics of the 1960s, the schools were *repressive* organizations that
   *resembled* (looked like) boot camps: teachers were obsessed with rules and
   regulations, and students were forced to obey without question.
   *repressive*
   Meaning: _____
   Clues you used: _____

   _____

   *resembled*
   Meaning: _____
   Clues you used: _____

   _____

2. *Resistance to change* is the tendency to reject new ideas and new ways of seeing or doing without examining them fairly.
   *resistance to change*
   Meaning: _____
   Clues you used: _____

   _____

3. Do you know the story of the six blind men and the elephant? Able to rely
   only on their sense of touch, they reached out and touched an elephant to
   learn about it. One touched its side and decided that an elephant was like a
   wall. The second touched its trunk and decided—a snake. The third, its
   tail—a rope; the fourth, its ear—a fan; the fifth, its leg—a tree; the last, its
   tusk—a spear. Now each had a clear picture of the elephant in mind. But
   because all the pictures were based on a limited *perspective*, all were
   wrong.
   *perspective*
   Meaning: _____
   Clues you used: _____

   _____

4. Often our expectations for students or their expectations for themselves can
   become a *self-fulfilling prophecy* because very often students will do as well
   as we expect them to do. Students' and teachers' expectations can set a student up to succeed or fail.
   *self-fulfilling prophecy*
   Meaning: _____
   Clues you used: _____

   _____

## LANGUAGE TIP

### *Following Directions*

Most people, no matter how much education they have, have difficulty following directions. For some reason we all think we understand what we're supposed to do before we carefully listen to or read directions. For example, how often have you filled out a form incorrectly only because you didn't take your time? How often have you answered a test question incorrectly because you didn't take the time to read the questions carefully, to be sure you understood before leaping on to the next step of actually writing? Let's see how well you follow directions now.

### Exercise **12**   Following Directions

Carefully follow all of the directions below. Be sure to read *all* the directions (1–7) before you do anything.

1. On a separate piece of paper, write your name in the top right corner.
2. Under your name, write today's date.
3. Put a circle around the date.
4. In the bottom right corner, write your birthday.
5. In the middle of the paper, draw a square.
6. Inside the square draw 5 zeros.
7. *Don't do any of the things listed in numbers 1–6.* Just sit and fold your hands on your desk.

How did you do following the directions? Congratulations if you read all the way to number 7 before you began to do anything!

# Applying Your Skills

## *In Praise of the F Word*

MARY SHERRY

*The following essay by Mary Sherry suggests a different approach for motivating students: a "healthy fear of failure." As you read look for main ideas and think about whether you agree or disagree with Sherry's suggestions.*

### Preparing to Read

1. Do you think that students get passing grades when they don't deserve them? Explain.
2. Do you think that students would do better if teachers were more strict about grades and flunked students more often? Explain.

1    Tens of thousands of 18-year-olds will graduate this year and be handed meaningless diplomas. These diplomas won't look any different from those awarded their luckier classmates. Their validity will be questioned only when their employers discover that these graduates are semiliterate.

**semiliterate** only able to read in a very limited way

2    Eventually a fortunate few will find their way into educational-repair shops—adult-literacy programs, such as the one where I teach basic grammar and writing. There, high-school graduates and high-school dropouts pursuing graduate-equivalency certificates will learn the skills they should have learned in school. They will also discover they have been cheated by our educational system.

3    As I teach, I learn a lot about our schools. Early in each session I ask my students to write about an unpleasant experience they had in school. No writers' block here! "I wish someone would have had made me stop doing drugs and made me study." "I liked to party and no one seemed to care." "I was a good kid and didn't cause any trouble, so they just passed me along even though I didn't read well and couldn't write." And so on.

I am your basic do-gooder, and prior to teaching this class I blamed the poor academic skills our kids have today on drugs, divorce and other impediments to concentration necessary for doing well in school. But, as I rediscover each time I walk into the classroom, before a teacher can expect students to concentrate, he has to get their attention, no matter what distractions may be at hand. There are many ways to do this, and they have much to do with teaching style. However, if style alone won't do it, there is another way to show who holds the winning hand in the classroom. That is to reveal the trump card of failure. 4

I will never forget a teacher who played that card to get the attention of one of my children. Our youngest, a world-class charmer, did little to develop his intellectual talents but always got by. Until Mrs. Stifter. 5

Our son was a high-school senior when he had her for English. "He sits in the back of the room talking to his friends," she told me. "Why don't you move him to the front row?" I urged, believing the embarrassment would get him to settle down. Mrs. Stifter looked at me steely-eyed over her glasses. "I don't move seniors," she said. "I flunk them." I was flustered. Our son's academic life flashed before my eyes. No teacher had ever threatened him with that before. I regained my composure and managed to say that I thought she was right. By the time I got home I was feeling pretty good about this. It was a radical approach for these times, but, well, why not? "She's going to flunk you," I told my son. I did not discuss it any further. Suddenly English became a priority in his life. He finished out the semester with an A. 6

I know one example doesn't make a case, but at night I see a parade of students who are angry and resentful for having been passed along until they could no longer even pretend to keep up. Of average intelligence or better, they eventually quit school, concluding they were too dumb to finish. "I should have been held back," is a comment I hear frequently. Even sadder are those students who are high-school graduates who say to me after a few weeks of class, "I don't know how I ever got a high-school diploma." 7

Passing students who have not mastered the work cheats them and the employers who expect graduates to have basic skills. We excuse this dishonest behavior by saying kids can't learn if they come from terrible environments. No one seems to stop to think that—no matter what environments they come from—most kids don't put school first on their list unless they perceive something is at stake. They'd rather be sailing. 8

Many students I see at night could give expert testimony on unemployment, chemical dependency, abusive relationships. In spite of these difficulties, they have decided to make education a pri- 9 ority. They are motivated by the desire for a better job or the need to hang on to the one they've got. They have a healthy fear of failure.

10      People of all ages can rise above their problems, but they need to have a reason to do so. Young people generally don't have the maturity to value education in the same way my adult students value it. But fear of failure, whether economic or academic, can motivate both.

11      Flunking as a regular policy has just as much merit today as it did two generations ago. We must review the threat of flunking and see it as it really is—a positive teaching tool. It is an expression of confidence by both teachers and parents that the students have the ability to learn the material presented to them. However, making it work again would take a dedicated, caring conspiracy between teachers and parents. It would mean facing the tough reality that passing kids who haven't learned the material—while it might save them grief for the short term—dooms them to long-term illiteracy. It would mean that teachers would have to follow through on their threats, and parents would have to stand behind them, knowing their children's best interests are indeed at stake. This means no more doing Scott's assignments for him because he might fail. No more passing Jodi because she's such a nice kid.

12      This is a policy that worked in the past and can work today. A wise teacher, with the support of his parents, gave our son the opportunity to succeed—or fail. It's time we return this choice to all students.

## Exercise **13**      Checking Your Understanding

Choose the best answer for each of the multiple choice questions.

1.  Why are some high school graduates' diplomas meaningless?
    _____ a.  Because teachers pass students who can't or wouldn't do the work.
    _____ b.  Because a policy that worked in the past can work today.
    _____ c.  Because flunking students is a useful tool to motivate them.
2.  How does Sherry suggest teachers get the attention of students who can't concentrate?
    _____ a.  Be a basic do-gooder.
    _____ b.  Teaching style alone will be enough of a motivator.
    _____ c.  Use effective teaching style and threaten failure.
3.  What effect does passing students who aren't qualified have on them?
    _____ a.  They become motivated.
    _____ b.  They'd rather be sailing.
    _____ c.  They and their employers feel cheated.

4. Overall, what is Sherry's main idea in this reading?

_____ a. The threat of flunking should be seen as a positive teaching tool.

_____ b. Students with meaningless diplomas are fortunate to go to adult literacy classes at night.

_____ c. It has been proven that people of all ages can rise above their problems.

**Exercise 14** **Vocabulary: Words in Context**

Based on the context clues in the essay, write the meaning of each of the *italicized* words below. If you need more information about the context for the words, go back to the paragraphs where they are located in the essay. The paragraph number is written at the end of each item.

1. Eventually a fortunate few will find their way into educational-repair shops—adult-*literacy programs*, such as the one where I teach basic grammar and writing. *(Para. 2)*

   *literacy programs:* _____

2. I am your basic do-gooder, and prior to teaching this class I blamed the poor academic skills our kids have today on drugs, divorce and other *impediments* to concentration necessary for doing well in school. *(Para. 4)*

   *impediments:* _____

3. Flunking as a regular policy has just as much *merit* today as it did two generations ago. We must review the threat of flunking and see it as it really is—a positive teaching tool. *(Para. 11)*

   *merit:* _____

4. It is an expression of confidence by both teachers and parents that the students have the ability to learn the material presented to them. However, making it work again would take a dedicated, caring *conspiracy* between teachers and parents. . . . It would mean that teachers would have to follow through on their threats, and parents would have to stand behind them, knowing their children's best interests are indeed at stake. *(Para. 12)*

   *conspiracy:* _____

**Exercise 15** **Making Connections**

1. Have you ever observed that people were positively motivated by the fear of failure? Give specific examples to support your answer.

2. Do you think you are sometimes motivated by fear of failure? Explain your answer.

3. What are some alternative methods of motivation that you think are more powerful than fear of failure?
4. How do you think Sherry's ideas (pages 89–91) about motivating people are different from Ruggiero's ideas (pages 82–84)?

**Exercise 16    Organizing to Learn**

Refer back to the article by Sherry (pages 89–91). Underline the main idea in each of the paragraphs indicated below.

1. Paragraph 3
2. Paragraph 8
3. Paragraph 11

## Chapter Review

**Exercise 17    Skills Review**

1. Explain how to identify a *topic* in a paragraph or longer reading.
2. Explain how to identify *main ideas* in a paragraph or longer reading.

**Exercise 18    Writing**

Explain in a paragraph how you like to be motivated. What things help you to be motivated to learn?

**Exercise 19    Collaborative Activity**

Brainstorm in a group. Have someone record all of the ways a teacher can help motivate students to learn. Then create a chart using your motivational approaches. On the left, list each method of motivation. On the right, list what the group thinks the outcomes, or results, would be of this method. Consider that some methods would offer rewards and positive reinforcements, while others would emphasize negative consequences for failure.

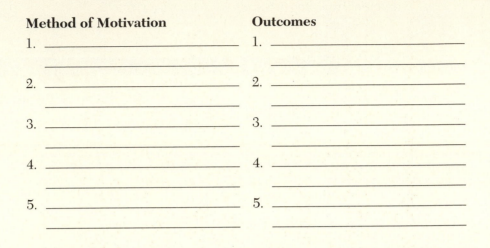

**Method of Motivation**          **Outcomes**

1. _____          1. _____
   _____             _____

2. _____          2. _____
   _____             _____

3. _____          3. _____
   _____             _____

4. _____          4. _____
   _____             _____

5. _____          5. _____
   _____             _____

**Exercise 20**    **Extension Activity**

What kinds of problems exist in your local high school or grade school? Find an article or other source of information about these problems. You might use any of the following:

- Article in a local newspaper or magazine
- Local Web site on the computer
- Local TV or radio news report
- Interview with high school students, parents, or school staff

Share the information you gather with your class group.

# Challenges in Education

## UNSTATED MAIN IDEAS

## IDENTIFYING UNSTATED MAIN IDEAS

In Chapter 3 you identified main ideas that were stated directly in the paragraph or passage. However, as a reader you will find that main ideas are not always so obvious. Sometimes the main idea is not stated at all, and you are expected to arrive at the main point that the writer is trying to make based on the information you are given. Follow these three steps to choose the main idea:

- Identify the topic
- List the main points made about the topic
- Add up the points listed above to arrive at the main idea

For example, read the following paragraph and see if you can decide what the unstated main idea is.

> Forty percent of Finns aged 24 to 65 have a college degree compared with 12 percent in the United States. Understandably, Finns are, per capita, the greatest consumers of literature in the world. School attendance is compulsory up to age 16, an earlier age than in Belgium, but schooling is rigorous. High school students attend classes 38 hours a week, compared with about 25 hours in the United States. Finnish students are also required to take more courses, including two foreign languages. All higher education is free, with most financial support coming from the state and the rest from private industries (Peltonen, 1993). (Alex Thio, *Sociology*)

The topic is "education in Finland." List the main points made about the topic:

- *40 percent of Finns have college degrees versus 12 percent in the United States*
- *Finns consume the most literature (read the most) in the world*
- *Schooling is rigorous (very demanding)*
- *High school students are in class 38 hours a week versus 25 in the United States*
- *Finns take more courses, including two foreign languages*
- *All higher education is free*

Add up the points listed above to arrive at the main idea:

When you combine all the points about education in Finland you might conclude that the main idea is "Finland has an outstanding educational system."

## Choosing the Main Idea

Sometimes authors seem to state more than one main idea within a single paragraph. Sometimes the ideas even contradict each other. As you read you must think actively about the ideas presented. If you are asked to identify the main idea in a paragraph where there appears to be more than one, your statement of the main idea may need to include both ideas. For example, read the following paragraph about the Japanese educational system.

> The Japanese youngsters' academic excellence cannot be attributed to the schools alone. Japanese mothers play a crucial role in their children's education, not only constantly encouraging hard work but also rendering help with homework. After-school classes, called jukus ("cram shops"), also contribute substantially, as they are attended by more than one-quarter of all primary pupils and more than one-half of all secondary students. Since so many students are involved in this supplementary learning, Francis McKenna concludes that the quality of Japanese schooling is actually lower than popularly believed. (Alex Thio, *Sociology*)

Which of the following sentences is the better statement of the main idea of this paragraph?

_____ 1. The success of Japanese students may be due to the time they spend studying outside of school rather than to the quality of the schools themselves.

_____ 2. Afterschool classes are the main reason why Japanese students are so successful academically.

*You should have chosen sentence 1 as the better statement of the main idea for this paragraph. Sentence 2 emphasizes the contribution of extra hours to Japanese students' success, but the paragraph as a whole does not try to prove that this is the main reason, or the only reason, for their success. Also, this statement does not include the doubts raised in the last sentence of the paragraph about the quality of regular Japanese schools.*

**Exercise 1**     **Identifying Unstated Main Ideas**

For each of the following paragraphs, choose the sentence that is the better statement of the paragraph's main idea.

1. The public schools, supported by public funds, have the responsibility to teach skills needed in public life—among them the use of the English language. They also must inculcate an appreciation of all the cultures that have contributed to this country's complex social weave. To set one ethnic group apart as more worthy of attention than others is unjust, and might breed resentment against that group. (Barbara Mujica, "Bilingualism's Goal")

____a. All cultures need to be appreciated by the schools and all students need to be given a good education which includes English.

____b. Special treatment of one ethnic group is not fair and causes resentments.

2. [His students'] life stories were amazing, and Crowfoot alone had heard every one. He struck up a conversation with a chunky kid in the front row and found himself listening to the dreams of a Salvadoran boy who hoped someday to become a cop. He complimented the artwork of the student who couldn't seem to shut up in class and found himself the confidant of a frustrated adolescent whose Guatemalan mother so feared the lure of gangs that she wouldn't let him out of the house. Someone stuck a wad of chewing gum into the hair of a tattooed class bully and, as he leaned forward to help remove it, he found himself unexpectedly moved by the gleam of hot tears welling in the boy's eyes. (Shawn Hubler, "Fledgling Teacher Gets Tough Lessons, Unexpected Rewards")

____a. There were a lot of students in Crowfoot's class.

____b. Crowfoot learned a lot about his students, and sometimes they did not fit the ideas that he had about them before he knew them better.

3. There has been phenomenal growth in the number of children who receive their formal education at home. Today there are about 500,000 such children, compared with only 12,500 in the late 1970s. Most of the home schooling parents are fundamentalist Christians who believe that religion is either abused or ignored in the public school. Other parents reject public education because of poor academic standards, overcrowding, or lack of safety. Most homeschooling parents have some college, with median incomes between $35,000 and $50,000. Over 90 percent are white. (From Alex Thio, *Sociology*)

____a. More parents are choosing homeschooling for their children, and they are doing so for a variety of reasons.

____b. Parents often reject public education because of the problems they observe there: poor academic standards, overcrowding, and lack of safety.

4. On a cloudy winter afternoon, Florann Greenberg, a teacher at P.S. 14 in New York City, noticed that her first-grade class was growing fidgety. One girl, dropping all pretense of work, stared at the snow falling outside the

schoolroom windows. Annoyed, Greenberg asked her, "Haven't you seen snow before?" The girl whispered, "No." Her classmates began shaking their heads. Then it dawned on Greenberg: of course these children had never seen snow; almost all were immigrants from Colombia and the Dominican Republic. Immediately, she changed the lesson plan. New topic: What is snow? How is it formed? How do you dress in the snow? What games do you play? (Paul Gray, "Teach Your Children Well")

_____ a. Many children have never seen snow and are surprised and fascinated when they see it in New York City for the first time.

_____ b. Teachers like Florann Greenberg need to recognize the diversity of their students' experience and to plan lessons accordingly.

5. Younger students sometimes have emotional problems in their educational environment. The stress of taking exams and of meeting deadlines can cause difficulty for those not used to responsibility and intense work. On the other hand, older students with children or with experience in jobs or the military adapt to pressure and stress more easily. A student who is also the parent of three children, for example, knows that grades, exams, and reports are not the most important aspects of life. Older students are also less likely to be intimidated by instructors or professors. (Deena R. Levine and Mara B. Adelman, *Beyond Language*)

_____ a. Younger students sometimes have emotional problems in their educational environment.

_____ b. Older students are likely to handle the stress of being a student better than young students.

## Writing Main Idea Sentences

When you identify an unstated main idea, you may need to write that idea in your own words. To do so, first you need to identify the topic of the reading and then you need to include that topic in the main idea statement. For example, read the following paragraph.

Among the students in continuing education programs are blue-collar workers seeking a promotion, a raise, or a new career; homemakers preparing to enter the job market at middle age; retired people seeking to pursue interests postponed or dormant during their working years; and people who want to enrich the quality of their personal, family and social lives. Most of these adults are serious students, as 60 percent are enrolled in a degree program. (Alex Thio, *Sociology*)

What Is the Topic?
*The topic is "adults returning to school" or, more specifically, "reasons why adults return to school."*
What Is the Main Idea?
*Because the main idea is not stated in this paragraph, you need to write it in a complete sentence of your own. Be sure to include the words you chose as the topic of the paragraph in your main idea statement. The main idea, as you remember, is simply a general statement, or assertion, the writer wants to make*

*about the topic. Your main idea for this paragraph might be worded like this: "Adults return to college for many different reasons."*

---

## LANGUAGE TIP

### Complete Sentences

When you are asked to write the main idea for a paragraph or for a longer piece you've read, be sure you write that idea as a complete sentence. A complete sentence is a subject/verb combination that can stand on its own. For example, the following group of words is a complete sentence: "I arrived at school early." It has a subject, "I," and a verb, "arrived," and it is a complete thought that makes sense by itself. However, if we change this group of words and say, "If I arrive at school early," "I" is the subject, and "arrive" is the verb, but this group of words is still not a complete sentence. The word *If* at the beginning sets up a condition that isn't completed in the sentence. It's not a complete thought, so it's not a sentence. The sentence would be complete if it were worded something like this: "If I arrive at school early, I will have time to review my work." Likewise, "Men riding in a car" and "Because he doesn't like anchovies" are groups of words that do not form a complete sentence. They would be sentences if they were worded something like this: "Three men were riding to work in the car," and "James won't eat the pizza because he doesn't like anchovies."

### Exercise **2**   Identifying Complete Sentences

Decide whether each of the following statements is a complete sentence or not. Write "C" on the blank before each complete sentence and "I" before an incomplete sentence. If your answer is "I," rewrite the words so that they are a complete sentence. The first one has been done for you.

___*I*___ 1. People who want to enrich the quality of their personal, family, and social lives. *This statement is incomplete. It has a subject "people" and it appears to have a verb "want," but the idea is still incomplete because the word "who" inserts another subject. To complete this idea, the writer might have said, "People who want to enrich the quality of their personal, family, and social lives often re-*

*(continued)*

*turn to college after many years." For another example of how this clause might be included in a complete sentence, find those words in the paragraph on page 98.*

_____ 2. How Matthew earned a degree in mathematics.

_____ 3. After the final exam was over.

_____ 4. The graduation ceremony was conducted with a great deal of dignity.

_____ 5. If you want to complete a B.A. degree in only four years.

_____ 6. Who continue to study after high school than in any other country.

# Organizing to Learn
## Working in Groups

One of the most beneficial ways for many people to organize what they've learned involves working in groups. If you already know that you learn best by discussing what you've read with other people or completing tasks—such as answering questions, organizing ideas graphically, or reviewing for a test—with a friend or two, working in groups may be a strategy that you want to use regularly to improve your understanding and ensure that you remember what you've learned. Many people find working in groups an excellent learning and studying technique. Researchers have identified a number of things that help small groups to be more effective, whether they are working together at school or at work. The following selection summarizes that advice.

### Participating in Small Groups

*As you read this article, notice that some paragraphs have a stated main idea and some do not. You will be asked to write some of the unstated main ideas in your own words.*

_____

### Preparing to Read

1. What experiences do you have working in small groups?
2. What are the advantages and disadvantages of working in groups in your classes?

1    Learning to work with other people is one of the most important skills you can develop for your college career and for your lifetime of work. More and more often, students are required to work with their peers—other students in the class—to carry out a variety of tasks. In any of your classes, you may be asked to discuss an article together, or to review information provided in a lecture. You may even be asked to do a project together or to write a paper together for which you will be graded as a group! Working collaboratively with other people will also be a skill that is required of you in your lifetime of work.

2    There are many advantages to working with other people because several minds are better than one. At the same time, there can be disadvantages if the group doesn't work well together.

3    Experts who write about small-group communication agree on certain guidelines, or rules, that are important for members of small groups to follow. First of all, *the members of the group must be motivated to do their best for their group.* So, it is important that everyone be prepared to contribute as much as they possibly can.

4    The two types of roles that all members of the group must play are: (1) task roles, and (2) supportive roles. *Task roles* are the responsibilities that group members have in order to work together and achieve their goal. *Supportive roles* are the things you need to do to make sure the people in your group can get along with each other and work well together.

5    The two types of roles that you play overlap: You may be doing both types at one time. For example, a group member might say, "That's a good idea. I think we should write it down as part of our answer." This person is helping the group carry out its assignment ("we should write it down as part of our answer"). And he or she is also being supportive of the other members of the group ("that's a good idea").

## Task Roles

6    If you perform the following functional and task roles, you and your group will benefit.

**functional** useful

7    1. Your group should decide on the steps you will follow to accomplish the assignment. If you are asked for the causes of a certain problem, concentrate on the causes. Don't allow yourselves to start talking about what might have happened if something had been different.

8    2. You need to be an active member of the group. Contribute as much as you can, but be brief and concise. Don't dominate your group by speaking more than everyone else or insisting that all

of your ideas be used. Make sure that everyone has an opportunity to talk.

**clarify** make clear

3.  By asking questions you can be sure that you are all understanding the discussion in the same way. You might clarify your understanding by making questions like: "I think that the author is saying that it helps children if they learn how to read in their first language before they try to learn how to read in a language that they don't understand. Do you think that was his point?" In this way, you both clarify what the author was saying, and you find out if your group needs to discuss the idea more before you all agree.  9

4.  Be a leader when your group needs it. Don't expect one member of the group to make all the decisions. All members of the group can be a leader at different times. No one person has all the answers. That's why you are working in a group.  10

## Supportive Roles

There are six maintenance and supportive roles that you should keep in mind when you are working in a group.  11

1.  All of us are different. Each member of your group will have his own personality and his own areas of strengths. Members of your group may also come from different cultural backgrounds. Show respect for everyone in your group.  12

2.  Even if everything that you say is polite, members of your group will also understand your body language. If you frown or make faces, or look at the ceiling when someone is talking, that person will understand that you disapprove or you are not interested in what he is saying.  13

3.  Your feedback should be clear. You should give verbal and nonverbal responses when your group members are talking. You can make friendly gestures like smiling or nodding your head so they know you are alert. You can also show that you are interested in what they are saying by interjecting supportive sounds ("uh-huh," "I see what you're saying.").  14

4.  Keep a positive and constructive atmosphere. Tell members of your group when they do something well. Encourage each other. Especially encourage the members of the group who do not speak up as much. They may be just as prepared and they may have something valuable to say, but you won't know if you don't give them a chance by encouraging their participation.  15

5.  Communication is a two-way process. Both the listener and the speaker are responsible. Listeners need to be alert and ask questions if they are unclear about what the speaker is trying to communicate. If there is someone in the group who disagrees with  16

everyone else, make every effort to understand that person's point of view.

6. You may at times need to (a) seek other people's opinions, (b) help the group decide what to do next, (c) help the group stop and evaluate its progress, (d) recognize when members of the group are close to agreement, and (e) help keep the group spirit up. (Adapted from Larry Samovar, *Oral Communication: Speaking Across Cultures*)    17

---

**Exercise 3** | **Writing the Main Idea in Your Own Words**

Write a main idea statement in your own words for each of the following paragraphs from the article above. The main idea may or may not be stated. In either case write the main idea in your own words so that the meaning of the paragraph is easier to understand. The first one has been done for you.

1. Paragraph 8

   The main idea is: *Be an active member of your group but be sure that everyone else has a chance to contribute as well.*

   *(When you add up the main points, you realize that the paragraph tells you to participate actively, but don't dominate the group: let everyone talk.)*

2. Paragraph 9
   The main idea is: _____
   _____

3. Paragraph 12
   The main idea is: _____
   _____

4. Paragraph 13
   The main idea is: _____
   _____

5. Paragraph 17
   The main idea is: _____
   _____

---

**Exercise 4** | **Checking Your Understanding/Collaborative Activity**

With your class group, review your answers to the above exercise. Choose the best main idea sentences.

| Exercise **5** | Making Connections/Collaborative Activity |

Based on the above reading, write three ways that you think you can improve the way your class groups function. Your suggestions can be for yourself, for members of your group, or for your group as a whole. Remember to keep your comments positive. Discuss your suggestions with your group.

## UNSTATED MAIN IDEAS IN LONGER PASSAGES

Identifying unstated main ideas in longer readings can appear challenging, but you will find it easier if you apply the same skills you used for shorter pieces.

- First, determine the topic of the reading.
- Second, ask yourself, "What is the point the writer is trying to make about the topic?" Add up all the significant information in the reading about the topic.
- Third, try to state that information in one carefully thought-out sentence. This sentence won't include all the specific details, but it will be a general statement that covers the main points.

### The Most Important Day (Helen Keller, The Story of My Life)

HELEN KELLER

*This is a short excerpt from Helen Keller's autobiography,* The Story of My Life. *When Keller was 18 months old, she became seriously ill and lost both her eyesight and her hearing. This part of her story tells about some important events in her life 5½ years later, just before she turned 7 years old. Keller considered this day "the most important day I remember in all my life." Read this piece to see what event happened that day to change her life and, consequently, the days and years that followed.*

**dumb** silent

On the afternoon of that eventful day, I stood on the porch,   1 dumb, expectant. I guessed vaguely from my mother's signs and from the hurrying to and fro in the house that something unusual was about to happen, so I went to the door and waited on the steps.

The afternoon sun penetrated the mass of honeysuckle that covered the porch and fell on my upturned face. My fingers lingered almost unconsciously on the familiar leaves and blossoms which had just come forth to greet the sweet southern spring. I did not know what the future held of marvel or surprise for me. Anger and bitterness had preyed upon me continually for weeks and a deep languor had succeeded this passionate struggle.

2    Have you ever been at sea in a dense fog, when it seemed as if a tangible white darkness shut you in, and the great ship, tense and anxious, groped her way toward the shore with plummet and sounding-line, and you waited with beating heart for something to happen? I was like that ship before my education began, only I was without compass or sounding-line, and had no way of knowing how near the harbor was. "Light! give me light!" was the wordless cry of my soul, and the light of love shone on me in that very hour.

3    I felt approaching footsteps. I stretched out my hand as I supposed to my mother. Someone took it, and I was caught up and held close in the arms of her who had come to reveal all things to me, and, more than all things else, to love me.

**reveal** show

4    The morning after my teacher came she led me into her room and gave me a doll. The little blind children at the Perkins Institution had sent it and Laura Bridgman had dressed it; but I did not know this until afterward. When I had played with it a little while, Miss Sullivan slowly spelled into my hand the word "d-o-l-l." I was at once interested in this finger play and tried to imitate it. When I finally succeeded in making the letters correctly I was flushed with childish pleasure and pride. Running downstairs to my mother I held up my hand and made the letters for doll. I did not know that I was spelling a word or even that words existed; I was simply making my fingers go in monkeylike imitation. In the days that followed I learned to spell in this uncomprehending way a great many words, among them *pin, hat, cup* and a few verbs like *sit, stand* and *walk.* But my teacher had been with me several weeks before I understood that everything has a name.

5    One day, while I was playing with my new doll, Miss Sullivan put my big rag doll into my lap also, spelled "d-o-l-l" and tried to make me understand that "d-o-l-l" applied to both. Earlier in the day we had had a tussle over the words "m-u-g" and "w-a-t-e-r." Miss Sullivan had tried to impress it upon me that "M-u-g" is *mug* and that "w-a-t-e-r" is *water,* but I persisted in confounding the two. In despair she had dropped the subject for the time, only to renew it at the first opportunity. I became impatient at her repeated attempts and, seizing the new doll, I dashed it upon the floor. I was keenly delighted when I felt the fragments of the broken doll at my feet. Neither sorrow nor regret followed my passionate outburst. I

**confounding** confusing

had not loved the doll. In the still, dark world in which I lived there was no strong sentiment or tenderness. I felt my teacher sweep the fragments to one side of the hearth, and I had a sense of satisfaction that the cause of my discomfort was removed. She brought me my hat, and I knew I was going out into the warm sunshine. This thought, if a wordless sensation may be called a thought, made me hop and skip with pleasure.

**sensation** feeling

We walked down the path to the well-house, attracted by the fragrance of the honeysuckle with which it was covered. Some one was drawing water and my teacher placed my hand under the spout. As the cool stream gushed over one hand she spelled into the other the word *water,* first slowly, then rapidly. I stood still, my whole attention fixed upon the motions of her fingers. Suddenly I felt a misty consciousness as of something forgotten—a thrill of returning thought; and somehow the mystery of language was revealed to me. I knew then that "w-a-t-e-r" meant the wonderful cool something that was flowing over my hand. The living word awakened my soul, gave it light, hope, joy, set it free! There were barriers still, it is true, but barriers that could in time be swept away. 6

I left the well-house eager to learn. Everything had a name, and each name gave birth to a new thought. As we returned to the house every object which I touched seemed to quiver with life. That was because I saw everything with the strange, new sight that had come to me. On entering the door I remembered the doll I had broken. I felt my way to the hearth and picked up the pieces. I tried vainly to put them together. Then my eyes filled with tears; for I realized what I had done, and for the first time I felt repentance and sorrow. 7

**repentence** regret

I learned a great many new words that day. I do not remember what they all were; but I do know that *mother, father, sister, teacher* were among them—words that were to make the world blossom for me, "like Aaron's rod, with flowers." It would have been difficult to find a happier child than I was as I lay in my crib at the close of that eventful day and lived over the joys it had brought me, and for the first time longed for a new day to come. 8

## Exercise **6**    Checking Your Understanding

1. What is the topic of this excerpt?
   *You probably identified the topic as "an important event in Keller's life."*
2. List three or more important points (things that happened to Keller).
   *You might have identified events such as a light came into her life; she understood that everything has a name; through "w-a-t-e-r" the mystery of lan-*

*guage was revealed to her; she became eager to learn; she began to enjoy life and "for the first time longed for a new day to come."*

3. Try to add up these significant events in one sentence that expresses the main idea.

   *Helen Keller herself stated her main idea in the paragraph that introduced this excerpt. (We didn't include that paragraph so that you could "discover" her main idea on your own.) Keller wrote, "The most important day I remember in all my life is the one on which my teacher, Anne Mansfield Sullivan, came to me." Certainly all the events that you listed above were a result of that momentous event in her life. They support the main idea that Keller stated in her introductory paragraph.*

## A Third of the Nation Cannot Read These Words

JONATHAN KOZOL

*In the following short passage Jonathan Kozol does not state his main idea. He begins by telling a story about a man who cannot read. The author wants to give the reader a chance to come to some of his or her own conclusions. Many times writers leave their main idea unstated to challenge their readers to think critically about the information presented.*

1    He is meticulous and well-defended.

2    He gets up in the morning, showers, shaves, and dresses in a dark gray business suit, then goes downstairs and buys a New York *Times* from the small newsstand on the corner of his street. Folding it neatly, he goes into the subway and arrives at work at 9 A.M.

3    He places the folded New York *Times* next to the briefcase on his desk and sets to work on graphic illustrations for the advertising copy that is handed to him by the editor who is his boss.

4    "Run over this with me. Just make sure I get the gist of what you really want."

5    The editor, unsuspecting, takes this as a reasonable request. In the process of expanding on his copy, he recites the language of the text: a language that is instantly imprinted on the illustrator's mind.

6    At lunch he grabs the folded copy of the New York *Times,* carries it with him to a coffee shop, places it beside his plate, eats a sandwich, drinks a beer, and soon heads back to work.

**meticulous** very neat

At 5 P.M., he takes his briefcase and his New York *Times,* waits 7 for the elevator, walks two blocks to catch an uptown bus, stops at a corner store to buy some groceries, then goes upstairs. He carefully unfolds his New York *Times.* He places it with mechanical precision on a pile of several other recent copies of the New York *Times.* There they will remain until, when two or three more copies have been added, he will take all but the one most recent and consign them to the trash . . . .

Then he returns upstairs. He opens the refrigerator, snaps the 8 top from a cold can of Miller's beer, and turns on the TV.

Next day, trimly dressed and cleanly shaven, he will buy another New York *Times,* fold it neatly, and proceed to work. He is a **solitary** lonely rather solitary man. People in his office view him with respect as someone who is self-contained and does not choose to join in casual conversation. If somebody should mention something that is in the news, he will give a dry, sardonic answer based upon the information he has garnered from TV.

He is protected against the outside world. Someday he will 10 probably be trapped. It has happened before; so he can guess that it **humiliation** em-barrassment will happen again. Defended for now against humiliation, he is not defended against fear. He tells me that he has recurrent dreams.

"Somebody says: WHAT DOES THIS MEAN? I stare at the page. A 11 thousand copies of the New York *Times* run past me on a giant screen. Even before I am awake, I start to scream."

If it is of any comfort to this man, he should know that he is 12 not alone. Twenty-five million American adults cannot read the poison warnings on a can of pesticide, a letter from their child's teacher, or the front page of a daily paper. An additional 35 million read only at a level which is less than equal to the full survival needs of our society.

**Exercise 7** | **Discussion Questions**

1. What is the man in this reading afraid of?
2. Why does he carry the *New York Times* around with him all the time?
3. What are his bad dreams about?

**Exercise 8** | **Making Connections**

1. Have you ever been afraid that someone will find out that you don't know how to do something that they expect you to know? Explain what happened.

2. Are there any services in your community that work to help adults learn to read? List them.
3. Have you ever helped an adult (or a child) learn to read? Explain how you helped.

---

**Exercise 9**     **Writing the Main Idea in Your Own Words**

Follow these three steps to help you arrive at the main idea for this passage. Suggested answers have been provided.

1. What is the topic? *People who can't read.*

2. List the main points made about the topic.
- *People who can't read have to be careful to keep their inability to read a secret;*
- *they make believe they read things (e.g., carry The New York Times newspaper around all the time);*
- *they get people at work who can read to explain things to them orally (like the editor);*
- *they watch TV to learn what's going on;*
- *they have nightmares about someone discovering their secret;*
- *the man in the story is not alone: 25 million American adults have trouble reading.*

3. Write the main idea in your own words (be sure that you write it as a complete sentence).

*It is difficult, and even painful, to have to hide the fact that you can't read.*

---

## The Best Teacher in America

A. JEROME JEWLER AND JOHN N. GARDNER

*The following excerpt is about Jaime Escalante, the math teacher who was made famous by the movie about his accomplishments,* Stand and Deliver.

## Preparing to Read

1. Who was your favorite teacher? Why did you like this teacher so much?
2. What qualities make a good teacher?

Jaime Alfonso Escalante Gutierrez was born in 1930 in Bolivia   1
and was educated in La Paz. Although he describes himself as "a
somewhat undisciplined young man," he nevertheless excelled in
school and went on to a teacher training college because his family
could not afford to send him to engineering school. For twelve
years as a high school teacher in La Paz, he gained a reputation for
excellence, creating a team of science students that consistently
won city-wide science contests.

In 1963 he and his family emigrated to the United States.   2
Barred from teaching because he did not hold a U.S. degree, he
worked as a cook and at other jobs while slowly earning night
school credits at California State University, Los Angeles. After ten
years, in 1974, he was finally hired to teach basic mathematics at
**predominantly**  Garfield High School, a predominantly Hispanic barrio school in
mostly  East Los Angeles.

In 1978 he began teaching an advanced placement (AP) calcu-   3
lus course. Four years later, when all eighteen of his students
passed the AP examination for college calculus (seven with perfect
scores), the Educational Testing Service, which administers the
test, concluded that some of his students had copied their answers
and forced twelve of them to retake the test. All twelve passed a
second time. With this incident, Escalante's program drew local,
state, and national attention, including the dramatization of the
story in the 1988 film *Stand and Deliver.* By 1988–89 over 200 students were enrolled in the AP calculus program.

Jaime Escalante believes that motivation is the key to learn-   4
ing. Here's what he has to say:

I do not recruit students by reviewing test scores or grades, nor are   5
they necessarily among the "gifted" or on some kind of "high IQ
**criterion** reason  track." . . . My sole criterion for acceptance in this program is that the
student wants to be a part of it and sincerely wants to learn math. I
tell my students, "The only thing you need to have for my program—
and you must bring it every day—is *ganas* [desire, or will to suc-
ceed]." If motivated properly, any student can learn mathematics. . . .

From the beginning, I cast the teacher in the role of the "coach"   6
and the students in the role of the "team." I made sure they knew that
we were all working together. . . .

I often break the students into groups to solve lecture prob-   7
lems. . . . After school, the students almost always work in teams. . . .

The film *Stand and Deliver* was based on the true story of Jaime Escalante's successes as a teacher in East Los Angeles.

8      The key to my success . . . is a very simple time-honored tradition: hard work, and lots of it, for teacher and student alike. . . . When students of any race, ethnicity, or economic status are expected to work hard, they will usually rise to the occasion. . . . They rise, or fail, to the level of the expectations of those around them, especially their parents and their teachers.

**status** level

## Exercise **10**  Checking Your Understanding

1. List the things about Escalante's teaching that made him such a special teacher.
2. Why did the authorities think his kids cheated on their advanced placement exam?

## Exercise **11**  Understanding Main Ideas

For each of the following paragraphs, choose the better main idea statement from the two sentences given. The main idea may be stated or unstated in the paragraph.

1. Paragraph 2

   _____a. After immigrating to the United States, Escalante worked hard many years before he got his job as a teacher at Garfield High School.

   _____b. He worked as a cook and at other jobs while slowly earning night school credits at California State University, Los Angeles.

2. Paragraph 3

   _____a. Escalante's program received nationwide attention when his students were accused of cheating on the AP calculus exam, but all passed it again when they had to take it over.

   _____b. In 1978 he began teaching an advanced placement (AP) calculus course.

3. Paragraph 5

   _____a. According to Escalante, any student can learn mathematics if motivated properly.

   _____b. Escalante does not recruit students by reviewing test scores or grades.

4. Paragraphs 6 and 7

   _____a. Escalante has his students work in teams because he feels they study and learn best in groups.

   _____b. Escalante finds it easy to focus student attention on the challenge of the AP test and its rewards of possible college credits.

5. The main idea of the whole article

   _____a. When students of any race, ethnicity, or economic status are expected to work hard, they will usually rise to the occasion.

   _____b. The film *Stand and Deliver* was based on the true story of Jaime Escalante's success as a teacher in East Los Angeles.

---

**Exercise 12**    **Making Connections**

1. Why do you think Escalante's students were so successful?
2. Have you ever had a class that you thought was hard but that you did very well in? How did you do it? What kind of help did you have?

• • • • • • • • • • • •

# Working with Words

## Understanding Words in Context

• • • • • • • • • • • • • • • • • • • • • • • • • • • • • • • • • • • •

### Contrast Clues

Sometimes you can figure out the meaning of a word by understanding what it is *not*. The sentence before or after the unfamiliar word may explain a word that is very different from or even the opposite of it. Some clue words that signal a contrast are:

*not, but, on the other hand, however, despite,* and *although.*

Read the following example and see if you can figure out what *ganas* means based on the contrast clue provided.

According to Escalante, if students have the "ganas" to learn, they will not give up easily to failure.

The word *not* should have been your signal that a contrast was being set up. Students with *ganas* "will *not* give up easily to failure." The opposite of people who give up easily are determined people, so *ganas* must mean "determination" or "desire [to achieve something]."

| **Exercise 13** | **Understanding Words in Context** |

Read the sentences and groups of sentences below and use context clues to identify the meaning of the *italicized* words. Use the three kinds of context clues you have learned so far: (1) definition clues (review on page 86), (2) explanation or example clues (review on page 86), and (3) contrast clues (see above). Then write what you think the meaning is and the clues you used. Your meaning does not have to be exact, just close enough so that you are understanding the sentences correctly. The first word has been done for you.

1. Despite having so many problems at home, motivated and self-confident students usually *excel* in their studies.

   *excel*

   Meaning: *do well*
   Clues you used: *the word "Despite" is a clue that indicates the unexpected. You would expect students with problems at home to have trouble with their studies, but despite indicates that the opposite is probably true.*

2. More and more often, students are required to work with their *peers*—other students in the class—to carry out a variety of tasks.

   *peers*

   Meaning: _____
   Clues you used: _____

3. If you don't raise your hands and ask questions, most teachers will *assume* that you understand.

   *assume*

   Meaning: _____
   Clues you used: _____

4. Experts who write about small-group communication agree on certain *guidelines,* or rules, that are important for members of small groups to follow.

   *guidelines*

       Meaning: _____

       Clues you used: _____

5. Sitting in a classroom and staring at words on a blackboard that were to me as foreign as *Egyptian hieroglyphics* is one of my early recollections of school. The teacher had come up to my desk and bent over, putting her face close to mine. "My name is Mrs. Newman," she said, as if the exaggerated mouthing of her words would make me understand their meaning. I nodded "yes" because I felt that was what she wanted me to do. But she just threw up her hands in despair and touched her fingers to her head to signify to the class I was *dense.* From that day on school became an *ordeal* I was forced to endure.

   *Egyptian hieroglyphics*

       Meaning: _____

       Clues you used: _____

6. *dense*

       Meaning: _____

       Clues you used: _____

7. *ordeal*

       Meaning: _____

       Clues you used: _____

8. After-school classes, called "jukus" (cram shops), also contribute substantially, as they are attended by more than one-quarter of all primary pupils and more than one-half of all secondary students.

   *jukus*

       Meaning: _____

       Clues you used: _____

9. Because the students did not sleep well before the exam, they expected to have *abysmal* scores, however, they did very well on the exam.

   *abysmal*

       Meaning: _____

       Clues you used: _____

## Blowing Up the Tracks

Patricia Kean

*In the following reading, educator Patricia Kean writes about "tracking" in the public schools, the practice of placing students in "ability groups." She begins with a description of two actual seventh-grade classes. Read her account and see what she thinks about tracking. She does not state her thesis, or main idea, at the beginning, but instead waits for you to join her in evaluating what she observed.*

---

## Preparing to Read

1. Were you ever placed in classes on the basis of ability groups? What was your experience like?
2. Do you think that all students of the same level should be grouped together? Or do you think students of mixed levels should be combined in a class?

1    It's morning in New York, and some seventh graders are more equal than others.

2    Class 7–16 files slowly into the room, prodded by hard-faced men whose walkie-talkies crackle with static. A pleasant looking woman shouts over the din, "What's rule number one?" No reply. She writes on the board. "Rule One: Sit down."

3    Rule number two seems to be an unwritten law: Speak slowly. Each of Mrs. H.'s syllables hangs in the air a second longer than necessary. In fact, the entire class seems to be conducted at 16 RPM. Books come out gradually. Kids wander about the room aimlessly. Twelve minutes into class, we settle down and begin to play "O. Henry Jeopardy," a game which requires students to supply one-word answers to questions like: "O. Henry moved from North Carolina to what state—Andy? Find the word on the page."

4    The class takes out a vocabulary sheet. Some of the words they are expected to find difficult include popular, ranch, suitcase, arrested, recipe, tricky, ordinary, humorous, and grand jury.

5    Thirty minutes pass. Bells ring, doors slam.

6    Class 7–1 marches in unescorted, mindful of rule number one. Paperbacks of Poe smack sharply on desks, notebooks rustle, and kids lean forward expectantly, waiting for Mrs. H. to fire the first question. What did we learn about the writer?

7    Hands shoot into the air. Though Edgar Allen Poe ends up sounding a lot like Jerry Lee Lewis—a booze-hound who married his 13-year-old cousin—these kids speak confidently, in paragraphs. Absolutely no looking at the book allowed.

We also have a vocabulary sheet, drawn from "The Tell-Tale 8 Heart," containing words like audacity, dissimulation, sagacity, stealthy, anxiety, derision, agony, and supposition.

As I sit in the back of the classroom watching these two very 9 different groups of seventh graders, my previous life as an English teacher allows me to make an educated guess and a chilling prediction. With the best of intentions, Mrs. H is teaching the first group, otherwise known as the "slow kids," as though they are fourth graders, and the second, the honors group, as though they are high school freshmen. Given the odds of finding a word like "ordinary" on the SAT's, the children of 7–16 have a better chance of standing before a "grand jury" than making it to college.

Tracking, the practice of placing students in "ability groups" 10 based on a host of ill-defined criteria—everything from test scores to behavior to how much of a fuss a mother can be counted on to make—encourages even well-meaning teachers and administrators to turn out generation after generation of self-fulfilling prophecies. "These kids know they're no Einsteins," Mrs. H said of her low-track class when we sat together in the teacher's lounge. "They know they don't read well. This way I can go really slowly with them."

With his grades, however, young Albert would probably be 11 hanging right here with the rest of lunch table 7-16. That's where I discover that while their school may think they're dumb, these kids are anything but stupid. "That teacher," sniffs a pretty girl wearing lots of purple lipstick. "She talks so slow. She thinks we're babies. She takes a year to do anything." "What about the other one?" a girl named Ingrid asks, referring to their once-a-week student teacher. "He comes in and goes like this: Rail (pauses) road. Rail (pauses) road. Like we don't know what a railroad means!" The table breaks up laughing.

Outside the walls of the schools across the country, it's slowly 12 become an open secret that enforced homogeneity benefits no one. The work of researchers like Jeannie Oakes of UCLA and Robert Slavin of Johns Hopkins has proven that tracking does not merely reflect differences—it causes them. Over time, slow kids get slower, while those in the middle and in the so-called "gifted and talented" top tracks fail to gain from isolation. Along the way, the practice re-segregates the nation's schools, dividing the middle from the lower classes, white from black and brown. As the evidence piles up, everyone from the Carnegie Corporation to the National Governors Association has called for change.

. . . Because tracking puts kids in boxes, keeps the lid on, and 13 shifts responsibility for mediocrity and failure away from the schools themselves, there is little incentive to change a nearly century-old tradition. "Research is research," the principal told me that day, "This is practice."

**homogeneity** sameness

**reflect** show

**mediocrity** something of low quality

**Exercise 14** | **Checking Your Understanding**

1. Which of the following statements best describes how Mrs. H. teaches the 7–16 group, the "slow group" of students?
   _____ a. Starts class promptly, teaches material at or above grade level, challenges students to excel
   _____ b. Takes 12 minutes to begin an activity, teaches material at about fourth-grade level, speaks slowly
   _____ c. Spends the entire class focusing on sitting down and other disciplinary activities

2. Which of the following statements best describes how Mrs. H. teaches the 7–1 group, the honors group of students?
   _____ a. Starts class promptly, expects students to be well prepared, teaches material at above grade level
   _____ b. Makes sure students are escorted to the room, emphasizes discipline throughout the lesson
   _____ c. Takes 12 minutes to begin an activity, teaches material at about seventh-grade level, speaks slowly

3. At the 7–16 lunch table students talk about the teacher's approach to their group. Which statement best describes their response to the class?
   _____ a. The students feel challenged by both Mrs. H. and her student teacher.
   _____ b. The students think the student teacher does a much better job of teaching them than Mrs. H. usually does.
   _____ c. They laugh at the teachers' slow speech and comment that they're being treated like "babies."

4. Which of the following statements best reflects the author's attitude toward tracking?
   _____ a. Tracking is very helpful because it reflects the differences between slow and gifted kids.
   _____ b. Tracking does not help either the slow or the gifted students, and it unnecessarily segregates students.
   _____ c. Tracking is secretly endorsed by researchers at UCLA, the Carnegie Corporation, and the National Governors Association.

**Exercise 15** | **Understanding Main Ideas**

For each of the following, choose the sentence that better states the main idea.

1. What is the main idea of paragraph 9?
   _____ a. With the best of intentions, Mrs. H. is teaching the first group, otherwise known as the "slow kids," as though they are fourth graders...

_____b. I sat in the back of the classroom watching these two very different groups of seventh graders and my previous life as an English teacher allowed me to make an educated guess and chilling prediction.

2. What is the main idea of paragraph 10?

_____a. These kids know they're no Einsteins.

_____b. Tracking . . . encourages even well-meaning teachers and administrators to turn out generation after generation of self-fulfilling prophecies.

3. What is the overall main idea of the reading?

_____a. The practice of tracking students does not benefit anyone and it should be stopped.

_____b. Tracking is OK for some students, but it is not so good for others; consequently, it is a necessary part of school programs.

## Exercise **16**  Working with Words

Using context clues decide what each of the following *italicized* words mean in these particular sentences. Write the meaning and the clues you used.

1. Class 7–16 files slowly into the room, prodded by hard-faced men whose walkie-talkies crackle with static. A pleasant looking woman shouts over the *din. . . . (Para. 2)*

   *din*

   Meaning: _____

   Clues you used: _____

2. Paperbacks of Poe smack sharply on desks, notebooks rustle, and kids lean forward *expectantly,* waiting for Mrs. H. to fire the first question. *(Para. 6)*

   *expectantly*

   Meaning: _____

   Clues you used: _____

3. *Tracking,* the practice of placing students in "ability groups" based on a host of *ill-defined* criteria—everything from test scores to behavior to how much fuss a mother can be counted on to make—encourages even well-meaning teachers and administrators to turn out generation after generation of *self-fulfilling prophecies.* "These kids know they're no Einsteins," Mrs. H. said of her low-track class when we sat together in the teacher's lounge. "They know they don't read well. This way I can go really slowly with them." *(Para. 10)*

   *tracking*

   Meaning: _____

   Clues you used: _____

4. Along the way, the practice *resegregates* the nation's schools, dividing the middle from the lower classes, white from black and brown. *(Para. 12)*

   *resegregates*

   Meaning: _____

   Clues you used: _____

5. Though some fashionably progressive schools have begun to reform, tracking *persists*. *(Para. 13)*

   *persists*

   Meaning: _____

   Clues you used: _____

## Exercise **17** Making Connections

1. According to the author, what kinds of effects does tracking have on students? Do you think her conclusions about the effects on students are accurate?
2. Have you ever been in a class of students that was obviously grouped by tracking? What were the advantages? What were the disadvantages?
3. The author suggests that there are a number of reasons why tracking is still used. Do you think that tracking should continue in our schools? Why or why not?

## Exercise **18** Organizing to Learn

Underline the main idea in each of the following paragraphs in the reading on pages 115–116.

1. Paragraph 11.
2. Paragraph 12.

# Chapter Review

## Exercise **19** Skills Review

Answer the following skills review questions individually or in a group.

1. List the three steps for identifying an *unstated* main idea.
2. Read the following excerpt. Then follow the three steps you identified above to arrive at and write an appropriate main idea for this paragraph.

> In a 1990 *Fortune* magazine poll of its list of the 500 largest industrial corporations and the 500 largest service corporations, 98 percent of the companies responding contributed to public education. The principal form of assistance was contributing money (78 percent of the companies). Sizable percentages also provided students with summer jobs (76 percent), contributed materials or equipment to schools (64 percent), participated in school partnerships (48 percent), and encouraged employees to run for school boards (59 percent) or to tutor or teach (50 percent). (Turley Mings, *The Study of Economics: Principles, Concepts, and Applications*)

Main idea: _____

_____

_____

---

**Exercise 20**   **Writing**

In a paragraph identify your strengths when working in a group. Also include ways you think you can *improve* your group participation.

---

**Exercise 21**   **Collaborative Activity**

In your group, list the task and supportive roles for effective groups.

**Task Roles**                          **Supportive Roles**

_____            _____

_____            _____

_____            _____

_____            _____

---

**Exercise 22**   **Extension Activity**

Find an article from a newspaper or magazine that describes someone who has successfully overcome a very difficult educational situation such as Helen Keller or someone from a different country. Clip out the article and share it with your class group.

Write a main idea sentence for your article to share with your class group and to turn in to your instructor. Be sure that your main idea sentence is (1) a complete sentence and (2) a sentence that includes the important points that add up in your article.

● ● ● ● ● ● ● ● ● ● ● ● ● ● ● ● ● ● ● ● ● ● ● ● ● ● ● ● ● ● ● ● ● ● ● ●

## Unit Review

● ● ● ● ● ● ● ● ● ● ● ● ● ● ● ● ● ● ● ● ● ● ● ● ● ● ● ● ● ● ● ● ● ● ● ●

## The Education of Berenice Belizaire

### JOE KLEIN

*The following excerpt from an article by Joe Klein appeared in* Newsweek *in August 1993. In it, he shares the remarkable educational achievements of a young Haitian girl and points out that immigrant students often do very well in American schools even though they have to struggle to learn the language at the beginning. In the second half of the reading, Klein discusses the contributions that immigrants—in particular, Haitian immigrants—have made to American society.*

### Preparing to Read

1. What changes in your life affected your education as you were growing up?
2. Have you ever moved from one state or country to another and changed schools as a result? What kinds of difficulties did you encounter?

1    When Berenice Belizaire arrived in New York from Haiti with her mother and sister in 1987, she was not very happy. She spoke no English. The family had to live in a cramped Brooklyn apartment, a far cry from the comfortable house they'd had in Haiti. Her mother, a nurse, worked long hours. School was torture. Berenice had always been a good student, but now she was learning a new language while enduring constant taunts from the Americans (both black and white). They cursed her in the cafeteria and threw food at her. Someone hit her sister in the head with a book. "Why can't we go home?" Berenice asked her mother.

**a far cry from** very different from

2    Because home was too dangerous. The schools weren't always open anymore, and education—her mother insisted—was the most important thing. Her mother had always pushed her: memorize everything, she ordered. "I have a pretty good memory," Berenice admitted last week. Indeed, the other kids at school began to notice that Berenice always, somehow, knew the answers. "They started coming to me for help," she says. "They never called me a nerd."

Within two years Berenice was speaking English, though not    3
well enough to get into one of New York's elite public high schools.
She had to settle for the neighborhood school, James Madison—
which is one of the magical American places, the alma mater of
Ruth Bader Ginsburg among others, a school with a history of un-
likely success stories. "I didn't realize what we had in Berenice at
first," says math teacher Judith Khan. "She was good at math, but
she was quiet. And the things she didn't know! She applied for a
summer program in Buffalo and asked me how to get there on the
subway. But she always seemed to ask the right questions. She understood the big ideas. She could think on her feet. She could explain difficult problems so the other kids could understand them.
Eventually, I realized: she wasn't just pushing for grades, she was
hungry for *knowledge* . . . And you know, it never occurred to me
that she also was doing it in English and history, all these other
subjects that had to be much tougher for her than math."

She moved from third in her class to first during senior year.    4
She was selected as valedictorian, an honor she almost refused
(still shy, she wouldn't allow her picture in the school's yearbook).
She gave the speech, after some prodding—a modest address
about the importance of hard work and how it's never too late to try
hard: an immigrant's valedictory. Last week I caught up with
Berenice at the Massachusetts Institute of Technology where she
was jump-starting her college career. I asked her what she wanted
to be doing in 10 years: "I want to build a famous computer, like
IBM," she said. "I want my name to be part of it."

Berenice Belizaire's story is remarkable, but not unusual. The    5
New York City schools are bulging with overachieving immigrants.

**burdens** extra
problems

The burdens they place on a creaky, corroded system are often
cited as an argument against liberal immigration policies, but
teachers like Judith Khan don't seem to mind. "They're why I love
teaching in Brooklyn," she says. "They have a drive in them we no
longer seem to have. You see these kids, who aren't prepared academically and can barely speak the language, struggling so hard.
They just sop it up. They're like little sponges. You see Berenice,
who had none of the usual, preconceived racial barriers in her
mind—you see her becoming friendly with the Russian kids, and
learning chess from Po Ching (from Taiwan). It is *so* exciting."

**reinvigorated**
brought back to
life

**Dreamy hothouse:** Indeed, it is possible that immigrant energy    6
reinvigorated not just some schools (and more than a few teachers)—but *the city itself* in the 1980s. "Without them, New York
would have been a smaller place, a poorer place, a lot less vital and
exciting," says Prof. Emanuel Tobier of New York University. They
restored the retail life of the city, starting a raft of small busi-

nesses—and doing the sorts of entry-level, bedpan-emptying jobs that nonimmigrants spurn. They added far more to the local economy than they removed; more important, they reminded enlightened New Yorkers that the city had always worked best as a vast, noisy, dreamy hothouse for the cultivation of new Americans.

7      The Haitians have followed the classic pattern. They have a significantly higher work-force participation rate than the average in New York. They have a lower rate of poverty. They have a higher rate of new-business formation and a lower rate of welfare dependency. Their median household income, at $28,853, is about $1,000 less than the citywide median (but about $1,000 higher than Chinese immigrants, often seen as a "model" minority). They've also developed a traditional network of fraternal societies, newspapers and neighborhoods with solid—extended, rather than nuclear—families.

**Exercise 1    Checking Your Understanding**

1. Why didn't Belizaire like living in the United States at first? *(Para. 1)*

2. Why couldn't Belizaire's family return to Haiti? *(Para. 2)*

3. Why does Judith Khan like to teach in Brooklyn? *(Para. 5)*

4. What does the author mean by "immigrant energy reinvigorated" the schools and the city of New York? *(Para. 6)*

**Exercise 2    Identifying Main Ideas**

Decide which sentence is the better statement of the main idea for each of the following paragraphs.

1. Paragraph 1.
    _____ a. Berenice and her family were not very happy at first living in New York.
    _____ b. She was learning a new language while enduring constant taunts from the Americans.
2. Paragraph 6.
    _____ a. Immigrant energy reinvigorated not just the schools but also the city of New York.
    _____ b. Immigrants started small businesses and did entry-level jobs that nonimmigrants spurn.

Answer the following questions with a complete sentence in your own words.

3. What is the main idea of paragraph 4?
4. What is the main idea of paragraph 5?
5. What is the main idea of the entire article, reading? (Don't forget to add up the important ideas of the whole piece.)

## Exercise 3    Working with Words

Read the following short passages from the article about Belizaire. Guess the meanings of the italicized words from context, then write down the clues you used.

1. Berenice had always been a good student, but now she was learning a new language while enduring constant *taunts* from the Americans (both black and white). They cursed her in the cafeteria and threw food at her.

   *taunts*

   Meaning: _____

   Clues you used: _____

2. She was selected as *valedictorian,* an honor she almost refused.

   *valedictorian*

   Meaning: _____

   Clues you used: _____

3. You see these kids, who aren't prepared academically and can barely speak the language, struggling so hard. They just *sop* it up. They're like little sponges.

   *sop*

   Meaning: _____

   Clues you used: _____

## Exercise 4    Making Connections

1. Why do you think Belizaire was able to do so well despite all the difficult challenges she faced?
2. What do you think other children can learn from the success of students like Belizaire?

**Exercise 5** | **Organizing to Learn**

Underline the main idea statement in each of the following paragraphs from the reading.

1. Paragraph 1
2. Paragraph 7

# UNIT
# 3
# Our Environment

## *Supporting Details*

*If we are going to live so intimately with these chemicals—eating and drinking them, taking them into the very marrow of our bones—we had better know something about their nature and their power.*

**Rachel Carson**

• • • • • • • • • • • •
# Protecting Our Environment
• • • • • • • • • • • • • • • • • • • • • • • • • • • • • • • • • • • • • • •

## *An Ill Wind*
------

NATIONAL GEOGRAPHIC

A cloud of the insecticide DDT billows over the beach—and beachgoers—in 1945 as part of a mosquito-control program at New York's Jones Beach State Park. Used in Europe to ward off bug-borne disease during World War II, DDT was once hailed as a miracle product. The photograph on page 127 was published in the October 1945 GEOGRAPHIC article "Your New World of Tomorrow." But by the time "tomorrow" came, evidence showed that birds from sprayed areas accumulated high levels of DDT, damaging their ability to reproduce. Other research pointed to the chemical as a human carcinogen. Use of DDT was banned in the United States in 1972.

### Preparing to Read

1. Look at the picture on page 127 and read "An Ill Wind." What is being sprayed on the beachgoers at New York's Jones Beach?
2. What do you know about DDT? What was it used for? What are the problems with using it?
3. Do you know of any chemicals that people use today that might cause problems similar to those caused by DDT?
4. What year was this picture taken? How many years did it take to realize that DDT was harmful?
5. Read the quotation under the insert. What does it mean? How does this statement relate to the picture?

## UNIT OBJECTIVES/SKILLS TO LEARN

In this unit you will learn how to

- Recognize supporting details
- Distinguish between major and minor supporting details
- Make an outline
- Write a summary
- Use the dictionary

In the process of acquiring these skills, you will read and use information about

- How human reproduction may be threatened by environmental pollution
- Pollution in our communities
- Solutions to environmental problems

### Key Terms and Concepts

**major supporting details**   additional information about the main idea

**minor supporting details**   more specific additional information about the major supporting details or less important additional information about the main idea

**toxic**   poisonous

**fertility**   the ability to have children

**pesticides**   materials used to kill pests such as insects

**extinct**   no longer in existence

• • • • • • • • • • • • •

# Raising Issues

## Change and the Environment

• • • • • • • • • • • • • • • • • • • • • • • • • • • • • • • • • • • • • • • •

Life for people at the turn of the twentieth century is in most ways easier than it was for our great-grandparents who lived 100 years ago. We have many conveniences today that people at that time would never have even dreamed of—automobiles; airplanes; electricity in just about every home; advances in farming, manufacturing, and health care; and information systems like the home and office computer. But, as we look around us, we can begin to see that many of the advances that people have made in the last century have had a negative impact on our environment.

In Chapters 5 and 6, you will be reading about how people and our advancing technology have affected the environment on Earth. At the same time you will be focusing on recognizing important supporting details and minor supporting details.

### Exposure to Chemicals and Human Fertility

Ruth Markowitz Heifetz, M.D.

*The following reading discusses the effects of chemicals in our environment, such as DDT, on human fertility. Fertility is the ability of men and women to have children. As you read the following article, consider the information carefully. Why is it important for employees to know as much information as possible about the chemicals in their workplace?*

Over 30 years ago, Rachel Carson wrote a book called *Silent* 1
*Spring.* She warned that DDT and other pesticides were killing birds
and other creatures and that the health of human beings was also
being threatened. At that time, the government and the chemical
producers said that DDT was perfectly safe to use on food, in
homes, and on public beaches without any type of warning. Carson
illustrated that the DDT had made the eggshells of birds so fragile
that offsrping could not survive, causing a decline of certain bird
populations.

As a result of Carson's book and the pressure of many citizens, 2
DDT was banned in the United States, although it was and continues to be produced in this country and shipped to countries around
the world. Years after the elimination of the use of DDT many of the
birds, like pelicans, have begun to increase in numbers.

Since the publication of *Silent Spring* many chemicals, espe- 3
cially certain pesticides, solvents and lead, have been identified as
causing problems such as miscarriages, birth defects and infertility
(inability to have children). One dramatic example of a workplace
chemical that caused a number of men to become sterile (unable to
father children) was the pesticide DBCP that was produced in a
chemical plant in Lathrop, California for a number of years, until its
use was banned in 1977. An extremely common substance that has
a variety of similar negative effects is lead, which is still used in
paints, construction, the auto industry and until recently as a component of most gasoline.

An increasing amount of evidence suggests that many of the 4
chemicals of modern industrial society can cause dangerous
changes in the processes that create new life, by interfering with
the chemical messages (hormones) that influence the normal
growth and development of many of the body's organs, including
the sex organs, the brain, the nervous system and the immune system. A number of studies, from many countries including the
United States, France, and Denmark, described the decrease in
sperm counts around the world. One of the reports based on a review of the world's medical literature calculates that there has been
a 50 percent decrease in the sperm counts during the past 40 years.
Not all reports confirm these findings, but at the present time the
multiple findings on decreased sperm counts and the data on increased infertility have convinced most scientists that we have a serious problem that requires careful attention.

In the past, most of the studies on the impact of chemicals on 5
human reproduction were focused on women during pregnancy.
Now we realize that these toxic exposures to men and women may
be just as important before they plan to have children, because the
cells that are in their bodies, sperm forming tissues (men) and eggs

**fragile** delicate
**decline** reduction

**defect[s]** some-
thing wrong

**confirm** agree
with

(women), can be affected. Also, during the early weeks of pregnancy before the mother realizes that she is pregnant, she can be seriously affected by certain chemicals.

6     It is important to know about the chemicals you are working with. You have the *right to know* this information. You should always carefully read the ingredients, directions, and caution statements of any products you use at home. At work, your employer has the responsibility under the Federal Hazard Communication regulation (1) to provide you with information on all the hazardous chemicals you are working with and, (2) to provide you with training concerning their safe use (ventilation, protective equipment you may need to wear, like a respirator). There are specific protective regulations concerning chemicals like lead, where employers must test for the chemical and provide alternative sites for you to work if you are exposed and pregnant or planning to have a child (man or woman). Know your rights and protect yourself and your future ability to have healthy children.

**alternative sites**
other locations

## Exercise 1    Discussion Questions

1. What was the warning that Carson voiced about DDT in her book *Silent Spring*?
2. What happened as a result of Carson's book?
3. What were the effects of the pesticide DBCP, and similar chemicals, on the people who worked with them?
4. Based on their use in the reading, what do you think each of the following words mean?
   a. sterile (para. 3)
   b. hormones (para. 4)
   c. infertility (para. 3)
5. What does the author say you should know about the chemicals in your work environment? What responsibilities does your employer have if you work with toxic chemicals?

## Exercise 2    Making Connections

1. Do you know of any couples that have had problems conceiving a baby?
2. Do you know what chemicals are used in your workplace or in workplaces you are familiar with? What are they?
3. What do you think could happen to the human population in the future if infertility continues to increase? What can we as individuals do to help solve this problem?

# *Our Environment, Our Future*

## MAIN IDEAS AND SUPPORTING DETAILS

In Unit Two you learned to identify main ideas in paragraphs and longer writings. A main idea is usually a general statement, or generalization, that provides an overall understanding of the reading; the supporting details give you additional information and are more specific. You can recognize the relationship between main ideas and supporting details in sentences, paragraphs, and longer readings.

### RECOGNIZING SUPPORTING DETAILS IN SENTENCES

For example, in paragraph 3 on page 130 of the reading "Exposure to Chemicals and Human Fertility," Heifetz is writing about examples of workplace chemicals that have caused problems for human reproduction. In the first sentence of that paragraph the author begins with a general idea (in **boldface**) and then gives more specific details (in *italics*):

Since the publication of *Silent Spring* **many chemicals,** especially some *pesticides, solvents and lead* **have been identified as causing problems** such as *miscarriages, birth defects and infertility.*

The general statement of the sentence is **Many chemicals have been identified as causing problems.** But more detailed, or specific, information is provided for the two key words, **chemicals** and **problems.**

**Chemicals**
The supporting details for chemicals are kinds of chemicals:

    pesticides

    solvents

    leads

**Problems**

The supporting details for problems are the examples of problems:

    miscarriages

    birth defects

    infertility

Another way to picture the relationship between these pieces of information is to use a map.

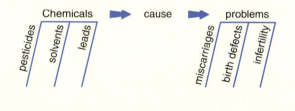

## LANGUAGE TIP

### General and Specific Details

We often call the main idea or the broadest statement of a passage a *general statement*. The details that are given for support or more information are called *specifics*. The more detailed the information, the more specific it is. Let's look at an example from the section "Raising Issues" on page 129.

> We have many conveniences today that people at that time would never have even dreamed of—automobiles; airplanes; electricity in just about every home; advances in farming, manufacturing, and health care; and information systems like the home and office computer.

The *general* statement is: "We have many conveniences today that people at that time would never have even dreamed of." The *specific* information is the lists of conveniences: "automobiles; airplanes; electricity in just about every home; advances in farming, manufacturing, and health care; and information systems like the home and office computer."

*(continued)*

We can organize this information in the following way:

**General statement:** *We have many conveniences today that people at that time would never have even dreamed of.*

**Specific statements:**
- automobiles
- airplanes
- electricity in almost every home
- advances in farming, manufacturing, and health care
- the information systems

**Exercise 3**    **General and Specific**

Read the following paragraphs, and then write down the general and specific statements. Part of the first one has been done for you.

1. Organic compounds are one type of hazardous waste. An organic compound is made of carbon, hydrogen and water; one example is dioxin. (Geoffrey C. Saign, *Green Essentials*)

   **General statement:** *Organic compounds are one type of hazardous waste.*
   **Specific statements:**

   - _____

   - *one example is dioxin* _____

2. Industries produce a wide variety of hazardous wastes (chemicals, toxins, metals, etc.) which are a problem to get rid of. Most of this waste is dumped on the site where it is produced. But some of it is buried in deep holes or encased in special containers. Sometimes, it is burned.

   **General statement:** _____
   **Specific statements:**

   - _____
   - _____
   - _____

# RECOGNIZING SUPPORTING DETAILS IN PARAGRAPHS

In paragraphs you often have the general statement or the main idea in the first few sentences, and then the writer develops the idea with more specific details. The best process for finding important supporting details would be to

- Identify the main idea
- Look for the additional important information about the main idea. These supporting details could be
  - examples
  - additional facts

For example, in the following paragraph from a *Time* article about the drop in human fertility, the main idea is stated in the first sentence. The author explains, "Just what these causes [for the drop in male fertility] might be is still largely a mystery." This statement is very general, but he goes on in the following sentences to tell us what the possible specific causes are. Read the paragraph below and see if you can identify the specific causes.

> Just what these causes might be is still largely a mystery. Stress, smoking and drug use are all known to be involved. So is the fact that men are having children later in life, . . . as well as the increase in sexually transmitted diseases. Even the shift in underwear fashion from boxers to briefs has been offered as an explanation. (Michael D. Lemonick, "What's Wrong with Our Sperm?")

## Exercise 4 — Identifying Supporting Details

List the possible causes for the drop in male fertility identified in the paragraph above. These causes are the important supporting details for the main idea.

1. _____
2. _____
3. _____
4. _____
5. _____
6. _____

*(Your answers should include (1) stress, (2) smoking, (3) drug use, (4) having children later in life, (5) the increase in sexually transmitted diseases, and (6) wearing briefs instead of boxers.)*

| Exercise **5** | **Identifying Supporting Details** |
|---|---|

For each of the following paragraphs (1) write the topic, (2) write the main idea, and (3) list the major supporting points. The first one has been done for you.

1. A number of measures have been taken to eliminate lead from our environment. In 1973, all new cars were required to use only unleaded gasoline. In 1986, that law was amended to make the requirement more rigid, reducing the amount of lead in unleaded gasoline from 2.5 grams per gallon to 0.1 grams per gallon. In 1976, a measure was enacted requiring paint manufacturers to reduce the amount of lead used in their products. Another requirement enacted to control the use of lead was a 1987 ruling requiring public water installations and private buildings to use plastic pipes instead of old lead pipes. (Curtis Byer, *Living Well: Health in Your Hands*)

   Topic: *Eliminating lead from the environment*

   Main idea: *A number of measures have been taken to eliminate lead from our environment.*

   Major supporting details:
   a. *required all new cars to use only unleaded gasoline*
   b. *reduced amount of lead that could be put in any gasoline*
   c. *reduced amount of lead in paint*
   d. *required use of plastic pipes instead of lead pipes*

2. Clean water, pure air, and productive soil are all essential for healthy living. Without clean air the human respiratory defenses against air pollutants can be overwhelmed. The water essential to our existence, if polluted, can become a carrier of disease producing organisms and toxic compounds. Contaminated soil pollutes ground water and reduces or destroys the productivity of the land. The contamination of these resources poses health hazards and limits the supply of these necessary resources. (Curtis Byer, *Living Well: Health in Your Hands*)

   Topic: _____

   Main idea: _____

   Major supporting details:
   a. _____
   b. _____
   c. _____

3. As individuals, we can take steps to reduce water pollution. We should never pour harmful chemicals down house or street drains or flush them down toilets. Waste crankcase oil drained from automobiles should be contained and taken to a nearby service station for recycling. Radiators should be drained away from water supplies. Insecticides, herbicides, paints, lacquers, thinners, and house-

hold cleaners should be disposed of according to instructions from local health or water departments. Reduced use of commercial fertilizers, detergents, and of water itself can help reduce water pollution. What steps are you taking to help reduce water pollution? (Curtis Byer, *Living Well: Health in Your Hands*)

Topic: _____

Main idea: _____

    Major supporting details:

      a. _____

      b. _____

      c. _____

      d. _____

      e. _____

4. The benefits of using chemicals on our lawns are numerous. The chemicals give us an easy way to fertilize lawns with apparently fantastic results. And other chemicals, namely pesticides, kill the pests that can sometimes destroy our lawns.

    Topic: _____

    Main idea: _____

       Major supporting details:

         a. _____

         b. _____

5. We dump too many chemicals on our lawns, and they can have bad effects as well as good ones. We spend about $1.5 billion on chemicals for 30 million acres of lawn. These chemicals kill the good insects, damage the soil, and cause human illness.

    Topic: _____

    Main idea: _____

       Major supporting details:

         a. _____

         b. _____

         c. _____

         d. _____

## *Pesticides*

CURTIS O. BYER

*The following reading from a college health textbook discusses the use of pesticides in food production and its possible negative effects on humans. As you read, notice how the author explains and supports his points with specific details.*

---

**beneficial** good, give benefits

**adversely** negatively

Pesticides are used to control pest organisms and improve crop yields by eliminating pests that attack crops. While pesticides are beneficial in killing these organisms, humans can be adversely affected by exposure to pesticides. In the United States, an estimated 45,000 illnesses and twenty-five deaths occur annually among farm workers using pesticides. The [negative health] effects of herbicide use in Vietnam have become public record.  1

**synthetic** man-made

In 1939, DDT, the first in a long list of synthetic organic pesticides, was developed. Since then, annual pesticide use has increased worldwide to an average of one pound of pesticide for each person on earth. While many of these products are used on plants, 92 percent of all American households use one or more types of pesticides. In fact, according to a study by the EPA, homeowners apply more pesticides per unit of land than do farmers.  2

Since 1972, DDT use has been officially banned in the United States. Yet a 1983 study showed that it is present in many fruits and vegetables. Some of this is due to illegal smuggling of DDT from Mexico; some of it is due to the fact that pesticides can contain up to 15 percent DDT by weight in spite of the 1972 ban.  3

**autopsies** examinations of dead bodies

The long-term effects of pesticides on human health have not been determined. Some pesticides are relatively new and information about effects of exposure are not yet known. Twenty-five different pesticides have been found to cause cancer, especially of the liver, in test animals. Human autopsies show that among victims of cancer, liver cirrhosis, hypertension, and cerebral hemorrhage, levels of DDT or its breakdown products in their bodies is fairly high.  4

---

## Exercise **6**    Checking Your Understanding

1. What are pesticides? _____

2. Write the sentence in paragraph 1 that best states the main idea of the paragraph.

   _____

   _____

3. Which of the following statements is *not* true?

   _____ a.  Most American households use pesticides.

   _____ b.  Pesticides are often dangerous for people.

   _____ c.  Scientists know the effects of all the pesticides that are available.

_____d.  Twenty-five pesticides are known to cause cancer.

_____e.  Long-term effects of pesticides are not yet known.

4.  Write "MI" before the statement that best describes the main idea for paragraph 4. Write "SD" before the statements that are supporting details.

     _____a.  Although scientists don't know all the long term effects of pesticides, they do know that pesticides are often dangerous to people.

     _____b.  Some pesticides are new and we don't know what their long term effects are.

     _____c.  Twenty-five different pesticides have been found to cause cancer, especially of the liver, in test animals.

     _____d.  Human autopsies show that among victims of cancer, liver cirrhosis, hypertension, and cerebral hemorrhage, levels of DDT or its breakdown products in their bodies is fairly high.

## Exercise 7  Identifying and Marking Important Supporting Points

Often, when you are studying a passage in a book, you will underline main ideas and number important supporting details. If you mark your text in this way, it will be easier to locate the important information when you are reviewing or studying for a test. To practice this skill, underline the sentences or parts of sentences from the passage that state the main idea, then number the important supporting details in the following paragraphs. The first one has been done for you.

1.  Pesticides are used to control pest organisms and improve crop yields by eliminating pests that attack crops. While pesticides are beneficial in killing these organisms, <u>humans can be adversely affected by exposure to pesticides.</u>① In the United States, an estimated 45,000 illnesses and twenty-five deaths occur annually among farm workers using pesticides.② The [negative health] effects of herbicide use in Vietnam have become public record.

2.  In 1939, DDT, the first in a long list of synthetic organic pesticides, was developed. Since then, annual pesticide use has increased worldwide to an average of one pound of pesticide for each person on earth. While many of these products are used on plants, 92 percent of all American households use one or more types of pesticides. In fact, according to a study by the EPA, homeowners apply more pesticides per unit of land than do farmers.

3.  Since 1972, DDT use has been officially banned in the United States. Yet a 1983 study showed that it is present in many fruits and vegetables. Some of this is due to illegal smuggling of DDT from Mexico; some of it is due to the fact that pesticides can contain up to 15 percent DDT by weight in spite of the 1972 ban.

4.  The long-term effects of pesticides on human health have not been determined. Some pesticides are relatively new and information about effects of ex-

posure are not yet known. Twenty-five different pesticides have been found to cause cancer, especially of the liver, in test animals. Human autopsies show that among victims of cancer, liver cirrhosis, hypertension, and cerebral hemorrhage, levels of DDT or its breakdown products in their bodies is fairly high.

## Exercise 8    Working with Words

Using the clues in the context of the reading on page 138, define the following words. Be sure to use your own words. The first one has been done for you.

1.  pesticides (para. 1): *chemicals used to kill pests that attack crops*
    *You probably used clues from the first and second sentences: "Pesticides are used to control pest organisms," and "pesticides are beneficial in killing these organisms."*
2.  beneficial (para. 1): _____
3.  adversely (para. 1): _____
4.  DDT (para. 2): _____

## Exercise 9    Making Connections

Where are the fresh fruit and vegetables you eat grown? Do you know whether or not they are sprayed with pesticides?

## LANGUAGE TIP

### Word Forms

Becoming familiar with various word forms can increase your comprehension of what you read, and it can also improve your spelling. Word forms are the shapes and spellings that English words assume as they change functions in a sentence. These different functions may be identified as the eight basic parts of speech. For now, we will look at four of these parts of speech and how they are used:

- Noun—name of a person, place, or thing—for example, woman, city, chemical.
- Verb—a word that shows action or existence (e.g., to be, is, are). All verbs can be written with a "to" in front of them—for example, *to go, to buy, to succeed, to be, to happen.*
- Adjective—a word that describes nouns. For example, in the sentence "It is a *hazardous* chemical," *hazardous* describes chemical.

- Adverb—a word that describes a verb or an adjective. For example, in the sentence "He plays *carelessly*," *carelessly* describes *how* he plays (*plays* is the verb in the sentence).

Notice how the meaning and form of the word *success* change in each of the following sentences.

1. The graduation party was a big *success*. (noun)
2. The graduation party was the most *successful* event this year. (*adjective*—it describes the party)
3. He *successfully* prepared all the food for the party. (*adverb*—it describes how he prepared)
4. They *succeeded* in doing everything they wanted to do. (verb in the past tense)

Notice that the word *success* has a noun form as well as verb, adverb, and adjective forms. Many words go through transformations like this as they change function. Recognizing these changes allows you to understand a word that looks unfamiliar at first. You know the meaning of the base word, *success*, so you have no trouble understanding its forms.

**Exercise 10**     **Understanding Language: Word Forms**

List below the other forms of the word that is given. Use your dictionary if you need help. Not all words may have a form in each part of speech. The forms of "nature" have been filled in for you. (In a couple of cases there is no adverb form of the word, so *"none"* has been printed in that column.)

| Noun | Verb | Adjective | Adverb |
|---|---|---|---|
| *nature, naturalist* | *naturalize* | *natural* | *naturally* |
| | *pollute* | | *none* |
| | | *respiratory* | |
| *explosion* | | | |
| | | | *hazardously* |
| | *elaborate* | | |
| | | *contaminated* | *none* |

• • • • • • • • • • • • •

# Working with Words
## Dictionary Skills

When you come across words while reading that you do not know, it is important to decide a few things before you look them up in the dictionary. To determine whether you should look a word up in the dictionary or the glossary of your book, ask yourself these questions:

• Do you need to know the exact meaning of the word to understand the reading?
• Is the word important? Will it be necessary to remember that word because it is key to understanding the subject?
• Have you tried to figure out the meaning of the word from the context but are still unsure about the meaning?

If you answered "yes" to these questions, then go to the dictionary.

### Parts of a Dictionary Entry

Let's say you read a few sentences that are similar to those on the opening page of this unit (page 127):

> Evidence showed that birds from areas where high levels of DDT had accumulated were unable to reproduce as well as birds from other areas. Other research pointed to DDT as a human *carcinogen.* Use of DDT was *banned* in the United States in 1972.

The words we want to focus on are *carcinogen* and *banned.* When you look carcinogen up in the dictionary (American Heritage Paperback), you will find the following entry. Notice that the dictionary entry gives you some very specific information:

• Pronunciation (in parentheses after the word)
• Part of speech (after each form given for the word)
• Definition
• Other forms of the word
• History of the word (in brackets after the first definition)

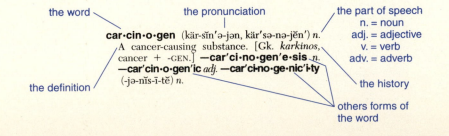

| Exercise **11** | **Working with Words** |
|---|---|

Looking at the dictionary entry, answer the following questions.

1. What does *carcinogen* mean?
2. What part of speech is *carcinogen*?
3. How many additional forms of the word *carcinogen* are in this dictionary entry?
4. What is the adjective form of *carcinogen*?

## Finding Your Word

Now, look at the dictionary entry you would find for *banned*. Notice that many times in the English language when you look in the dictionary for a word you will not find it exactly as it was written in your reading because there are many forms for the same word; *banned* is one example. To find it in the dictionary, you must look under *ban*. Read the following dictionary entry.

**ban**[1] (băn) *v.* banned, ban-ning. To prohibit, esp. officially. —*n.* A prohibition imposed by law or official decree. [< OE *bannan,* to summon, and < ON *banna,* to prohibit.]

| Exercise **12** | **Working with Words** |
|---|---|

1. What does *banned* mean?
2. What parts of speech can *ban* be?
3. What two other forms of the verb *ban* does the dictionary give?

## Organizing to Learn
### Outlining

When you are reading information that includes a lot of details, it is helpful to organize that information in some way so it will be easier to understand. Making an outline is one good method. Outlines provide you with a visual framework for studying and remembering information. To set up your outline, first identify the main ideas and supporting details for those ideas. For example, as you read the following passage pay particular attention to (1) the main idea and (2) important supporting points. Notice that the supporting details in this article are the three cities that have environmental problems. The details about the cities tell us what the problems are and the results of those problems.

## Toxins in Our Backyards

*Are there any areas of your city or county with a lot of industries that pollute the environment with toxic chemicals? Where are they located? As you read the following article, try to determine the main problem of each of these communities.*

---

Many of the production and disposal facilities of toxic materials—and their possible disastrous consequences—are located in or near our local communities. Texas City, Texas, Baton Rouge, Louisiana, and Chicago, Illinois are three examples of American communities that are now facing some of the severe consequences of toxic pollution.  1

**severe** very serious

### Texas City, Texas

Texas City is home to a part of a group of petroleum and chemical plants that surrounds Houston. These industries dump millions of tons of wastewater into Galveston Bay. The waters are so polluted that fishermen are not allowed to take shrimp from the bay. But, many families who live near the bay in Galveston County rely on seafood for much of their diet and among these people, there has been an unusually high number of cases of mental retardation and learning disabilities. In addition, there are reports of some clusters of some very rare cancers in Texas City itself.  2

### Baton Rouge, Louisiana

In 1989, there was a huge explosion at the Exxon refinery in Baton Rouge. Propane, ethane and diesel fuels burned for almost 15 hours, and more than 50,000 people were either hurt or suffered property damage. Baton Rouge has seven major petrochemical plants, and 10 hazardous waste sites that are polluting the region. Samples of mother's milk from this city revealed high levels of toxic chemicals such as chloroform, dichlorobenzene and other synthetic chemicals.  3

### Chicago, Illinois

The area around the Altgeld Gardens housing project is called a "toxic donut" because it includes a circle of 100 factories, 50 hazardous waste landfills, and 103 toxic waste dumps. The residents of the area who are mostly black, Hispanic, and older white citizens  4

Smokestacks from a Shell Oil refinery tower over homes in Martinez. Residents of San Francisco Bay's "toxic triangle" are increasingly concerned.

suffer from higher rates of cancer and infant mortality than people in the rest of the United States. (Adapted from *Greenpeace Quarterly*, "Homestreet USA")

**infant mortality** babies dying before reaching 1 year old

## WRITING AN OUTLINE

An outline begins with a title which names the topic. Next, the main idea of the whole section is written in a complete sentence. For "Toxins in Our Backyards," the title and the main idea statement would look like this:

*Toxins in Our Backyards*

*Main idea: Many of the production [factories] and disposal facilities of toxic materials— and their possible disastrous consequences—are located in or near our local communities.*

Next, look at the important supporting details. In this article, these details are the examples of the three areas of the country where the production and disposal of toxins have had a bad effect on the people living in those regions. List each of these areas using roman numerals (I, II, III, IV, etc.). Under each of these roman numerals use capital letters (A, B, C, D, etc.) to show the important details for each of the examples. In this case, the rest of the outline will list the regions of the country, the environmental problems of those regions, and the results of those environmental problems. Try completing the parts that are left blank.

I. *Texas City, Texas* _____
   A. *Problems:* _____
   B. *Results: More mental retardation and learning disabilities, higher rates of cancer*

II. _____
   A. *Problems: Refinery explosions, 7 big petrochemical plants, 10 hazardous waste sites*
   B. *Results:* _____

III. *Chicago, Illinois* _____
   A. *Problems:* _____
   B. *Results:* _____

The whole outline should look something like this:

*Toxins in Our Backyards*

*Main idea: Many of the production (factories) and disposal of toxic materials—and their possible disastrous consequences—are located in or near our local communities.*

I. *Texas City, Texas* _____
   A. *Problems: Petrochemical plant explosions and dumping wastewater into bay*
   B. *Results: More mental retardation and learning disabilities, higher rates of cancer*

II. *Baton Rouge, Louisiana*
   A. *Problems: Refinery explosions, 7 big petrochemical plants, 10 hazardous waste sites*
   B. *Results: Mothers' milk was toxic (full of dangerous chemicals)*

III. *Chicago, Illinois*
   A. *Problems: Circle of factories, hazardous waste landfills, abandoned toxic waste dumps*
   B. *Results: Higher levels of cancer and infant deaths*

## Exercise **13**  Making Connections

1. What kinds of industry does your town or city have? Do people in these industries work with toxic chemicals?
2. Where are the industries that deal with toxic chemicals located in your city? Are they near neighborhoods?

• • • • • • • • • • • • • • •

# Applying Your Skills
• • • • • • • • • • • • • • • • • • • • • • • • • • • • • • • • • • • • • • • •

## *Toxic Metals, Dioxins, and PCBs*

CURTIS O. BYER AND LOUIS SHAINBERG

*The following passage from a health textbook describes some of the toxic materials that pollute our environment. Some of these chemicals can be found in our houses, others in our communities. Some of them make people sick. There is a good chance that some even affect our ability to have children. No one knows for sure whether or not many of them are bad for our health. Notice that the authors of this textbook selection have defined important words in the margins for you. Be sure you understand these words.*

### Preparing to Read

Do you use any toxic chemicals in your home or garden? Check your cleaning supplies and make a list of the products that you think may be toxic.

1    Various metallic elements or their compounds have been found to be hazardous to our health. These metals include mercury and lead.

**compounds** combinations of metal

### Mercury

2   Mercury is a by-product of coal and industrial wastes. As mercury is produced, it is released into the air and water, and travels into sewers and surface waters. Mercury is also a by-product of natural

sources produced from vapors from the earth's crust and from ocean bottom sediments. Consumption of any foods containing mercury, such as fish living in contaminated waters, can be hazardous.

Methyl mercury is an extremely toxic form of mercury. Methyl  3 mercury remains in the body for months, and can affect the central nervous system, kidneys, liver, and brain tissues. It is known to be responsible for birth defects. In the late 1950s, 649 Japanese people died and 1385 suffered mercury poisoning after methyl mercury was released into bay waters.

## Lead

We are exposed to lead every day in our water, food, and air. Sev-  4 enty-seven percent of the United States population has unsafe levels of lead in their blood, according to a 1986 EPA study. This lead comes from many sources, most of them unnatural.

A number of measures have been taken to eliminate lead from  5 our environment. In 1973, all new cars were required to use only unleaded gasoline. In 1986, that law was amended to make the requirement more rigid, reducing the amount of lead in unleaded gasoline from 2.5 grams per gallon to 0.1 gram per gallon. In 1976, a measure was enacted requiring paint manufacturers to reduce the amount of lead in their products. Another requirement enacted to control the use of lead was a 1987 ruling requiring public water installations and private buildings to use plastic pipes instead of the old lead pipes.

There are measures that individuals can take to protect them-  6 selves. If you are occupying an old building at work, school, or at home, run the water for two to three minutes in order to clean out most of the lead. Also, look into the safest and most effective way to remove leaded paint and apply new, unleaded paints instead.

Since the bodies of young children easily absorb lead, their in-  7 gestion of lead products can be fatal. About 200 children in America die yearly from lead poisoning, and another 12,000 to 16,000 children are treated for it each year. Survivors of lead poisoning often suffer from palsy, blindness, partial paralysis, and mental retardation. Studies show that lead in the blood can lower intelligence in children; even low levels of lead contamination can cause hearing loss and elevated blood pressure.

## Dioxins

**herbicide** a chemical that kills plants

**dioxin** family of over 75 toxic chemicals

Dioxins are a group of seventy-five chemicals, some of which are  8 formed during the manufacture of the **herbicide** 2,4,5-T. One by-product of 2,4,5-T production, usually referred to as TCCD, is a highly toxic **dioxin**. TCCD can cause liver cancer, birth defects, and

The oceans are prized as places of solitude, recreation, and industry. Yet, the ocean has become a place to dump wastes. A pandora's box of discarded items may be washed ashore by the relentless tides. Alarmingly, this debris has included hazardous and pathogenic medical throw-aways.

death of laboratory animals when administered at very low levels. Workers exposed to TCCD in industrial accidents may suffer from headaches, hair and weight loss, liver disorders, irritability, insomnia, nerve damage in the arms and legs, loss of sex drive, and disfiguring acne.

**exposed to** open to, having experience with

9     Major cases of dioxin contamination have been found in Times Beach, Missouri. In 1971 in this St. Louis suburb, dioxin-contaminated oil was sprayed on dirt roads to control dust. The resulting contamination was so severe that in 1983, the EPA bought the town for a cost of $36.7 million and relocated all of its 2200 people.

Other dioxin contamination has been found in fish taken from the Great Lakes and from rivers flowing into these lakes.

Although some federal agencies have established maximum 10 exposure levels for dioxins, these levels are not universally accepted as representing hazardous levels. Researchers do not agree on the level of dioxins or exposure time that is hazardous to humans.

## PCBs

**polychlorinated biphenyls (PCBs)** mixtures of at least 70 widely used compounds containing chlorine that can be biologically magnified in the food chain with unknown effects

**Polychlorinated biphenyls (PCBs)** are mixtures of almost seventy 11 different, but related chlorinated hydrogen compounds that were manufactured in the United States before 1979. PCBs were widely used in consumer products such as plastics, paints, rubber, waxes, and adhesives. They have also been used as insulation and cooling fluids in electrical transformers. In 1968, PCB-contaminated food was accidentally eaten in Japan. Victims suffered from liver damage, kidney damage, reproductive disorders, and skin lesions; there was also an unusually high incidence of stomach and liver cancer.

PCBs enter the body through food, the skin, and the lungs, and 12 accumulate in the fatty tissues. PCBs are very resistant to biological and chemical breakdown. As a result, the PCBs that have been dumped in landfills, sewers, and along roadsides have found their way into the food chain.

Although PCBs are no longer manufactured in this country, 13 they are still present in existing electrical transformers. Fires involving PCB filled electrical transformers in public facilities have exposed many people to these hazardous chemicals. In 1985 the EPA ordered the removal of PCBs from all transformers in apartment and office buildings, hospitals, and shopping malls by 1990. Until their removal, however, the transformers still in use will pose serious threats if they leak, explode, or catch on fire.

**Exercise 14**　　**Checking Your Understanding**

1. Which sentence best states the main idea of paragraphs 1–6?
2. In this reading the authors explain the hazards of two metallic elements and two types of chemicals. Use the headings of the four major divisions of the reading to complete the listing below.

   Toxic metals

   a. _____

   b. _____

Hazardous chemicals

a. _____

b. _____

3. What can individuals do to protect themselves and their children from lead poisoning? (Para. 6)
4. What is TCCD? What symptoms do workers have who have been exposed to TCCD? *(Para. 8)*
5. What did the EPA (Environmental Protection Agency) do in response to the dioxin contamination in Times Beach, Missouri? *(Para. 9)*

| Exercise **15** | **Identifying Important Supporting Details** |
| --- | --- |

1. In paragraph 3, the main idea is that methyl mercury is an extremely toxic form of mercury that can remain in the human body for months. In the sentences that follow the authors identify six possible effects of mercury. List the parts of the body that are affected and other effects. The first one has been done for you.

a. *the central nervous system* _____

b. _____

c. _____

d. _____

e. _____

f. _____

2. The main idea of paragraph 5 is stated in the first sentence: "A number of measures have been taken to eliminate lead from our environment." List below the measures that were taken from 1973 to 1987.

a. _____

b. _____

c. _____

d. _____

3. The main idea of paragraph 6 is "There are measures that individuals can take to protect themselves" from lead poisoning. List the detailed suggestions from paragraph 6 below.

a. _____

b. _____

c. _____

| Exercise **16** | **Working with Words** |

Read the following sentences and then choose the best meaning for the *italicized* words based on their context. If you cannot understand these words from their context, use your dictionary.

1. *Consumption*—i.e., eating or drinking—of any foods containing mercury, such as fish living in waters *contaminated* with this toxic substance, can be extremely dangerous to human health.

   *consumption*

   _____a. eating

   _____b. discarding

   _____c. watching

   *contaminated*

   _____a. clear

   _____b. made toxic

   _____c. safe

2. Since the bodies of young children easily absorb lead, their *ingestion* (eating or inhaling) of lead products can be *fatal*, that is, lead to death.

   *ingestion*

   _____a. playing with

   _____b. buying

   _____c. taking into their bodies

   *fatal*

   _____a. deadly

   _____b. interesting

   _____c. important

3. *Measures* in the form of laws and regulations have been taken to reduce the amount of lead in the environment.

   *measures*

   _____a. feet and inches

   _____b. actions

   _____c. laws and regulations

4. There are *measures* that individuals can take to protect themselves. If you are occupying an old building at work, school, or at home, run the water for two to three minutes in order to clean out most of the lead.

   *measures*

   _____a. feet and inches, meters and millimeters

_____ b. laws and regulations

_____ c. things you can do to protect yourself

In the following sentences, which are taken directly from the reading, key words are defined for you. Underline the definitions of the italicized words.

5. *Dioxins* are a group of seventy-five chemicals, some of which are formed during the manufacture of the herbicide 2,4,5-T.
6. *Methyl mercury* is an extremely toxic form of mercury.

**Exercise 17**  **Making Connections**

1. Do you know of any places in or near your neighborhood that might use toxic chemicals? What are they? Do you think they are handled safely?
2. Why is it important to you to be careful to not throw toxic chemicals down the drain? Explain.

**Exercise 18**  **Organizing to Learn**

Complete the following outline of the article.

*Toxic Metals, Dioxins, and PCBs*

*Main idea: Various metals, chemicals, and their compounds have been found to be hazardous to our health.*

I. *Mercury*
   A. *Product of industry and natural sources—hazardous if consumed*
   B. *Methyl mercury—extremely toxic, known to cause birth defects*

II. *Lead*
   A. *77% in U.S.—unsafe level in blood*
   B. *Measures to eliminate from environment*
   C. *Measures to protect yourself*
   D. *Young children's danger from lead*

III. *Dioxins*
   A. _____
   B. _____
   C. _____

IV. *PCBs*
   A. _____
   B. _____
   C. _____

# Chapter Review

• • • • • • • • • • • • • • • • • • • • • • • • • • • • • • • • • • • • • • • • • • • • •

| Exercise **19** | Skills Review |

1. Complete the steps to identify important supporting details.

   *How to Identify Important Supporting Details*

   Identify the main idea.

   _____

   • _____

   • additional facts

2. Complete the following outline on how to prepare an outline.

   *How to Prepare an Outline*

   *Main idea: Write the main idea, or thesis, of the passage here.* _____

   I. *State, in a few words, or as a topic, the first main idea or category* _____

      A. _____

      B. _____

   II. _____

      A. *Important supporting detail* _____

      B. _____

3. Pick out two words from any of the readings in this chapter and look them up in the dictionary. Then (1) write the definition of the word which is appropriate to the context in which you found it, (2) write the part of speech of the word, and (3) write the other forms of the word and their parts of speech as they are listed in your dictionary.

4. What two techniques have you learned in this chapter that can help you organize material and learn it? Briefly describe each technique.

| Exercise **20** | Writing |

Make a list of the things you can do to reduce your own exposure to toxic chemicals at your home, in your community, and with the food you eat.

| Exercise **21** | Collaborative Activity |

Discuss the lists that you wrote describing ways to reduce your exposure to toxic chemicals. Combine your lists into one that includes all the important points that you each made.

**Exercise 22** **Extension Activity**

Find a newspaper or magazine article about pollution problems and/or solutions. On a separate piece of paper, write out the main idea of the article and the important supporting points. Bring the article to class to share with your class group.

# CHAPTER 6

# *Protecting Our Environment*

## MAJOR AND MINOR SUPPORTING DETAILS

In addition to recognizing main ideas and supporting details, it is important to know how to identify minor supporting details. As you know, the main idea is the overall general statement or point the author is trying to make, and the major supporting details are the details, examples, or reasons that the author gives to support the main idea statement or thesis. The minor supporting details are additional points that either (1) give more information to explain the major supporting details, (2) give examples, or (3) give additional information to make the material more interesting. Depending on the reading, minor supporting details can either offer important information essential to your understanding or just extra information that you need not remember. The following passage is an example of a paragraph with important major and minor supporting details about dangers of exposure to certain materials in the workplace.

> With less ozone in the atmosphere, increasing amounts of ultraviolet (UV) radiation reach the Earth's surface. This can have disastrous effects on human health. UV exposure affects the skin, causing premature aging, wrinkling, and various forms of skin cancer. UV rays can make the lens of the eye cloud up with cataracts, which, if untreated, can lead to blindness. Excess UV radiation may also affect human immune systems, making the body unable to fight off disease. But human life is not the only kind of life at risk from UV exposure. High doses of UV radiation can reduce the yield of basic food crops, such as soybeans, and UV-B, the most dangerous form of UV light, penetrates below the surface of the ocean. There it can kill the plankton (one-celled plants) and krill (tiny shrimplike animals) that serve as food for larger fish. (Susan Stempleski, *Focus on the Environment*)

When we look carefully at the paragraph, we can see that its main focus is on the "disastrous effects" of UV exposure, both to human health and to other kinds of life. Because there is not a single sentence in the article that makes this point directly, we have to write an unstated main idea sentence.

> *Main Idea* (unstated): Increasing amounts of ultraviolet radiation can have disastrous effects for humans and other life on earth.

Looking carefully at the paragraph, we find that the first major supporting detail, is the discussion of human health. It is explained further by the information on *how* human health will be affected—it affects the skin, the eyes, and the immune system. The next major supporting detail describes the effects on other kinds of life. "But human life is not the only kind of life at risk from UV exposure." Crops and ocean life are also affected.

## USING AN OUTLINE

Using an outline (see page 143) to organize information with a few levels of detail is helpful because it shows how the details relate to each other. Use capital letters to indicate minor supporting details under the roman numerals, which indicate major supporting details. If still more detail is needed, use regular numbers under the capital letters. Using the example above about the effects of ultraviolet radiation, we can identify the major and minor supporting details as follows.

*Effects of UV Radiation on Life*      (Topic or title)

Main idea: *Increasing amounts of ultraviolet radiation can have disastrous effects for humans and other life on earth.*

I. *Human health* — Major supporting detail
   A. *Affects the skin* — Minor supporting details
      1. *Wrinkling*
      2. *Cancer* — Additional details
   B. *Affects the eyes (cataracts)*
   C. *Affects immune system (reduces body's ability to fight disease)*

II. *Other life at risk* — Major supporting detail
   A. *Reduces crop yields*
   B. *Penetrates ocean (can kill plankton and krill which are food for larger fish)* — Minor supporting details

**Exercise 1**    **Outlining Major and Minor Supporting Details**

For the paragraphs below, complete the following short outlines by writing in the appropriate places the stated or unstated main idea, the major supporting points, and the minor supporting points. Some of the information has been provided.

1. Probably one of the best-known manifestations [or examples] of occupational disease is the decreased lung function that results from breathing certain dusts and fibers. Coal miners have long been known to suffer from pneumoconiosis, or black lung disease. This condition leaves the miners' lungs permanently scarred and their respiratory function drastically reduced. Since the early part of this decade, inhaled asbestos has been known to cause a scarring of the lungs called asbestosis. It is caused by breathing asbestos particles over long periods of time. (Adapted from Warren Boskin, *Health Dynamics*)

Main Idea: *One example of occupational disease is the decreased lung function that results from breathing certain dusts and fibers.*

(Major supporting detail)
(Minor supporting details)

 I. *Coal miners suffer from pneumoconiosis or black lung disease.*
  A. *Lungs permanently scarred*
  B. *Respiratory function drastically reduced*

(Major supporting detail)
(Minor supporting detail)
(Minor supporting detail)

 II. *Asbestos*
  A. _____
  B. _____

2. As the twentieth century comes to a close, people around the globe have developed programs to save endangered wildlife. To this end, there has been some very promising cooperation between countries. American schoolchildren participate in programs to buy and protect areas of the rain forest in Costa Rica. In 1988, the United States and the former Soviet Union worked together to save gray whales that were trapped in the Alaskan ice. The San Diego Zoo has a program to work with the Chinese government to help preserve the endangered panda bear. People have also developed the technological means to help endangered wildlife. Zoos have breeding programs which have aided many forms of wildlife to reproduce in captivity. And the movement of endangered whales can be tracked by satellite.

Main Idea: _____

(Major supporting detail)
(Minor supporting details)

 I. *Cooperation between countries*
  A. _____
  B. _____
  C. _____

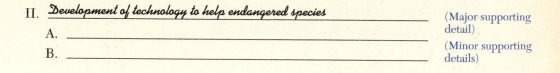

II. *Development of technology to help endangered species* (Major supporting detail)

   A. _____ (Minor supporting details)

   B. _____

• • • • • • • • • • • • • •

# Organizing to Learn
## Using a Map

Another way to organize the same information is to create a visual pattern that shows the relationships between the information, such as the map below. Notice how the information in a paragraph or in any kind of reading passage can be organized visually so that you immediately understand the relationships between the main idea, the important supporting details, and the minor supporting details.

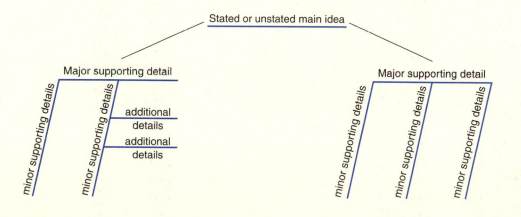

The information from the paragraph about ultraviolet radiation (page 156) would follow the above pattern in a map like this one:

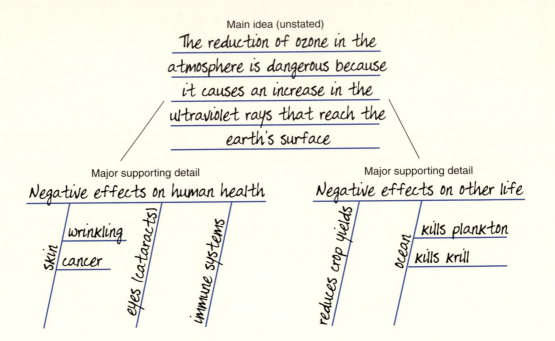

Main idea (unstated)

The reduction of ozone in the atmosphere is dangerous because it causes an increase in the ultraviolet rays that reach the earth's surface

Major supporting detail
Negative effects on human health

skin — wrinkling, cancer
eyes (cataracts)
immune systems

Major supporting detail
Negative effects on other life

reduces crop yields
ocean — kills plankton, kills krill

Here, the information is organized to show its relationship in a spatial way. The main idea is at the top. The two major supporting details are diagramed next to each other, below the main idea. The minor supporting details branch off from the major supporting details, just below them. Because there are three minor supporting details for the effects on human health, there are three branches under it. (Notice that the further details that explain the two kinds of skin problems are recorded as branches to the minor supporting detail of "skin.") Because there are two supporting details for the effects on other life, there are only two branches under it. It is important that you change your diagram to suit the information you are working with.

## Exercise 2    Mapping Major and Minor Supporting Details

For the following paragraphs, complete the maps which show the relationships between the main idea and the major and minor supporting details.

1. One of the most interesting problems facing environmentalists today is the disposal of all the trash and garbage that our society produces. There are basi-

cally three ways to handle this problem: (1) it can be put in landfills (dumps), (2) it can be burned, or (3) the amount of trash that we generate can be reduced. When we put trash in landfills, we very soon find that we are running out of acceptable locations for these dumps. In addition, landfills often produce leachate, which is a kind of toxic run-off that becomes absorbed into the soil and into our groundwater supply. Burning trash would seem like a good solution; however, when trash is burned, severe air pollution is created and toxins are released into the atmosphere. The third measure, creating less trash to begin with, is the best solution to the problem, but it is difficult to implement because, in addition to recycling, people would have to learn to live more modestly, consume less, and consequently throw away less.

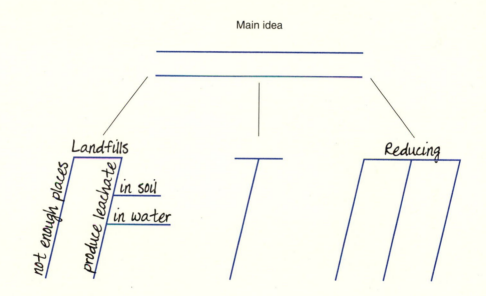

2. Studies carried out over the last 20 years have revealed some surprising information about landfills. We have learned that most of the garbage and trash in landfills tends not to biodegrade, that is, break down by bacteria into basic elements and compounds. William Rathje, an archeologist whose life work has been studying American trash in landfills, has found 40-year-old hot dogs, a head of lettuce that was in almost perfect condition after 25 years, and an in-tact order of guacamole next to a newspaper dated 1967. The biodegradation that does occur is extremely slow. It takes hundreds of years for garbage and trash in landfills to break down. According to Rathje, landfills are "vast mummifiers."

Main idea

Studies have revealed
some surprising information
about landfills.

Garbage in landfills tends
not to biodegrade

Biodegradation that does
happen is very slow

"Vast mummifiers"

3. Discarded materials that pose a threat to human health or to the environment are called **hazardous wastes.** These wastes may be solid, liquid, or gaseous, and include many toxic, corrosive, and ignitable substances. Until a little more than a decade ago, an estimated 6 billion tons of hazardous wastes were being dumped in 26,000 designated sites around the country. These sites included municipal landfills, farm fields, and chemical dump sites from which chemicals leached into surrounding water supplies. Love Canal in Niagara Falls, New York, a neighborhood of almost a thousand homes, was affected by toxic and carcinogenic chemicals from an abandoned chemical dump nearby. The government declared the area a federal disaster area and was forced to relocate people, demolish homes, and pay settlements to many of the families affected by the disaster. (Curtis O. Byer, *Living Well: Health in Your Hands*)

Main idea

Hazardous wastes are a
big problem for our country.

Huge quantities: 6 billion tons
of hazardous wastes dumped
in 26,000 sites

Chemical dump sites

Love Canal, a very
important example
relocated people

dump with toxic &
carcinogenic chemicals

4. A wide range of health problems can be caused or aggravated by workplace exposures. Certain solvents can cause heart arrhythmias (irregular heartbeats), which can precipitate heart failure and trigger a heart attack. Certain solvents can cause neurological problems, such as tremors, weakness, or even paralysis. Exposure to lead can cause convulsions in children and mercury can make people seem crazy. In fact, the character of the Mad Hatter in Alice in Wonderland is based on the experiences of hat makers who used mercury in the felting process. Many of them went "mad" because of their exposure to toxic levels of mercury. (Warren Boskin, *Health Dynamics*)

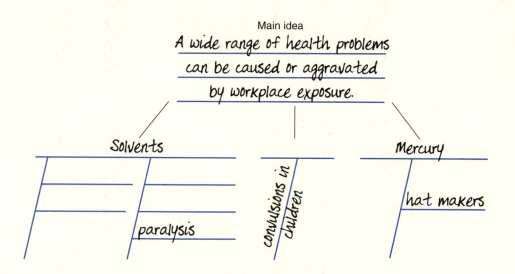

## MARKING MAIN IDEAS AND MAJOR AND MINOR SUPPORTING DETAILS

Very often when you are studying a large section of a textbook, you will not have time to outline or map all the information. Another way to handle this situation, and the one used most often by students who have to study huge amounts of material, is to mark the textbook itself. In addition to underlining the main ideas, you can indicate important supporting points by writing numbers next to them, and you can indicate minor supporting details by writing letters next to them. You would only be concentrating on minor supporting details when you are studying for a class for which you have to understand and remember that level of detail. For example, read the following paragraph:

People have always had the problem of how to dispose of their trash; the problem is not new to the twentieth century. One way to deal with trash is to cover it up. In ancient Troy, some articles of trash were simply dropped on the floor. When the floor got too cluttered, families would simply mud over them so that the trash became a layer in the floor. They did this over and over again until the doors became too low. Then they would raise their ceilings and make higher doors. In nineteenth-century cities of Europe and America trash was often just dumped out into the streets or rivers. In London, people dumped their garbage and waste into the River Thames. In Paris, people simply threw their garbage out the window. It was polite for a man to walk on the outside of the walkway if he was with a woman because if trash were thrown out of a window, it would be more likely to hit him.

First, underline the main idea of this paragraph, "People have always had the problem of how to dispose of their trash." Then write "1" and "2" above the two major details, which describe the two ways that trash was dealt with historically. Next, write "a" and "b" above the examples of these major details, otherwise known as minor supporting details. When we finish marking the paragraph, it will look like this:

People have always had the problem of how to dispose of their trash; the problem is not new to the twentieth century. ① One way to deal with trash is to cover it up. ⓐ In ancient Troy, some articles of trash were simply dropped on the floor. When the floor got too cluttered, families would simply mud over them so that the trash became a layer in the floor. They did this over and over again until the doors became too low. Then they would raise their ceilings and make higher doors. ② In nineteenth-century cities of Europe and America trash was often just dumped out into the streets or rivers. ⓐ In London, people dumped their garbage and waste into the River Thames. ⓑ In Paris, people simply threw their garbage out the window. It was polite for a man to walk on the outside of the walkway (to the left) if he was with a woman because if trash were thrown out of a window, it would be more likely to hit him.

| Exercise **3** | **Marking Major and Minor Supporting Details** |

In the following paragraphs, underline the main idea, number major supporting details, and use letters for minor supporting details.

1. [The passenger pigeon is a good example of a common species that became extinct. It] was a large pigeon that lived in the forests of North America. When the first settlers arrived on the continent, the total number of passenger pigeons was certainly in the billions, and they migrated northward and southward across the continent in flocks of more than 100 million birds. When they flew across the sky, the sun would vanish, and night would seem to fall. They could do considerable damage to a forest just by settling onto the branches of its trees, and when they moved on, the ground would be buried under several feet of droppings. When they flew together, the flapping of their wings was "like the roar of distant thunder," according to the famous naturalist John James Audubon. (Christopher Lampton, *Endangered Species*)

2. Recycling paper in the United States makes good sense. Every American uses an average of 699 pounds of paper each year, or about eight times the world average per person. One Sunday edition of the *New York Times* alone requires the weekly consumption of 150 acres of forest to produce the needed

paper. About three-quarters of U.S. paper products end up as trash. This is more significant since paper also makes up over 40 percent of the volume of urban solid waste produced each year. Americans spend about 10 percent of their grocery dollars on paper packaging, which they throw out. (Curtis O. Byer, *Living Well: Health in Your Hands*)

3. Pesticides in our water supply are cause for concern. Pesticides seep into our well-water supply when they are applied to crops nearby. In Iowa, Minnesota and Wisconsin, in farming areas, 1/3 of all wells tested are toxic because they contain pesticides. In fact, an EPA (Environmental Protection Agency) study reported that 10 percent of all community drinking wells have traces of pesticides. In addition, there are pesticide problems in major North American rivers. The entire Mississippi River is contaminated with herbicides. It dumps tons of pesticide into the Gulf of Mexico. (Adapted from Geoffrey C. Saign, *Green Essentials*)

· · · · · · · · · · · ·

# Working with Words

## Dictionary Skills

· · · · · · · · · · · · · · · · · · · · · · · · · · · · · · · · · · · · · · · · · · · · · · · · · ·

When you look up a word in your dictionary—because you have decided that it's an important word and you cannot figure it out from context—remember that you must choose the correct definition. Words often have many definitions, so you must be sure that you pick the definition that fits the way the word is being used in the reading.

For example:

The Edsel, produced by Ford Motor Company in the 1950s, was probably the biggest lemon of any car every made.

If you don't understand how the word *lemon* is being used, you might decide to look it up in the dictionary. You will find three definitions for lemon, which are numbered 1.a., 1.b., and 2. *Slang*.

**lem·on** (lĕm′ ən) *n.* **1**. **a.** An egg-shaped yellow citrus fruit with acid, juicy pulp. **b.** A tree bearing such fruit. **2**. *Slang.* Something chronically defective or unsatisfactory. [< Pers. *līmūn.*]

The first definition (1.a.) is for the fruit itself. The second definition (b.), which is related to the first, is for the lemon tree. And the third definition (2. *Slang*) is "something chronically defective or unsatisfactory."

Which definition is correct for the meaning of lemon in the above sentence? You know that somehow "lemon" refers to the car named Edsel; therefore, the fruit and the tree definitions are not possible. On the other hand, something that is unsatisfactory makes sense.

**Exercise 4    Dictionary Definitions**

Find the correct definitions for the *italicized* words in the following sentences using the dictionary definitions provided on page 167.

1. Plastic trash and grocery bags, insecticides, computers, televisions, styrofoam cups and fast-food containers, synthetic fabrics and paint—the seemingly *benign* list of common products belies the danger inherent in the expansion of the petrochemical industry. . . . (Warren Boskin, *Health Dynamics*)

   *benign* _____

   _____

2. According to a history *current* residents have been able to piece together, the land . . . became a municipal and chemical disposal site until 1953. (Aubrey Wallace, *Eco-Heroes*)

   *current* _____

   _____

3. For many years, hazardous wastes were disposed of on the land, under the assumption that they would *degrade* into harmless products or would be contained in landfills. (Warren Boskin, *Health Dynamics*)

   *degrade* _____

   _____

4. At the same time, some twenty-two thousand tons of poisons were bubbling underground, beginning to cause cancer, *miscarriages*, deformed babies, and illness and death among children and adults.

   *miscarriages* _____

   _____

5. Most hazardous substances are *organic* chemicals.

   *organic* _____

   _____

For the following sentences, look the meaning up in your dictionary and write it on the lines provided. Remember to find the correct meaning for the way the word is used in the sentence.

6. The oryx no longer exists in the wild except in special *reserves*, where it is protected from machine gun–wielding hunters. (Christopher Lampton, *Endangered Species*)

*reserves* _____

_____

7. The *dawn* of the twenty-first century will see one million fewer species [types of plants and animals] on this planet than did the *dawn* of the twentieth. (Christopher Lampton, *Endangered Species*)

    *dawn* _____

_____

**ab•er•ra•tion** (ăb′ ə-rā′shən) *n.* **1.** A deviation from the normal, usual, or expected. **2.** *Optics.* A defect of focus, as blurring or distortion, in an image [Lat. *aberratio,* diversion.] **—ab•er′rant** *adj.*

**be•nign** (bǐ-nīn′) *adj.* **1.** Of a kind disposition. **2.** *Pathol.* Not malignant. [< Lat. *benignus.*] **—be•nign′ly** *adv.*

**cur•rent** (kûr′ ənt. kûr′-) *adj.* **1.** Belonging to the present time; present-day. **2.** Commonly accepted; prevalent. *—n.* **1.** A steady and smooth onward movement, as of water. **2.** The part of a body of liquid or gas that has a continuous onward movement. **3. a.** A flow of electric charge. **b.** The amount of electric charge that passes a point in a unit of time. [< Lat. *currere,* to run.] **—cur′rent•ly** *adv.*

**de•grade** (dǐ-grād′) *v.* -grad•ed, -grad•ing. **1.** To reduce in rank, status, or position. **2.** To debase; corrupt. **3.** *Chem.* To decompose (a compound) by stages. **— de•grad′able** *adj.* **—deg′ra•da′tion** (děg′re-dā′shən) *n.* **—de•grad′ed•ly** *adv.* **—de•grad′ed•ness** *n.* **—de•grad′er** *n.*

**de•pres•sion** (dǐ-prěsh′ ən) *n.* **1.** The act of depressing or condition of being depressed. **2.** A mental condition of gloom or sadness: dejection. **3.** An area that is sunk below its surroundings; hollow. **4.** A region of low barometric pressure. **5.** A period of drastic decline in the national economy. **—de•pres′sive** *adj.*

**mis•car•riage** (mis-kar′ĭj) *n.* **1.** Mismanagement. **2.** Premature expulsion of a non-viable fetus from the uterus.

**or•gan•ic** (ôr-găn′ĭk) *adj.* **1.** Of, relating to, or affecting an organ of the body. **2.** Of, relating to, or derived from living organisms. **3.** Using or grown with fertilizers consisting only of natural animal or vegetable matter. **4.** Like an organism in organization or development: *an organic whole.* **5.** Of or constituting an integral part of something; fundamental. **6.** *Chem.* Of or relating to carbon compounds. **—or•gan′i•cal•ly** *adv.*

## WRITING A SUMMARY

Very often, students and professional workers are asked to write summaries of important information. You might, for example, be asked to research a topic— such as the market for a new product—and report your *summarized* findings to your employer or to your fellow students. This means that you would be required to use the skills you have just practiced—you would need to identify the main ideas and major and minor supporting details and to decide whether or not to include details in your summary. Sometimes minor details are very important, but very often they are not necessary. Writing a summary is also an excellent way to *organize* the material that you have read for future review and testing.

To write an effective summary, follow these steps:

- Carefully read and understand the material you are going to summarize.
- Determine the main idea or thesis. Write that main idea in a sentence using your own words. Very often, when you write the main idea sentence, you will give credit to the author whose work you are summarizing and will mention the title of the passage or article or book.
- Decide on what major supporting details you need to include.
- Decide whether or not to include minor supporting details.
- Write the summary in your own words beginning with your main idea sentence and including the major supporting details. Use complete sentences.
- Remember, it is easier to use your own words if you are not looking directly at the passage while you write! Don't copy! If you use the author's language, be sure to put quotation marks around it.

## Writing the Main Idea Sentence for a Summary

You can begin a summary different ways but an effective method gives the main idea and the source information in the first sentence. Many professors and employers want to know the main idea of the text you're summarizing, who wrote it, and where it was published at the very beginning of the summary. Remember, it is very important to use your own words. Once you have figured out how to write the main idea in your own words, you can write the first sentence of the summary by using the phrase "According to *(name of author)* in the *(article, passage, or book)* entitled *(title here)* *(main idea here)*.

For example, you may have decided that the main idea of an article, written in your own words, is:

It is important to recycle your old newspapers because the paper can be used again.

That information may be based on an article by John Smith entitled "All That Paper" in *The Daily News*. Then your summary main idea sentence could be:

According to John Smith, in his *Daily News* article, "All That Paper," it is important to recycle your old newspapers to save our environment.

Of course your summary could begin with an introduction divided into two sentences, such as the following:

In his *Daily News* article entitled "All That Paper," John Smith discusses the advantages of recycling newspapers. We must recycle old newspapers to save our environment.

In this case, the first sentence states the source and the topic and the second sentence states Smith's main idea.

| Exercise **5** | **Adding Your Source to Main Idea Sentences for Summaries** |
|---|---|

Rewrite the following main idea sentences to give credit to the author and refer to the source. Use the format, *According to* _____. The first one is done for you.

1. People are often exposed to toxic materials at work and doctors and scientists don't have enough information about those materials. (a textbook excerpt by John Boskin called "Occupational and Environmental Risks")
   *According to J. Boskin, in the excerpt "Occupational and Environmental Risks,"*
   *people are often exposed to toxic materials at work and doctors and scientists don't*
   *have enough information about those materials.*

2. Getting rid of trash has always been a problem for people. (Based on an article by John Doe entitled "Trash Is Not News.")

   _____

   _____

   _____

3. When an animal or plant becomes extinct, there is nothing that we can do to bring it back. (Based on the book by Christopher Lampton entitled *Endangered Species.*)

   _____

   _____

   _____

4. Americans throw away more trash than people in any other country of the world. (Based on a book by Jane Smith entitled *American Trash.*)

   _____

   _____

   _____

5. There are many things we can each do to help prevent water pollution (Based on the article by Jane Doe entitled "What You Can Do.")

   _____

   _____

   _____

## Identifying Major Supporting Details for Summaries

Decide what the *major supporting details* are for the entire reading and whether you need to include minor supporting details in your summary. Because you want to find the major supporting details for the whole reading, you may not be mentioning the main idea of every single paragraph. (For practice, you may want to write down the major supporting details under the main idea in outline form. Try to do this from memory, then check back to the reading to make sure that you got the general points.)

### L A N G U A G E   T I P

#### Put It in Your Own Words

When you need to summarize a reading or to explain an idea or information from another writer, it is very important that you use your own words. If you take words directly from another text you must use quotation marks (" ") and include the source of your information. If you use other people's sentences or phrases without giving them credit, you may be accused of "copying" or "plagiarizing" work. One of the most important rules in American colleges and universities is: *Don't copy other people's work!*

Many students say, "But I can't explain it as well as this writer." This may be true, but the only way you can learn is if you practice.

Some tips on using your own words:

1. First read and understand the sentence that you want to put into your own words.
2. Try to substitute words that are familiar to you for words that are not familiar.
3. Write down only one or two of the very important words that help explain the idea.
4. Turn your paper over and try to write the sentence in your own words.
5. Don't get discouraged. This skill takes a lot of practice. You won't sound like a professional writer to begin with, but you're not supposed to be!

Let's look at a few examples. If the following is your original sentence, then what words are absolutely necessary?

Many of the production (factories) and disposal facilities of toxic materials—and their possible disastrous consequences—are located in or near our local communities.

You would probably pick *factories* and *toxic*. So you might state this idea in your own words by writing:

*Toxic dumps and factories that produce toxins are in or near our neighborhoods, and they may be dangerous for people living near them.*

When pathologist Dr. Russell Sherwin began examining the lungs of inner-city Los Angeles youths who had died from accidents or violence, he discovered a curious thing: eight of ten had lung abnormalities that were probably caused by breathing the city's filthy air.

What words are absolutely necessary? Probably you would pick *examine, lungs,* and *air.* So you might state this idea in your own words by writing:

*A doctor in Los Angeles who examines bodies after people die found out that even young people had special lung problems from breathing the city's bad air.*

### Exercise 6    Put It in Your Own Words

Rewrite the following sentences in your own words.

1. For more than two decades, archaeologist William L. Rathje has sorted through numerous garbage cans and landfills. (Brian Williams, *Healthy for Life*) (*Clue: What's another word you can use for garbage cans and landfills?*)

   _____

   _____

2. The dawn of the twenty-first century will see *one million fewer species on this planet* than did the dawn of the twentieth. (Christopher Lampton, *Endangered Species*)

   _____

   _____

3. When a species becomes extinct, no power on earth can bring it back, just as nothing can bring back the dinosaurs. (Christopher Lampton, *Endangered Species*)

   _____

   _____

# Changing the Balance of Life in the Water

## MARY O'NEILL

*The following reading explains the types of life that live in rivers and lakes and how each form of life depends on others. Read it carefully and prepare to write a summary of it.*

**organisms** living beings

**link** tie or connection

We see only a tiny number of the plants and animals that live   1
in lakes and streams. We're of course familiar with fish, frogs, otters, and water lilies. But perhaps even more important to the life of the water are billions of tiny organisms. They are the bottom link in the chain of water life.

## Phytoplankton

The smallest plants in the water are called phytoplankton. Phyto-   2
plankton may be as small as a single cell. But they are able to live on sunlight, minerals in the water, and carbon dioxide. They take in these simple substances and are themselves food for other kinds of life in the water.

## Zooplankton: The Bottom of a Delicate Chain of Life

Zooplankton are the tiniest animals in the water. Many feed on the   3
phytoplankton. These zooplankton, in turn, become food for larger animals. *This chain of "eating and being eaten" continues all the way up to larger animals such as the fish-eating otters. Each member of this "food chain" is important to all the other members. If one member dies off or grows out of control, all the others may be in danger. The balance of life can be easily disturbed by human activities.*

## Detergent Dump

In the 1950s fishermen began to notice that fish were getting harder   4
to find. Many lakes and streams were covered with a thick green film—a type of phytoplankton called algae. The water underneath was nearly lifeless. What had killed off life there?

It was clear that the algae were doing too well. They were   5
choking off all other life forms. Scientists found that the algae were getting too much food. But where was it coming from?

## Changing the Balance of Life in the Water

We see only a tiny number of the plants and animals that live in lakes and streams. We're of course familiar with fish, frogs, otters, and water lilies. But perhaps even more important to the life of the water are billions of tiny organisms. They are the bottom link in the chain of water life.

The smallest plants in the water are called phytoplankton. Phytoplankton may be as small as a single cell. But they are able to live on sunlight, minerals in the water, and carbon dioxide. They take in these simple substances and are themselves food for other kinds of life in the water.

Zooplankton are the tiniest animals in the water. Many feed on the phytoplankton. These zooplankton, in turn, become food for larger animals. This chain of "eating and being eaten" continues all the way up to larger animals such as the fish-eating otters. Each member of this "food chain" is important to all the other members. If one member dies off or grows out of control, all the others may be in danger. The balance of life can be easily disturbed by human activities.

PHYTOPLANKTON  ZOOPLANKTON  BEARS  HUMANS  SMALL FRY  LARGE FISH  OTTERS

Each member of this "food chain" is important to all the other members. If one member dies off or grows out of control, all the others may be in danger.

6    The substance that seemed to be too plentiful was a group of nutrients called phosphates. Used in both detergents and fertilizers, phosphates were being dumped in sewers by washing machines in the home and by industries. Run-off water from farms was also carrying fertilizer with it.

7    With so much food, the algae grew out of control. When the algae finally died and sank to the bottom, bacteria that break down rotting algae used up the water's oxygen. And as more oxygen was used up, fish and other animals couldn't breathe.

## One Solution

Today many detergents no longer contain phosphates. Their boxes    8
are labeled "phosphate-free."

## WRITING A SUMMARY

If we think carefully about the reading and notice the italicized sentences in
paragraph 3, we can identify the main idea for our summary. Then, by looking at
the important supporting points under the headings "Phytoplankton," "Zooplankton," "Detergent Dump," and "One Solution," we can identify the important supporting details we need to include as well. (For the purpose of this summary, it is not necessary to include all of the minor supporting details.) To make it
clearer to ourselves, we can write a brief outline or diagram.

Changing the Balance of Life in the Water

Main idea: The balance of life in the water, or the "food chain" (of eating and being eaten), can be disturbed by human activity.

I.  The delicate food chain
   A.  Phytoplankton (smallest plants)
   B.  Zooplankton (smallest animals—eat phytoplankton)
   C.  Large animals eat zooplankton, etc.
II.  Problem for small plants and animals—whole food chain affected
   A.  Too much algae in streams from fertilizers (phosphates)
   B.  Rotting algae use up water's oxygen
   C.  Fish and other animals can't breathe, so they die
   D.  One step toward a solution: Use detergents that don't have phosphates

Once we have the main idea and major supporting points, we can write the summary, which will look something like this.

     According to Mary O'Neill, in her book *Water Squeeze*, the balance of life
in the water, or the "food chain" (of eating and being eaten), can be disturbed by
human activity. Phytoplankton are the smallest plants in the water and often they
are eaten by zooplankton which are the smallest animals in the water. Other,
larger animals eat the zooplankton, and this process continues up to the largest
fish or otters. If anything happens to the small plants and animals, the whole food
chain will be affected. In the 1950s many lakes and streams became covered with
too much algae because phosphates from detergents and fertilizers were being

dumped in the streams. Because there was too much "food" for the algae, it multiplied and rotted and used up the water's oxygen. Without enough oxygen, fish and other animals couldn't breathe. One solution to this problem is to use detergents that don't have phosphates.

## An Assessment of Risks

PETER H. RAVEN, LINDA R. BERG, AND GEORGE B. JOHNSON

*The following reading discusses the different kinds of risks we take when making decisions about how to treat our bodies. The author points out that when it comes to our health occasionally we get overly concerned about things over which we have little control, yet we often make irresponsible decisions about things we can control directly.*

1    Each of us takes risks every day of our lives. Walking on stairs involves a small risk, but a risk nonetheless, because some people die from falls on stairs. Using household appliances is slightly risky, because some people die from electrocution when they operate appliances with faulty wiring or use appliances in an unsafe manner. Driving in an automobile and flying in a jet offer risks that are easier for most of us to recognize. Yet few of us hesitate to fly in a plane, and even fewer hesitate to drive in a car because of the risk.

2    Estimating the risks involved in a particular action so that they can be compared and contrasted with other risks is known as risk assessment. Risk assessment helps us estimate the probability that an event will occur and enables us to set priorities and manage risks in an appropriate way.

**assessment** evaluation

**probability** likelihood

3    As an example, consider a person who smokes a pack of cigarettes a day and drinks well water containing traces of the cancer-causing chemical trichloroethylene (in acceptable amounts as established by the Environmental Protection Agency). Without knowledge of risk assessment, this person might buy bottled water in an attempt to reduce his or her chances of getting cancer.

4    However, this person is 180 million times more likely to get cancer from smoking than to get it from drinking such low levels of trichloroethylene. Knowing this, the person in our example would, we hope, be induced to stop smoking.

**induced** led to

**dilemmas** situations that require you to make difficult choices

One of the most perplexing dilemmas of risk assessment is that people often ignore substantial risks but get extremely upset about minor risks. The average life expectancy of smokers is more than eight years shorter than that of nonsmokers; almost one-third of all smokers die from diseases caused or exacerbated by their habit. Yet many people get much more upset over a one-in-a-million chance of getting cancer from pesticide residues on food than they do over the relationship between smoking and cancer. Perhaps part of the reason for this attitude is that behaviors such as diet, smoking, and exercise are parts of our lives that we can control *if we choose to.* Risks over which most of us have no control, such as pesticide residues, tend to evoke more fearful responses. 5

## A Balanced Perspective on Risks

Threats to our health, particularly from toxic chemicals in the environment, make big news. Many of these stories are more sensational than factual. If they were completely accurate, people would be dying left and right, whereas, in fact, human health is better today than at any time in our history, and our life expectancy continues to increase rather than decline. 6

This does not mean that we should ignore human-made chemicals in the environment. Nor does it mean we should discount the stories that are sometimes sensationalized by the news media. These stories serve an important role in getting the regulatory wheels of the government moving to protect us as much as possible from the dangers of our technological and industrialized world. 7

People cannot expect no-risk foods, no-risk water, or no-risk anything else. Risk is inherent in all our actions and in everything in our environment. We do, however, have the right to expect the risks to be minimized. For example, given the fact that we consume some natural carcinogenic substances in our food, we should try to avoid consuming uncontrolled amounts of human-made carcinogens in addition. Simply stated, we should not ignore small risks just because larger ones exist. 8

**Exercise 7**    **Outline and Summary Practice**

1. Fill in the outline.

   Main idea (in your own words): _____

   _____

Major supporting details (you decide how many supporting points you will have and remember to label them with roman numerals)

_____

_____

_____

2. Now, using the main ideas from your outline, write a summary.

• • • • • • • • • • • • •

# Applying Your Skills

• • • • • • • • • • • • • • • • • • • • • • • • • • • • • • • • • • • • •

## *How Species Become Extinct*

CHRISTOPHER LAMPTON

*The following excerpt, which gives some of the reasons that species became extinct in the past few hundred years, discusses what happened to a very common bird—the passenger pigeon— after the Europeans came to this continent.*

### Preparing to Read

1. What animals do you know of that have become extinct?
2. What causes or possible causes of extinctions do you know about?

## Overhunting

1    . . . humans still hunt—for food, for sport, and for animal by-products such as furs and oils. At least one animal, the rhinoceros, is hunted because superstitious people believe that parts of its body will cure diseases—they will not—or improve their love lives, which is even less likely. Because of the proficiency and skill of human

The passenger pigeon, once the most common bird in North America, was hunted to extinction in the nineteenth century. The last passenger pigeon died in captivity in 1914. This engraving is from a watercolor executed by the nineteenth-century wildlife artist John J. Audubon.

hunters, any hunted animal is in danger of extinction, unless extraordinary steps are taken to control the hunters. And hunters are notoriously difficult to control!

2  The most spectacular example of an animal hunted to extinction occurred within the memory of people alive today. The victim was the passenger pigeon, once the most common bird in North America, and possibly the most common bird on Earth.

3  The passenger pigeon was a large pigeon that lived in the forests of North America. When the first settlers arrived on the continent, they found what Samuel de Champlain, the French explorer, called "an infinite number of pigeons," an estimate that wasn't as farfetched as it sounds. The total population of passenger pigeons was certainly in the billions, and they migrated northward and

southward across the continent in flocks of more than 100 million birds. When they flew across the sky, the sun would vanish, and night would seem to fall. They could do considerable damage to a forest just by settling onto the branches of its trees, and when they moved on, the ground would be buried under several feet of droppings. When they flew together, the flapping of their wings was "like the roar of distant thunder," according to the famous naturalist John James Audubon.

4    Obviously, the passenger pigeon was a successful species, well adapted to its environment. But, in a world dominated by human beings, it had made a crucial evolutionary mistake: it was delicious to eat. Purveyors of gourmet food were willing to pay cash on the barrelhead for dead passenger pigeons, and greedy hunters were more than willing to supply the carcasses.

5    The birds had not evolved to resist that modern weapon of destruction, the gun. As the passenger pigeons migrated, parties of hunters would wait for them in their nesting grounds and slaughter them wholesale as they alighted amid the trees. The dead and dying pigeons could then be bagged and carried off. A party of hunters could easily kill fifty thousand birds in a week.

**resist** defend themselves against

6    But even wholesale slaughter seemed insufficient to exterminate a species as common as the passenger pigeon. How could mere human beings armed with guns threaten the future of a species that numbered in the billions?

7    Quite easily, as it turned out. No one knows when the slaughter of the passenger pigeon began, though it was probably shortly after settlers began to arrive in the sixteenth and seventeenth centuries. But the end of the slaughter is quite easy to pinpoint. On March 24, 1900, a young hunter shot the last passenger pigeon ever seen in the wild. For some years afterward, a few of the birds survived in zoos, but on September 1, 1914, the last passenger pigeon in captivity died in the Cincinnati Zoo. The species was extinct.

8    The story of the passenger pigeon is extraordinary, but it isn't all *that* extraordinary. Many other species have met the same fate: overhunted into extinction. In fact, it is a sad refrain that recurs throughout human history. Other animals hunted into oblivion in recent centuries include the quagga (a close relative of the zebra), the aurochs (a relative of the bison), and Steller's sea cow (a relative of the manatee, probably responsible for some reported sightings of "mermaids"). In the last century, the American bison, sometimes incorrectly called the American buffalo, was nearly hunted into extinction. Fortunately, most varieties of this animal have managed to recover from overhunting and are, at least temporarily, out of risk.

**recurs** repeats itself

**Exercise 8**    **Checking Your Understanding**

1. Choose the best main idea sentence for the reading.
   _____ a. The birds had not evolved to resist that modern weapon of destruction, the gun.
   _____ b. Hunters are responsible for many of the extinctions that have occurred in recent times as well as today: the extinction of the passenger pigeon is one example.
   _____ c. They [the pigeons] could do considerable damage to a forest just by settling onto the branches of its trees, and when they moved on, the ground would be buried under several feet of droppings.

2. For the following statements, mark "T" if the statement is true and "F" if the statement is false.
   _____ a. Mass extinctions are always caused by natural disasters.
   _____ b. Extinction of large land animals still takes place today.
   _____ c. Because of the advances of science, we may be able to bring back animals that are now extinct.
   _____ d. The passenger pigeon is an example of an animal that was able to survive after the arrival of Europeans on the North American continent.
   _____ e. The correct word for what we call the American buffalo is the American bison.

**Exercise 9**    **Main Ideas and Major and Minor Supporting Points**

1. Read the following paragraph. Write letters above the minor supporting details that make the information more interesting by describing the effects that the pigeons had when they flew overhead or landed in a forest.

   The passenger pigeon was a large pigeon that lived in the forest of North America. When the first settlers arrived on the continent, they found what Samuel de Champlain, the French explorer, called "an infinite number of pigeons," an estimate that wasn't as farfetched as it sounds. The total population of passenger pigeons was certainly in the billions, and they migrated northward and southward across the continent in flocks of more than 100 million birds. When they flew across the sky, the sun would vanish, and night would seem to fall. They could do considerable damage to a forest just by settling onto the branches of its trees, and when they moved on, the ground would be buried under several feet of droppings. When they flew together, the flapping of their wings was "like the roar of distant thunder," according to the famous naturalist John James Audubon.

2. In your own words, write the main idea of paragraphs 6 and 7.

   _____

   _____

3. Complete the following map for paragraph 8.

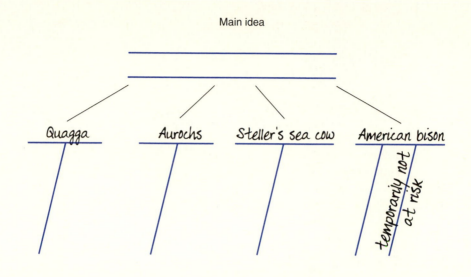

Main idea

Quagga          Aurochs          Steller's sea cow          American bison

temporarily not at risk

---

**Exercise 10** | **Working with Words**

Find the correct dictionary definition for the following words. Be sure to check the context in which they appear in the excerpt.

1. infinite (para. 3) _____
2. evolved (para. 5) _____
3. wholesale (para. 6) _____

Determine the meanings for the following words by going back and reading them in the paragraph in which they appear. Write their meaning in your own words.

4. vanish (para. 3) _____
5. pinpoint (para. 7) _____
6. quagga (para. 8) _____

---

**Exercise 11** | **Making Connections**

What kinds of things do you think people can do in order to protect animals that are in danger of extinction?

## Exercise **12** | Organizing to Learn: Outlining and Summarizing

1. Write a brief outline of the reading "How Species Become Extinct."
2. Write a brief summary of the reading "How Species Become Extinct."

# *Chapter Review*

## Exercise **13** | Skills Review

1. Why is it important for you to know the difference between major and minor supporting details?
2. What are minor supporting details? What kinds of minor supporting details are there?
3. List the six steps to take when writing a summary.

## Exercise **14** | Writing

Write a letter to the editor of your local or school newspaper in which you discuss the environmental problem addressed by your group and make suggestions for how that problem could be resolved.

## Exercise **15** | Collaborative Activity

Discuss an environmental problem that exists in or near your community (e.g., endangered animals; noise, land, or air pollution; toxic waste disposal; trash disposal). Take notes of your group's discussion to answer the following questions:

- What is the problem?
- What is the cause of the problem?
- What are some solutions for the problem?

## Exercise **16** | Extension Activity

1. Go to the library and find a magazine or newspaper article about animals that are in danger of becoming extinct. Underline or write out the main idea of the article. Number the major supporting details and write letters for the minor supporting details. Bring the article to class to share with your class group and/or to turn into your instructor.
2. Write an outline or a map for the article you brought in about animals that are in danger of becoming extinct.
3. Write a summary for the article you brought in about animals that are in danger of becoming extinct.

# *Unit* Review

## The Garbage Crisis

KATHLYN GAY

*Many people believe that Americans throw away too much trash
and that our landfills are rapidly filling. At the same time, a great
deal of toxic material is carelessly discarded. Some say we will
have a problem for many generations to come if we are not more
careful about how we handle our wastes now. In the following
selection Kathlyn Gay presents an overview of the problem.*

### Preparing to Read

1. Preview the reading.
2. Write two reader's questions that you think will be answered.

1    People in the United States produce more waste than any
other society in the world. In one year, for example, Americans
throw out 1.6 billion disposable pens, 240 million tires, 2 billion disposable razors and blades, and about 18 billion disposable diapers.
Enough aluminum is discarded each year to rebuild all of the commercial airplanes in the United States—every three months.

**discarded** thrown away

2    In just one metropolitan area, Los Angeles County, the
garbage produced every nine to ten days would fill Dodger Sta-
dium. The daily flow of solid waste from New York City is 27,000
tons. Each Chicagoan produces between five and six pounds of
garbage daily. The refuse from other major cities and smaller communities brings the nation's total garbage heap from industrial,
commercial, and residential sources to an estimated 250 million
tons annually. Of that total, commercial and residential waste ac-
counts for 160 million tons. It would take a lineup of trucks reaching
halfway to the moon to hold all the garbage generated each year by
American consumers!

**ton** two thousand pounds

**generated** cre-ated, produced

3    Where does all that stuff go? In the past, communities got rid
of their garbage by tossing it into a river and letting the water carry
the refuse downstream. As urban areas developed, people threw

In most communities, garbage and trash collectors pick up the waste and haul it to a landfill, where the throwaways are covered over with dirt and compacted. Well-designed landfills have safeguards to prevent toxic materials from seeping into soils and waterways.

their garbage into an open dump at the edge of town. These dump sites attracted rats and other pests and eventually were outlawed. Today, municipal or private trash collectors haul garbage away and dispose of it in a landfill, areas that local governments have set aside for waste disposal and decomposition.

A landfill usually begins as an excavated area or pit. Garbage is dumped in the pit and covered over with a layer of soil. Bacteria in the soil can biodegrade, or break down, materials such as food scraps in a relatively short time. Decomposed materials then become part of the earth. But bacteria need oxygen and water to work efficiently. At most modern landfills, machines crush and tightly compact refuse, then pack down the dirt cover. Thus, the rate of decomposition slows down, and refuse may stay intact for many months or years. A milk carton can last five years; nylon cloth may be around for thirty to forty years; aluminum cans take from two hundred to five hundred years to decompose; and some glass and plastics may last millions of years.

4

**decompose** to rot, to break down into components

5  Not only do these materials add to the heaps of waste that fill up disposal sites, but an increasing amount of trash contains toxic substances such as weed and pest killers, cleaning fluids, paint strippers, and used car oil. Some throwaways contain heavy metals like lead and mercury, proven health hazards. Lead may seep from corroding batteries, for example. Children exposed to low levels of lead can suffer brain damage, nervous system disorders, and other developmental problems.

6  Toxic compounds become part of the leachate, the liquid that percolates through or seeps from solid waste as it decomposes. If a landfill is not properly designed, leachate can run off into streams or seep through the soil into groundwater, the source of drinking water for at least half of the U.S. population. This is a particular problem in areas where there are high levels of precipitation and soils are sandy and porous.

7  In 1976, the U.S. Congress passed the Resource Conservation Recovery Act that requires states to construct safer landfills. New ones must be underlined with thick layers of clay or vinyl materials or both, so that leachate will not percolate through the soil. In some areas, landfills can be constructed on clay beds that are a natural part of the land; in other areas, layers of clay soil must be laid down and compacted. However, only about 900 of the 6,000 landfills in the United States are lined.

---

**Exercise 1**  **Checking Your Understanding**

1. Choose the best main idea statement for the reading.
   _____ a. The management of American landfills needs to be improved because Americans produce more waste than any other country.
   _____ b. Children exposed to low levels of lead can suffer brain damage, nervous system disorders, and other developmental problems.
   _____ c. Americans produce more waste than any other country in the world.
   _____ d. In one year . . . Americans throw out 1.6 billion disposable pens, 240 million tires, 2 billion disposable razors and blades, and about 18 billion disposable diapers.

2. For the following sentences, write "*Major*" for the major supporting details and "*Minor*" for the minor supporting details. (The minor supporting details provide additional information or make the information more interesting.)
   _____ a. Industrial, commercial, and residential sources of waste make up about 250 million tons annually.
   _____ b. It would take a lineup of trucks reaching halfway to the moon to hold all the garbage generated each year by American consumers!

_____ c. Most waste is dumped in landfills.

_____ d. Materials in landfills don't break down for a long time.

_____ e. An increasing amount of trash contains toxic substances which are health hazards.

_____ f. In some areas landfills can be constructed on natural clay beds.

_____ g. The U.S. Congress passed legislation to construct safer landfills, but much more work needs to be done to make them all safe.

**Exercise 2**    **Working with Words**

Find the correct dictionary definitions for the *italicized* words in the following sentences and write them on the lines provided.

1. At most modern landfills, machines crush and tightly *compact refuse,* then pack down the dirt cover.

   *compact* _____

   *refuse* _____

2. [Leachate] is a particular problem in areas where there are high levels of *precipitation* and soils are sandy and porous.

   *precipitation* _____

Find out the meanings of the following *italicized* words from the context of the sentences and write their meanings on the lines provided.

3. Today, municipal [city] or private trash collectors haul garbage away and dispose of it in a *landfill,* areas that local governments have set aside for waste disposal and decomposition.

   *landfill* _____

4. Bacteria in the soil can *biodegrade,* or break down, materials such as food scraps in a relatively short time.

   *biodegrade* _____

5. Toxic compounds become part of the *leachate,* the liquid that percolates through or seeps from solid waste as it decomposes.

   *leachate* _____

**Exercise 3**    **Making Connections**

1. Make a list of the things that you throw away that you might be able to recycle.
2. Call your local landfill and find out how much they charge to dump materials there.

3. Where do people in your neighborhood get rid of stuff that they don't want any more (old beds, refrigerators, clothes, etc.)? List the different possible places.
4. Why do you think it is important to think about how much we throw away?

**Exercise 4**   **Organizing to Learn**

1. Write an outline or map of the reading.
2. Write a summary of the reading, remembering to use your own words and include only major supporting details.

# 4
# Our Changing Families

## *Patterns of Organization*

*All happy families resemble one another; every unhappy family is unhappy in its own fashion.*

Leo Tolstoy

## Preparing to Read

1. Who are the people in the picture on page 189? What do you think their relationship is to each other? What are they doing?
2. What do you think is the meaning of the quotation under the picture? Do you agree? Why or why not?

## UNIT OBJECTIVES/SKILLS TO LEARN

In this unit you will learn how to

- Recognize patterns of organization, including examples, chronological order, definition, comparison and contrast, and cause and effect
- Interpret transitional words and phrases in sentences, between sentences and between paragraphs

In the process of acquiring these skills, you will read and use information about

- Housework 100–150 years ago
- Families in history and in the United States today

### Key Terms and Concepts

**patterns of organization**    the way ideas and information are organized
**transitional words and phrases**    clues that help you recognize patterns of organization
**extended family**    a family that includes relatives besides parents and children (such as grandparents, aunts, and uncles)
**nuclear family**    a family that includes only the parents and children
**single-parent family**    a family headed by an unmarried mother or father
**patriarchal family**    a family in which a male is given most authority
**matriarchal family**    a family in which a female is given most authority
**monogamy**    marriage with one husband and wife
**polygamy**    practice of having more than one spouse at a time

# Raising Issues

## What Is a Family?

Recently there has been a lot of talk about families. Some politicians like to point to the different types of American families as a problem in our society; others feel that our families are fine the way they are, but that government needs to help them more.

What do you think a family should be like? If you think about your own family, your friends' families, and other families you know, you will probably realize that there are lots of different kinds of families. Who are the members of these families? You probably know some single-parent families, some stepfamilies, some families that include grandparents, and some families made up of both biological parents and their children. In Chapter 7 we will be reading about family life in the United States and how it has changed over the past few centuries. In Chapter 8 we will read about families in the United States today, the challenges of family life, and what makes a successful family.

## *My Husband's Nine Wives*

ELIZABETH JOSEPH

*In the following selection, Elizabeth Joseph writes about her experience in a rather unusual marriage relationship. Her family practices polygamy; that is, her husband had six other wives when she married him, and now he has nine wives. Read to see why she thinks this is an ideal relationship for herself and her children.*

1    I married a married man.

2    In fact, he had six wives when I married him 17 years ago. Today, he has nine.

3    In March, the Utah Supreme Court struck down a trial court's ruling that a polygamist couple could not adopt a child because of their marital style. Last month, the national board of the American Civil Liberties Union, in response to a request from its Utah chapter, adopted a new policy calling for the legalization of polygamy.

4    Polygamy, or plural marriage, as practiced by my family is a paradox. At first blush, it sounds like the ideal situation for the man and an oppressive one for the women. For me, the opposite is true. While polygamists believe that the Old Testament mandates the practice of plural marriage, compelling social reasons make the life style attractive to the modern career woman.

**paradox** something that is different from what is expected

**mandates** requires

5    Pick up any women's magazine and you will find article after article about the problems of successfully juggling career, motherhood, and marriage. It is a complex act that many women struggle to manage daily; their frustrations fill up the pages of those magazines and consume the hours of afternoon talk shows.

In a monogamous context, the only solutions are compromises. The kids need to learn to fix their own breakfast, your husband needs to get used to occasional microwave dinners, you need to divert more of your income to insure that your preschooler is in a good day-care environment. 6

I am sure that in the challenge of working through these compromises, satisfaction and success can be realized. But why must women only embrace a marital arrangement that requires so many trade-offs? 7

When I leave for the 60-mile commute to court at 7 A.M., my 2-year-old daughter, London, is happily asleep in the bed of my husband's wife, Diane. London adores Diane. When London awakes, about the time I'm arriving at the courthouse, she is surrounded by family members who are as familiar to her as the toys in her nursery. 8

My husband, Alex, who writes at night, gets up much later. While most of his wives are already at work, pursuing their careers, he can almost always find one who's willing to chat over coffee. 9

I share a home with Delinda, another wife, who works in town government. Most nights, we agree we'll just have a simple dinner with our three kids. We'd rather relax and commiserate over the pressures of our work day than chew up our energy cooking and doing a ton of dishes. 10

Mondays, however, are different. That's the night Alex eats with us. The kids, excited that their father is coming to dinner, are on their best behavior. We often invite another wife or one of his children. It's a special event because it only happens once a week. 11

Tuesday night, it's back to simplicity for us. But for Alex and the household he's dining with that night, it's their special time. 12

The same system with some variation governs our private time with him. While spontaneity is by no means ruled out, we basically use an appointment system. If I want to spend Friday evening at his house, I make an appointment. If he's already "booked," I either request another night, or if my schedule is inflexible, I talk to the other wife and we work out an arrangement. One thing we've all learned is that there's always another night. 13

**intimacy** closeness

Most evenings, with the demands of career and the literal chasing after the needs of a toddler, all I want to do is collapse into bed and sleep. But there is also the longing for intimacy and comfort that only he can provide, and when those feelings surface, I ask to be with him. 14

**confining** restricting

Plural marriage is not for everyone. But it is the life style for me. It offers men the chance to escape from the traditional, confining roles that often isolate them from the surrounding world. More important, it enables women, who live in a society full of obstacles, to fully meet their career, mothering, and marriage obligations. 15

Polygamy provides a whole solution. I believe American women would have invented it if it didn't already exist.

| Exercise **1** | **Discussion Questions** |

1. Why does Joseph think that polygamy is an attractive lifestyle for the modern career woman?
2. What does she mean when she says her husband is already "booked"?
3. What does Joseph mean when she says, "Polygamy provides a whole solution"?

| Exercise **2** | **Making Connections** |

1. How do women or men you know manage the responsibilities of marriage, family, and career?
2. Do you think that polygamy is a good way for women to manage the responsibilities of marriage, family, and career? Explain why or why not.

# CHAPTER 7

# Families in History and Around the World

## EXAMPLES, CHRONOLOGICAL ORDER, AND DEFINITIONS

In Unit Three you learned to distinguish between main ideas and the many supporting ideas in paragraphs and essays. These supporting ideas are often organized according to certain *patterns of organization.* Writers choose a particular pattern of organization because it helps them present their ideas and information in a clear way. Recognizing these patterns makes it easier for readers to understand what the writer is trying to tell us. Three of the most common ways to organize information are by examples, chronological order, and definitions.

## EXAMPLES

### In Sentences

Sentences often explain an idea by offering examples. For instance, when discussing families today, an author might first identify the different types of families.

> Families in America today include a wide variety of models, such as the traditional extended family, the single-parent family, the nuclear family, and the stepparent family.

Each of the underlined terms in this sentence is a separate example of a kind of family in today's society.

**Clues.**   Watch for the following clues to help you recognize examples in sentences or in longer passages.

1. Lists of examples are often separated by commas, semicolons, or numbers.
2. The following words are often used to introduce lists:
   - such as
   - for example
   - for instance
   - in addition
   - moreover

## In Paragraphs

In a paragraph or a longer passage an example could be one sentence or several sentences long. Examples in sentences—which can be major or minor supporting details—are often used to support the main idea statement of a paragraph. In the following paragraph, the main idea is stated in the first sentence, "Historically, in most cultures the family has been patriarchal or male-dominated." The writer then goes on to use two examples, one from the Old Testament and one from ancient Rome, to support her main idea. Notice that she introduces the first example with the words, "One *example* is given." The second example, however, is introduced only by the words "In ancient Rome."

> Historically, in most cultures the family has been patriarchal or male-dominated. One example is given in the Old Testament, where male heads of a clan were allowed several wives, as well as concubines. In ancient Rome, the family was also patriarchal, but polygamy was not practiced. The Roman family was an extended one, and the patriarch had the authority even to kill his sons. (UN Chronicle)

When we recognize that the paragraph is organized to give examples, we can organize that information into a map, showing the major and minor supporting details. It would look like this:

Main idea

**In most cultures, the family has been patriarchal or male-dominated.**

(Example 1)
**Old testament-heads of clans**

- several wives
- concubines

(Example 2)
**Ancient Rome-patriarchal**

- no polygamy
- extended family
- father authorized to kill sons

Another way for a writer to use examples is to simply provide a list. In the following paragraph, the clues are the words "such as" and the list using numbers separated by semicolons.

In many parts of the world, the extended family, in which grandparents, aunts, uncles, and children all live together, is the most common family structure. The extended family structure has been successful because it provides many benefits for families such as: (1) economic advantages because it is cheaper to house and to feed many people who all live together; (2) work distribution advantages because there are more people to share in household tasks such as cooking, cleaning, and taking care of children; and, (3) social advantages because there are so many family members around, no family members are lonely or left alone if they need help taking care of themselves due to sickness or old age.

Another way to organize information that is presented as examples is to use an outline. For the above paragraph, a brief outline might look like this:

Benefits of Extended Families

Main idea: The extended family structure has been successful because it provides many benefits for families.

   I. Economic
     A. Cheaper to live together
     B. Cheaper to eat together
  II. Work distribution; share in tasks
     A. Cooking and cleaning
     B. Taking care of children
 III. Social
     A. No one lonely
     B. If sick or old, taken care of

**Exercise 3**    **Identifying Examples**

In the following paragraphs, underline the main idea and circle the clue words or punctuation that signals the use of examples. Then on a separate sheet of paper, make a map or outline that includes the important information in the paragraph.

1. In traditional European peasant societies, the firstborn son inherited the family land, so second and third sons had to look for other ways to earn a living. In sixteenth-century Spain there were more options open to them. First, they could join the church. Second, they could become a paid soldier. And finally, they could join the expeditions of exploration to the New World.
2. Historically, men's most important role within the family structure was to provide food for the family. This they did by hunting, fishing, and raising sheep or cattle. In addition, they were frequently responsible for the agricultural tasks that required heavy physical labor.

3. First of all, the family, because of the strong feelings it generates, is a powerful source not just of love and care but *also* of pain and conflict. . . . In most families, there are instances of conflict and violence, such as anger, physical punishment of children, or spouses poking and slapping each other. In fact, the family is one of the few groups in society empowered by law or tradition to hit its members. It is, for example, legal for parents to spank their children as a form of punishment. Moreover, many husbands who strike their wives to "keep them in line" are not arrested, prosecuted, or imprisoned. (Alex Thio, *Sociology*)

## LANGUAGE TIP

### Coordination

Coordination is one of the ways that information and ideas are combined in sentences. Read over the following list of conjunctions and the explanations of how they coordinate ideas.

- And—indicates additional information
- But—indicates a contradiction, an exception, or unexpected information
- Either/Or—indicates that a choice must be made between two possibilities
- Neither/Nor—indicates that the items that follow are *not* included

Items listed in a series within a sentence are *coordinated* by the above conjunctions. For example:

Families in America include a wide variety of models, such as the traditional extended family, the single-parent family, the nuclear family, and the stepparent family.

Here the list of examples is marked by a comma after each item and then by "and" between the last two items in the series.

Independent clauses—subject/verb combintions that can stand alone as a sentence—can also be *coordinated,* or linked together, in a sentence. For example, the following is a compound sentence:

The Roman family was an extended one, and the patriarch had the authority even to kill his sons.
(subject)  (verb)                          (subject)  (verb)

*(continued)*

As a reader you should recognize that two independent clauses joined by "and" are considered equally important. Watch for the conjunctions that link ideas in a sentence because these small words can completely change the meaning of the entire thought. For example, notice the different meanings in the following sentences which are emphasized by the use of "and" or "but."

> Roman fathers had the right to kill their sons, but they almost never killed a child.

In this sentence, the emphasis is on how rare it was for a father to kill a son.

> Roman fathers had the right to kill their sons, and they occasionally did kill their own offspring.

In this sentence, the emphasis is on the fact that sometimes fathers actually did kill a son.

**Exercise 4** | **Coordination**

Read each of the following similar sentences. Underline the conjunctions. Notice how changing the conjunction changes the meaning of the sentence. (Not all of the sentences are true, of course.)

1. In Brazil, the joint extended family was typical and the oldest male was in charge.
2. In Brazil, the extended family was typical, but the oldest male was not in charge.
3. In Brazil, families were either extended families or the oldest male was in charge.
4. In Brazil today, families are neither extended families nor is the oldest male in charge.

# CHRONOLOGICAL ORDER

## In Sentences

Chronological order organizes information according to the time at which an event occurred. It often shows how something developed over time or explains its history. For example, the writer of the following sentence is concerned about the changes in the baby boom generation's attitude towards family between the 1960s and the 1970s.

The large baby boom generation, which had been active in the 1960s, was moving on to marriage and parenthood by the end of the 1970s. (Arlene and Jerome Skolnick, *Family in Transition*)

**Clues**    Watch for the following clues to help you recognize that the author is focusing on chronological order.

1. Dates, such as: in 1970, in the 1800s, etc.
2. Transitional words indicating time changes such as:
   - then
   - when
   - after
   - before
   - later
   - while

## In Paragraphs

The use of chronological order to organize information is also obvious in paragraphs. For example, in the following paragraph each sentence begins with dates to keep the reader's focus on the changes in the family from one decade to another. In fact, the main idea of the paragraph is: "The American family has been changing over time," or "The American family has changed since the 1950s." The time clues—which help you figure out the main idea—have been underlined for you.

During the 1950s the Cleavers on the television show "Leave It to Beaver" epitomized the American family. In 1960, over 70 percent of all American households were like the Cleavers: made up of a breadwinner father, a homemaker mother and their kids. Today, "traditional" families with a working husband, an unemployed wife, and one or more children make up less than 15 percent of the nation's households. (James Kirby Martin et al., *America and Its People*)

• • • • • • • • • • • • • •

# Organizing to Learn
## Time Lines

• • • • • • • • • • • • • • • • • • • • • • • • • • • • • • • • • • •

One good way to organize information based on chronological order is to set it up as a time line. With a time line, you can see the chronological relationship between events. For example, for the above paragraph, a time line might look like this:

Main idea: The American family has changed since the 1950s.

| 1950s | Family like the Cleavers |
|---|---|
| 1960 | 70 percent like Cleavers (breadwinner father, homemaker mother) |
| Today | Only 15 percent of families with working father and unemployed wife (full-time homemaker) |

---

**Exercise 5**    **Identifying Chronological Order/Using Time Lines**

In the following paragraphs underline dates and clue words or phrases that indicate chronological order. Write the main idea and complete the time lines. The clues in the first sentence have already been underlined for you.

1. The Dating Ritual. Developed largely <u>after World War I came to an end in 1918</u>, the U.S. custom of dating has spread to many industrial countries. It has also changed in the United States in the last two decades. <u>Before the 1970s</u>, dating was more formal. Males had to ask for a date at least several days in advance. It was usually the male who decided where to go, paid for the date, opened doors, and was supposed to be chivalrous. The couple often went to an event, such as a movie, dance, concert, or ball game.

   <u>Today</u>, dating has become more casual. In fact, the word "date" now sounds a bit old-fashioned to many young people. (Alex Thio, *Sociology*)

   Main idea: _____

   _____

   Time line

   | 1918 | _____ |
   |---|---|
   | Before 1970s | _____ |
   | Today | dating has become casual |

2. Families and individual family members have at certain times in history decided to move away from the areas where they were born. At the beginning of the nineteenth century (early 1800s), German peasants began migrating to the United States. In the 1840s, people from Ireland migrated because there was not enough food due to the failed potato crops. Later in the nineteenth century, Scandinavians came. Finally, in the 1890s and early twentieth century, many Eastern European families moved to the "New World," looking for better opportunities.

Main idea: _____

_____

Time line

Beginning of 1800s (early 19th century)    _____

1840s | people from Ireland because of Irish potato crop failure

Late 1800s | _____

End of 1800s, early 20th century | _____

# DEFINITIONS

## In Sentences

A definition answers the question, "What is it?" For example, the following sentence explains what "monogamy" is. The term is in **bold face** to attract our attention to its importance, and the meaning is provided between the dashes.

> **Monogamy**—the marriage of one man to one woman—is the most common form in the world. (Alex Thio, *Sociology*)

**Clues.**    Watch for the following clues to help you recognize that the author has provided a definition.

1. Words such as:
   * means
   * refers to
   * consists of
   * is (often indicates that the meaning of a word or phrase will follow)
2. Sometimes definitions are included
   * in parentheses: Polygamy (the practice of having more than one spouse at a time) is not very common in Western countries.
   * between dashes: Polygamy—the practice of having more than one spouse at a time—is not very common in Western countries.
   * immediately after the term between commas: Polygamy, the practice of having more than one spouse at a time, is not very common in Western countries.

## In Paragraphs

Sometimes a writer will expand his or her definition to a paragraph or more in length. For example, in the following reading the authors try to define *family*. In fact, the main idea is the definition of the family. Notice that *family* is not an easy word to define and the authors use different terms to explain its meaning.

What is a family? In everyday conversation we make assumptions about what families are or should be. Traditionally, both law and social science specified that the family consisted of people related by blood, marriage, or adoption. Some definitions of the family specified a common household, economic interdependence, and sexual and reproductive relations. . . .

Burgess and Locke defined the family as "a group of persons united by the ties of marriage, blood, or adoption; constituting a single household; interacting and communicating with each other in their respective social roles (husband and wife, mother and father, son and daughter, brother and sister); and creating and maintaining a common culture." This definition goes beyond earlier ones to talk about family relationships and interactions. (Mary Ann Lamanna and Agnes Riedmann, *Marriages and Families*)

Another way to organize this information is to map or to outline it.

### Definition of the Family

Main idea: A family is defined as people related by blood, marriage, or adoption, although some experts have added additional characteristics to that list.

Additional characteristics (major supporting details):
  I. Single household
 II. Economic interdependence
III. Sexual and reproductive relations
 IV. Communicating with each other in their roles (Burgess and Locke)
  V. Maintaining a common culture (Burgess and Locke)

**Exercise 6   Identifying Definitions**

Circle the clues that indicate definitions in the following paragraphs. Underline the definition of each boldfaced word. Then complete the maps that follow.

1. A few societies have placed the mother at the head of the family. This type of family is called **matriarchal.** The husband usually goes to live with the wife's family. Women may own the property, and pass it on to their daughters. A few tribes today are matriarchies. (*World Book Encyclopedia*)

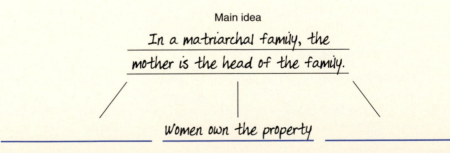

Main idea

In a matriarchal family, the mother is the head of the family.

Women own the property

2.  There are also norms governing the number of spouses a person may have. **Monogamy**—the marriage of one man to one woman—is the most common form in the world. But many societies, especially small, preindustrial ones, approve of **polygamy,** marriage of one person to two or more people of the same sex. It is rare for a society to allow the practice of **polyandry,** marriage of one woman to two or more men. . . . A new variant of polygamy has become increasingly common in the United States. Rather than having several spouses at the same time, many have one spouse at a time, going through a succession of marriage, divorce, and remarriage. Such practice is not really polygamy, but **serial monogamy,** marriage of one person to two or more people but only one at a time. (Alex Thio, *Sociology*)

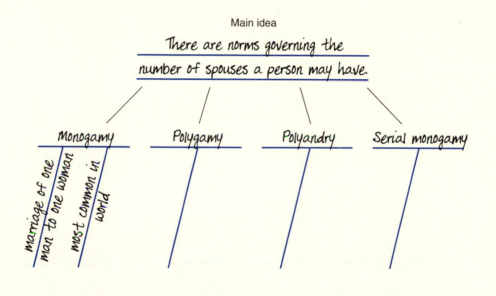

Main idea

There are norms governing the number of spouses a person may have.

Monogamy — Polygamy — Polyandry — Serial monogamy

marriage of one man to one woman

most common in world

---

**Exercise 7    Identifying Patterns of Organization**

Decide whether each of the following sentences is primarily organized by examples, chronological order, or definition. Underline the clues that you used to decide. The first one has been done for you.

1.  As families have become less traditional, the legal <u>definition</u> of a family has become much more flexible and nonspecific and <u>is not limited to</u> people linked by legal marriage, by blood, or by adoption. (Mary Ann Lamanna and Agnes Riedmann, *Marriages and Families*)

    Pattern of organization: *Definition* _____ (*The writers' focus in this sentence is on the different parts of "the legal definition of a family."*)

2. In the United States and Canada, the term *family* commonly means a group of related persons who share a home. (Nona Glazer, *The World Book Encyclopedia*)

   Pattern of organization: _____

3. The rate of divorce has more than doubled since 1965, peaking in 1979 and dropping slightly since then. (Mary Ann Lamanna and Agnes Riedmann, *Marriages and Families*)

   Pattern of organization: _____

4. The study of the family does not fit neatly within the boundaries of any single scholarly field: genetics, physiology, archeology, history, anthropology, sociology, psychology, and economics all touch upon it. (Arlene Skolnick and Jerome Skolnick, *Family in Transition*)

   Pattern of organization: _____

5. [Between] 1960 and 1993 the percent of children in one-parent families who were living with a never-married mother grew from 4 percent to 35 percent. (Robin Wolf, *Marriages and Family in a Diverse Society*)

   Pattern of organization: _____

6. Single-parent families, one-earner nuclear families, two-earner families and stepfamilies reflect the diversity of American families today.

   Pattern of organization: _____

7. A society with the women in charge is called **matriarchal** (from words meaning "mother" and "ruler"). (Ruth Shonle Cavan, "Family")

   Pattern of organization: _____

**Exercise 8  Identifying Patterns of Organization**

Decide whether each of the following paragraphs is primarily organized by examples, chronological order, or definition. Find the main ideas in the following examples and write them on the lines provided (they may be stated or unstated). Circle the clues that you used to identify the pattern of organization. A paragraph may have more than one pattern of organization, so identify the one that is more important for supporting the main idea. The first one has been done for you.

1. It was not enough for a housewife to know how to use a cast-iron stove. She also had to know how to prepare unprocessed foods for consumption. Prior to the 1890s, there were few factory-prepared foods. Shoppers bought poultry that was still alive and then had to kill and pluck the birds. Fish had to have scales removed. Green coffee had to be roasted and ground. Loaves of sugar had to be pounded, flour sifted, nuts shelled, and raisins seeded. (James Kirby Martin et al., *America and Its People*)

   Pattern of organization: *Examples* _____

*(This paragraph is chiefly organized to provide examples of the various tasks—such as killing and plucking birds, raosting and grinding coffee, and seeding raisins—that housewives had to perform 100 years ago. Although the date 1890 is included, the pattern is not chronological because the writers' primary purpose is not to trace changes through time, but to provide specific examples of tasks housewives had to undertake many years ago.)*

Main idea: *Housewives had to do a lot of different chores to prepare a meal prior to the 1890s.*

2. Families have been changing gradually over time, but in much of the world, the changes have followed the same basic steps. When families lived on farms, they were large because people needed children to help them work. Mothers spent their time taking care of the household. But in the last few hundred years people have been moving to urban areas where families have fewer children. Jobs have increasingly become available to women, and fewer women were able to stay at home and pass up the possibility of an added income to help support the family. Today, in most developed countries, the vast majority of women work.

Pattern of organization: _____

Main idea: _____

3. A primary group is a small group marked by close, face-to-face relationships. Group members share experiences, express emotions, and, in the ideal case, know they are accepted and valued. In many ways, teams and families are similar primary groups: joys are celebrated spontaneously, tempers can flare quickly, and expression is often physical. (Mary Ann Lamanna and Agnes Riedmann, *Marriages and Families*)

Pattern of organization: _____

Main idea: _____

4. In American society, life in many families is organized primarily around the *nuclear* family. A nuclear family is made up of parents and their children and spans only two generations. Nuclear families do not include extended family members such as aunts, uncles, and grandparents.

Pattern of organization: _____

Main idea: _____

5. In a few societies the mother or grandmother has the stronger voice in making decisions. For example, among the Hopi Indians in the southwestern United States, the women of the family own the land. When a woman marries, her husband moves in with her family or into a house nearby. But the men work the land and also carry out important religious ceremonies. (Ruth Shonle Cavan, "Family")

Pattern of organization: _____

Main idea: _____

_____

6. *Cohabitation* refers to two people living together in a sexual relationship without marriage. Two decades ago cohabitation was rare. In 1970 only 11 percent of people who married for the first time had prior experience with cohabitation. Today, almost half of people who enter first marriages have previously cohabited. The U.S. Bureau of the Census estimates that today there are 5 million cohabiting couples in the United States. . . . Of the cohabiting couples, 1.2 million have children under age fifteen living with them. (Robin Wolf, *Marriages and Family in a Diverse Society*)

Pattern of organization for the first sentence: _____

Pattern of organization for the rest of the paragraph: _____

Main idea: _____

## Patterns of Organization in Longer Selections

Very often when you read a longer selection you will find that it contains more than one thought pattern. This happens because different thought patterns support different kinds of main ideas. Different kinds of textbooks, however, do tend to organize most of their information around a dominant pattern. The following excerpt, for example, is from a history book. Overall, in this case, information is organized in chronological order, but individual paragraphs use different patterns to support the main idea.

### *Housework in Victorian America*

JAMES KIRBY MARTIN, ET AL.

*Part of the definition of a family is a group of people who live together in a household. When we live together in a household, we usually divide up the roles that each member of the family has. During some periods and in some places in the past the woman's role was to take care of the house (cook, clean, shop, etc.) and the children. The men were expected to go to work and earn enough money to support the family. The following excerpt from a college history textbook describes what life was like for the American housewife of 100 years ago.*

## Preparing to Read

1. How many women do you know that are full-time housewives?
2. What are the responsibilities of the women in your family? To cook? To clean? To take care of children? To work outside the home?
3. What are the responsibilities of the men in your family? To cook? To clean? To take care of children? To work outside the home?
4. As you read the following passage from a history textbook, think about the differences between doing housework 100 years ago and doing housework today.

1      Housework in nineteenth-century America was harsh physical labor. Preparing even a simple meal was a time- and energy-consuming chore. Prior to the twentieth century, cooking was performed on a coal- or wood-burning stove. Unlike an electric or a gas range, which can be turned on with the flick of a single switch, cast-iron and steel stoves were exceptionally difficult to use.

2      Ashes from an old fire had to be removed. Then, paper and kindling had to be set inside the stove, dampers and flues had to be carefully adjusted, and a fire lit. Since there were no thermostats to

regulate the stove's temperature, a woman had to keep an eye on the contraption all day long. Any time the fire slackened, she had to adjust a flue or add more fuel.

Throughout the day, the stove had to be continually fed with new supplies of coal or wood—an average of 50 pounds a day. At least twice a day, the ash box had to be emptied, a task which required a woman to gather ashes and cinders in a grate and then dump them into a pan below. Altogether, a housewife spent four hours every day sifting ashes, adjusting dampers, lighting fires, carrying coal or wood, and rubbing the stove with thick black wax to keep it from rusting. 3

It was not enough for a housewife to know how to use a cast-iron stove. She also had to know how to prepare unprocessed foods for consumption. Prior to the 1890s, there were few factory-prepared foods. Shoppers bought poultry that was still alive and then had to kill and pluck the birds. Fish had to have scales removed. Green coffee had to be roasted and ground. Loaves of sugar had to be pounded, flour sifted, nuts shelled, and raisins seeded. 4

**arduous** difficult

Cleaning was an even more arduous task than cooking. The soot and smoke from coal- and wood-burning stoves blackened walls and dirtied drapes and carpets. Gas and kerosene lamps left smelly deposits of black soot on furniture and curtains. Each day, the lamp's glass chimneys had to be wiped and wicks trimmed or replaced. Floors had to be scrubbed, rugs beaten, and windows washed. While a small minority of well-to-do families could afford to hire cooks at $5 a week, waitresses at $3.50 a week, laundresses at $3.50 a week, and cleaning women and choremen for $1.50 a day, in the overwhelming majority of homes, all household tasks had to be performed by a housewife and her daughters. 5

Housework in nineteenth-century America was a full-time job. Gro Svendsen, a Norwegian immigrant, was astonished by how hard the typical American housewife had to work. As she wrote her parents in 1862: 6

> We are told that the women of America have much leisure time but I haven't yet met any woman who thought so! Here the mistress of the house must do all the work that the cook, the maid and the housekeeper would do in an upper class family at home. Moreover, she must do her work as well as these three together do it in Norway.

Before the end of the nineteenth century, when indoor plumbing became common, chores that involved the use of water were particularly demanding. Well-to-do urban families had piped water or a private cistern, but the overwhelming majority of American 7 families got their water from a hydrant, a pump, a well, or a stream located some distance from their house. The mere job of bringing water into the house was exhausting. According to calculations made in 1886, a typical North Carolina housewife had to carry water from a pump or a well or a spring eight to ten times each day. Washing, boiling, and rinsing a single load of laundry used about 50 gallons of water. Over the course of a year she walked 148 miles toting water and carried over 36 tons of water.

8    Homes without running water also lacked the simplest way to dispose of garbage: sinks with drains. This meant that women had to remove dirty dishwater, kitchen slops, and, worst of all, the contents of chamberpots from their house by hand.

9    Laundry was the household chore that nineteenth-century housewives detested most. Rachel Haskell, a Nevada housewife, called it "the Herculean task which women all dread" and "the great domestic dread of the household."

**detested** hated

10    On Sunday evenings, a housewife soaked clothing in tubs of warm water. When she woke up the next morning, she had to scrub the laundry on a rough washboard and rub it with soap made from lye, which severely irritated her hands. Next, she placed the laundry in big vats of boiling water and stirred the clothes about with a long pole to prevent the clothes from developing yellow spots. Then she lifted the clothes out of the vats with a washstick, rinsed the clothes twice, once in plain water and once with bluing, wrung the clothes out, and hung them out to dry. At this point, clothes would be pressed with heavy flatirons and collars would be stiffened with starch.

11    The last years of the nineteenth century witnessed a revolution in the nature of housework. Beginning in the 1880s, with the invention of the carpet sweeper, a host of new "labor-saving" appliances were introduced. These included the electric iron (1903), the electric vacuum cleaner (1907), and the electric toaster (1912). At the same time, the first processed and canned foods appeared. In the 1870s, H. J. Heinz introduced canned pickles and sauerkraut; in the 1880s, Franco-American Co. introduced the first canned meals; and in the 1890s, Campbell's sold the first condensed soups. By the 1920s, the urban middle class enjoyed a myriad of new household conveniences, including hot and cold running water, gas stoves, automatic washing machines, refrigerators, and vacuum cleaners.

12    Yet despite the introduction of electricity, running water, and "labor-saving" household appliances, time spent on housework did not decline. Indeed, the typical full-time housewife today spends just as much time on housework as her grandmother or great-grandmother. In 1924, a typical housewife spent about 52 hours a week in housework. Half a century later, the average full-time

**decline** go down

housewife devoted 55 hours to housework. A housewife today spends less time cooking and cleaning up after meals, but she spends just as much time as her ancestors on housecleaning and even more time on shopping, household management, laundry, and childcare.

How can this be? The answer lies in a dramatic rise in the stan- 13 dards of cleanliness and childcare expected of a housewife. As early as the 1930s, this change was apparent to a writer in the *Ladies Home Journal*:

> Because we housewives of today have the tools to reach it, we dig every day after the dust that grandmother left to spring cataclysm. If few of us have nine children for a weekly bath, we have two or three for a daily immersion. If our consciences don't prick us over vacant pie shelves or empty cookie jars, they do over meals in which a vitamin may be omitted or a calorie lacking.

## Exercise **9**    Checking Your Understanding

Answer the following questions based on the previous reading.

1. Choose the best main idea statement for the reading:
   _____ a. Cleaning was even harder work than cooking for housewives in the nineteenth century.
   _____ b. Housework in nineteenth-century America required harsh physical labor, and even the introduction of laborsaving devices did not lessen the workload significantly.
   _____ c. The last years of the nineteenth century witnessed a revolution in the nature of housework.
   _____ d. Standards of cleanliness have risen dramatically in American households.
2. Preparing unprocessed foods for meals included all of the following *except*:
   _____ a. Removing scales from fish
   _____ b. Defrosting a frozen entree
   _____ c. Killing a chicken or other poultry
   _____ d. Roasting and grinding coffee beans
3. Before the end of the nineteenth century, the majority of American families got their household water from
   _____ a. A hydrant
   _____ b. A pump
   _____ c. A well
   _____ d. A nearby stream
   _____ e. All of the above

4. According to this reading the household chore that women hated most was
   _____a. Keeping a fire going in the stove
   _____b. Emptying the chamberpots
   _____c. Laundry
   _____d. Scrubbing floors
5. Despite the introduction of laborsaving devices, time spent on household work did not decline because:
   _____a. Standards of cleanliness rose dramatically in American homes.
   _____b. It took a lot of time to learn to use the new devices.
   _____c. Women didn't want to use the toasters, vacuum cleaners, and electric irons.
   _____d. The devices seldom worked as well as expected.

**Exercise 10    Making Connections**

1. How do you divide up the housework in your home? How many hours a week do the members of your household spend on housework? Is this more or less than the average of 52 hours in 1924 or 55 hours in 1974 reported in this reading?
2. List a number of the household duties you and members of your household regularly perform. How do those tasks compare to the duties of a housewife in the nineteenth century?
3. How do you think housework will change in the next 50 years? What new labor-saving device would you most like to see invented?

**Exercise 11    Identifying Patterns of Organization**

First, decide which is the primary thought pattern for the two following excerpts from the reading. Write your answer—examples, chronological order, or definition—in the space after each excerpt. Then write out the main idea. Finally, design your own map or write an outline of the excerpt.

1. The last years of the nineteenth century witnessed a revolution in the nature of housework. Beginning in the 1880s, with the invention of the carpet sweeper, a host of new "labor-saving" appliances were introduced. These included the electric iron (1903), the electric vacuum cleaner (1907), and the electric toaster (1912). At the same time, the first processed and canned foods appeared. In the 1870s, H. J. Heinz introduced canned pickles and sauerkraut; in the 1880s, Franco-American Co. introduced the first canned meals; and in the 1890s, Campbell's sold the first condensed soups. By the 1920s, the urban middle class enjoyed a myriad of new household conve-

niences, including hot and cold running water, gas stoves, automatic washing machines, refrigerators, and vacuum cleaners.

Pattern of organization: _____

Main idea: _____

Map or outline:

2. Cleaning was an even more arduous task than cooking. The soot and smoke from coal- and wood-burning stoves blackened walls and dirtied drapes and carpets. Gas and kerosene lamps left smelly deposits of black soot on furniture and curtains. Each day, the lamp's glass chimneys had to be wiped and wicks trimmed or replaced. Floors had to be scrubbed, rugs beaten, and windows washed.

Pattern of organization: _____

Main idea: _____

Map or outline:

· · · · · · · · · · · · · · ·

# Working with Words
## Word Parts: Prefixes
· · · · · · · · · · · · · · · · · · · · · · · · · · · · · · · · · · · · · ·

One way to multiply the number of words in your vocabulary rather quickly is to become aware of word parts. Known as *prefixes, roots,* and *suffixes,* these word parts can be put together to form words.

- Prefixes appear at the beginning of a word.
- Roots can be at the beginning, middle, or end of a word.
- Suffixes appear at the end of a word.

Knowing the meaning of many common word parts can greatly increase your vocabulary. For example, if you know that "gamy" is a root that means "marriage," you can understand many words relating to marriage. Some examples are *monogamy, bigamy,* and *polygamy.* In each case, a common prefix has been added to the front of the root. The prefix "mono" means "one," so "monogamy" means "marriage to one person." "Bi" means two, so "bigamy" means "marriage to two people," a man married to two women is called a bigamist. "Poly" means many, so "polygamy" means "marriage to more than one partner at a time."

Below is a list of 32 common prefixes, their meanings, and examples of words that use that prefix with that meaning. The first group of prefixes identifies number, the next prefixes mean "no" or "not," the third group identifies time, and the fourth group indicates place or position.

| Exercise **12** | **Working with Words: Prefixes** |

As you go through these prefixes, many of which you are already familiar with, write your own examples in the space provided. If you can't think of other examples, use the dictionary to find some.

### Number

| Prefix | Meaning | Example | Your Examples |
|--------|---------|---------|---------------|
| mono | one | monogamy | _____ |
| uni | one | uniform | _____ |
| bi | two | bigamy | _____ |
| tri | three | tricycle | _____ |
| quad | four | quadruplet | _____ |
| penta | five | pentagon | _____ |
| multi | many | multitalented | _____ |
| poly | many | polygamy | _____ |
| dec | ten | decimal | _____ |
| cent | hundred | centimeter | _____ |

### Negative

| Prefix | Meaning | Example | Your Examples |
|--------|---------|---------|---------------|
| anti | against | antiabortion | _____ |
| dys | ill, difficult | dysfunctional | _____ |
| il | not | illegible | _____ |
| im | not | immature | _____ |
| in | not | inaccurate | _____ |
| ir | not | irresponsible | _____ |
| un | not | unmarked | _____ |

**Time**

| Prefix | Meaning | Example | Your Examples |
|---|---|---|---|
| ante | before | anteroom | _____ |
| post | after, behind | postpartum | _____ |
| pre | before | prebirth | _____ |
| proto | first | prototype | _____ |
| re | again | return | _____ |

**Place or Position**

| Prefix | Meaning | Example | Your Examples |
|---|---|---|---|
| circum | around | circumcise | _____ |
| co | with, together | cooperate | _____ |
| com, con | with, together | communicate | _____ |
| dis | apart, away | disappear | _____ |
| en | in, into | entrap | _____ |
| epi | on, above | epicenter | _____ |
| ex | out of, from | exhale | _____ |
| sub | under, below | submarine | _____ |
| tele | far off, distant | telephoto | _____ |
| trans | across | translate | _____ |

**Exercise 13** | **Prefixes**

For any five of the prefixes above find examples of sentences in newspapers, magazines, or textbooks that use words that begin with this prefix. Copy the original sentence. Then write the meaning of the word as it's used in that sentence. Here is an example:

From "Housework in Victorian America":

*"She also had to know how to prepare unprocessed foods for consumption." (Actually two of the prefixes on our list are in this sentence—"pre" and "un.") "Prepare" means to do before or ahead of time. "Unprocessed" foods are foods that have not been processed or prepared ahead of time.*

• • • • • • • • • • • • • •

# Applying Your Skills

• • • • • • • • • • • • • • • • • • • • • • • • • • • • • • • • • • • • • • •

## *Marriage and Family: An Overview*

Robin Wolf

*The following excerpt from a sociology textbook explains how our society has changed in the past 50 years and how those changes have affected the American family. As you read this selection, think about the patterns of organization that are used and the main ideas of the passage.*

### Preparing to Read

1. Look at the headings of this selection. What topics will be covered?
2. Write three reader's questions that you think will be answered in this selection.

### From Industrial to Postindustrial Society

1 The United States changed from an industrial society based on factory production, which had its heyday in the 1940s and 1950s, to a postindustrial society in the 1960s that is organized around information processing, advanced technology, and services jobs. A number of factors associated with this change altered American families.

**altered** changed

2 **Female Employment**. The expansion of service jobs drew married women into the work force. Female employment and financial independence made divorce possible for a greater number of people.

3 **Delayed Marriage**. In modern society, well-paid jobs for both men and women require higher education. Extended education is incompatible with early marriage, so three decades ago the marriage age began to rise. This encouraged cohabitation and premarital sexual expression.

4 **The Sexual Revolution**. Attitude change associated with the sexual revolution of the the 1960s and 1970s encouraged cohabitation and probably also contributed to the rising divorce rate by making sexual relationships outside of marriage more acceptable.

In addition, the oral contraceptive and legalized abortion separated sexual pleasure from reproduction.

**Life Cycle Change.** During the twentieth century the life cycle 5 changed as life expectancy increased, fertility declined, and the number of years that women spent raising children also declined. This made it possible for more married women to seek paid employment and probably also contributed to the rise in the divorce rate. It is a challenge to choose a mate with whom to share a half century of married life.

**Changes in Technology.** Changes in technology made divorce 6 and the employment of married women easier. Washing machines, fast food restaurants, microwave ovens, and prepared frozen entrees freed women to enter the labor force. Antibiotics and vaccinations reduced the time women spent caring for children with childhood diseases.

### Was There a Golden Age?

**nostalgically** thinking about the past pleasantly

Traditionalists observe these social changes and look nostalgically 7 back at the family of the 1950s in which the mother kept house and looked after the needs of the children and husband. However, social observers in every era look at family change, lament the discomfort it causes, and long for an earlier golden age when family life seemed more appealing. In reality, all periods of history challenge family members with problems and troubles. In the so called "golden age" of the 1950s, many wives felt frustrated by their inability to develop their talents in activities outside the home. It would probably be a mistake to judge the health of a family by the presence or absence of family tensions. Rather, the hallmark of a strong family is its ability to cope with difficult situations.

### Harbor Not Haven

**image** picture

The family has traditionally been viewed as a "haven" or retreat from 8 a harsh world. However, it is probably expecting too much of families to assume that they can satisfy all of the personal needs of their members. Schvaneveldt and Young suggest that it is more useful to view the family as a "harbor" rather than a "haven." A safe harbor provides its members with rest and security, but they can also set sail into the outside world and experience themselves as independent people. Marriage is coming to be seen as an institution that combines intimacy with autonomy, or self-direction. This image of the family is particularly useful for two-earner marriages and for stepfamilies in which children must relate to a complex array of family members in several nuclear families. Social change associated with the shift from an industrial to a postindustrial society often appears chaotic. Yet family change may represent a normal adjustment to new economic

Families must change in response to new environments and new economic realities, but they may retain important rituals and traditions. Here, a Laotian family eats dinner in the traditional Laotian fashion in their New York City apartment.

realities. Also, family change may, in part, reflect the attempts of family members to find a balance between autonomy on one hand and commitment and self-sacrifice on the other. In these changing times, it is not surprising that we have a growing diversity of family forms.

## Structural Diversity Among Families

9   Families in the United States are becoming increasingly diverse in their structure. One-parent families, stepfamilies, two-earner families, and families with extended kin are becoming increasingly important. These family forms have increased in number in response to the recent social change discussed earlier.

### One-Parent Families

10   Thirty percent of all families with children are one-parent families. Moreover, one-parent families are often a transitional state between first and second marriages, so that the number of people who have lived in one-parent families is far greater than the number who currently reside in one. It is estimated that over one-half of all children born in the early 1980s will live in a one-parent family before they reach age eighteen. One-parent families make up a significant portion of all families: one-fifth of white families, one-third of Hispanic families, and six-tenths of African American families.

**hampered** made
more difficult

The loss of well-paid blue-collar (manual labor) jobs in the postindustrial era has hampered the ability of many men, particularly men of color, to support a family. The result has been a rising divorce rate and an increasing number of nonmarital pregnancies. . . .

[B]etween 1960 and 1993 the percent of children in one-parent 11 families who were living with a never-married mother grew from 4 percent to 35 percent. In fact, the 5 million children living with never-married mothers in 1993 equaled the total number of children living in all one-parent families in 1960. Among low-income persons, non-marital parenthood, sometimes combined with cohabitation, has become an important family form.

Recently, the make-up of one-parent families has undergone a 12 small but interesting change. Over the last two decades the number of one-parent families headed by fathers has tripled, so that father-headed families now make up 13 percent of all one-parent families. Fathers are becoming more likely to seek custody of their children, particularly when those children are older boys.

### Stepfamilies

**traits** characteristics

Stepfamilies are becoming an increasingly important family form. 13 Half of all divorces involve a child under age eighteen. Three-fourths of divorced persons remarry, often bringing children with them. It has been estimated that one-third of all children will live in a stepfamily at some time before they reach age eighteen. Many of the traits that children exhibit in one-parent families are carried over into stepfamilies, such as taking responsibility for household chores. However, the autonomy that adolescents typically experience in one-parent families tends to disappear in stepfamilies. Children in stepfamilies are generally more closely supervised than those in one-parent families. The high school completion rate of children in stepfamilies is higher than that of children in one-parent families.

Although stepfamilies experience a good deal of stress as 14 family members adjust to new roles in the family, most couples who remarry report that they are satisfied with their marriages. Moreover, some aspects of stepfamily life that were previously considered to be social problems, such as low cohesion (which refers to loose emotional connections between stepparents and stepchildren), are now considered to be a creative adaptation to the demands of relating to two families.

### Two-Earner Families

**norm** usual, standard

The typical married couple today forms a two-earner family. In addition, cohabitors are most often found in a two-earner partnership. 15 The working mother has become the norm even in families with young children. Because the purchasing power of wages earned by men declined after 1973, only with the entry of wives into the labor force have families been able to maintain their standard of living.

Even families from traditional cultures, in which the wife was expected to remain at home to care for the family, tend to undergo change when they immigrate to the United States. Mexican-American wives and Southeast-Asian wives often find it necessary to seek employment in order to help support the family.

### Families That Include Extended Kin

16   In American society, life in many families is organized primarily around the *nuclear family.* A nuclear family is made up of parents and their children and spans only two generations. In contrast, traditional societies consider the *extended family* to be of primary importance. The extended family includes those kin who extend outward from the nuclear family, such as grandparents, aunts, and uncles. Extended kin relationships have always been central in immigrant families, which were coping with a new environment, but have diminished in importance among white middle-class families. However, today extended kin relationships are once more growing in importance. Families are increasingly likely to provide housing to extended kin who have fallen on financial hard times. One-third of African-American families and one-fourth of white families include other adults in the household. Most often this other adult is a relative.

## Cultural Diversity Among Families

17   It is not possible to study one version of "the family" in the United States as if it represented all families. Marital patterns and household compositon vary with race and ethnicity, as does the meaning of "the family." For example, multiple roles have traditionally been the norm in African-American marriages, with women being wives, mothers and employees. In addition, the extended family is likely to be far more important to the functioning of African-American, Hispanic, and Asian families than to white families of European extraction. The economic marginality of many minority families means that they must rely on extended kin for security, for information on how to adjust to residence in a new country, and for such services as child care. Because family experiences of racial and ethnic groups vary, an examination of families in the United States would not be complete without taking into account ethnic and racial variation.

**Exercise 14**   **Checking Your Understanding**

1. Choose the best main idea sentence for the entire reading.
   _____ a.  The typical married couple today forms a two-earner family.
   _____ b.  The extended family includes those kin who extend outward from the nuclear family, such as grandparents, aunts and uncles, and these types of families have always been central in immigrant families.

_____c. The traditional American family has been changing over the past 50 or 60 years and today's families are incresingly diverse in their structure.

Underline the best main idea sentences for the following paragraphs.

2. Paragraph 9.
3. Paragraph 10.
4. Paragraph 11.
5. Which of the following statements would the author agree with? *(Para. 1)*
   _____a. The families of the 1950s were better than the families of today.
   _____b. People always think change is uncomfortable.
   _____c. In the 1950s women were not necessarily always happy with their roles as housewives.
   _____d. Families always face challenges.
6. According to the author, which of the following statements is *not* true? *(Paras. 2 and 3)*
   _____a. Families in the United States are more diverse than they were before.
   _____b. Families are changing because the times are changing.
   _____c. The changes in families are OK because families are adjusting to new realities.
   _____d. Family members should be dependent on their families for everything that they do.

---

**Exercise 15**   **Identifying Patterns of Organization**

Read the passages below and identify the pattern of organization used for each sentence or paragraph—examples, chronological order, or definition. What clues helped you identify the pattern of organization? The first one has been done for you.

1. **Changes in Technology.** Changes in technology made divorce and the employment of married women easier. Washing machines, fast food restaurants, microwave ovens, and prepared frozen entres freed women to enter the labor force. Antibiotics and vaccinations reduced the time women spent caring for children with childhood diseases.
   Pattern of organization: *Examples*
   Clues: *list of examples divided by commas, use of the word "and"*

2. The United States changed from an industrial society based on factory production, which had its heyday in the 1940s and 1950s, to a postindustrial society in the 1960s that is organized around information processing, advanced technology, and services jobs. A number of factors associated with this change altered American families.

Pattern of organization: _____

Clues: _____

3. Between 1960 and 1993 the percent of children in one-parent families who were living with a never-married mother grew from 4 percent to 35 percent. In fact, the 5 million children living with never-married mothers in 1993 equaled the total number of children living in all one-parent families in 1960. Among low-income persons, non-marital parenthood, sometimes combined with cohabitation, has become an important family form.

Pattern of organization: _____

Clues: _____

4. One parent families, stepfamilies, two-earner families, and families with extended kin are becoming increasingly important.

Pattern of organization: _____

Clues: _____

5. A nuclear family is made up of parents and their children and spans only two generations.

Pattern of organization: _____

Clues: _____

## Exercise **16**  Working with Words

Reread the first six paragraphs of "Marriage and Family: An Overview." Underline five words that use one of the prefixes from pages 213–214. On the lines below, write the words you chose and the appropriate definitions. An example has been done for you.

1. Postindustrial society—This means society *after* industrial society of *after* society based on factory production.

2. _____
   _____

3. _____
   _____

4. _____
   _____

5. _____
   _____

6. _____
   _____

| Exercise **17** | Making Connections |
|---|---|

Briefly describe two families that you know. Who are the members of the family, and what is their relationship to one another? Into which category of family described in the above selection do they fit?

| Exercise **18** | Organizing to Learn |
|---|---|

1. Write a time line for the following paragraph which is organized by chronological order.

   Over the last 50 years in China, family life has improved because more Chinese babies are living past the first year of life. The number of births has remained fairly constant, but in the early decades of the twentieth century, 27 to 30 infants died out of 1,000 births. In 1952, 18 infants died out of 1,000 births, and by the early 1970s, that figure had fallen to about 15 per 1,000 and was continuing to fall. (*Encyclopedia Britannica,* "China")

2. Design a map or outline that shows the main idea and the supporting details (examples) of the following paragraph.

   Changes in technology made divorce and the employment of married women easier. Washing machines, fast food restaurants, microwave ovens, and prepared frozen entrees freed women to enter the labor force. Antibiotics and vaccinations reduced the time women spent caring for children with childhood diseases. (Robin Wolf, *Marriages and Family*)

## *Chapter Review*

| Exercise **19** | Skills Review |
|---|---|

In your class groups or alone fill in the blanks below about patterns of organization.

| Pattern of Organization | Characteristics | Clues |
|---|---|---|
| Examples | _____ | *Word clues:* "such as," "for example," "for instance," "in addition," "moreover" |
| | | *Other clues:* _____ |

| Pattern of Organization | Characteristics | Clues |
|---|---|---|
| _____ | Organizes information according to time | *Word clues:* "then," "when," "after," "before," "later," "while" <br><br> *Other clues:* _____ <br> _____ |
| _____ | Answers the questions, "What is it?" or "What does it mean?" | *Word clues:* _____ <br> _____ <br><br> *Other clues:* definitions are provided in parentheses, between dashes, or between commas immediately after the term |

## Exercise 20 — Writing

1. Write a short paragraph about your family history that you organize by chronological order.
2. Write a paragraph that begins with one of the following topic/main idea sentences. Use examples to support the first sentence.
   a. Some families I know have similar problems.
   b. Successful families I know have certain things in common.
3. Write a definition paragraph answering the question, "What is, in your opinion, a happy family?"

## Exercise 21 — Collaborative Activity

Share your chronological order, example, or definition paragraph with your class group. Together you and your group will (1) check your pattern of organization, (2) find the clues in your writing that help identify the pattern of organization, and (3) make an outline, map, or time line of your paragraph.

## Exercise 22 — Extension Activity

Find an article about families in a newspaper or magazine. Write out the main idea, the pattern of organization, and the clues you used to identify it. Then, map, outline, or make a time line of your article. Bring your article and your paper to class to share with your class group or to turn in to your instructor.

# The Family in the Community

## COMPARISON/CONTRAST AND CAUSE/EFFECT

### COMPARISON/CONTRAST

Comparing and contrasting are two of the most common ways writers organize their ideas. A comparison answers the question, "How are two things alike or different?" Notice as you read the following paragraph that it is comparing how families use the television. If you read carefully you will notice two very different approaches to television use. This paragraph emphasizes the *contrast* between them.

> In the United States today, families basically have two contrasting attitudes towards television. Many families allow the television to be on at any time of the day or night. Very often, members of these families watch television alone or don't interact with other family members while they are watching. The TV is used to have some kind of background noise in the house, or as a kind of electronic babysitter. Parents often turn it on to entertain "bored" children. In contrast, other families strictly control when the television will be watched and what programs can be watched. More often these families watch programs together and discuss them together. In these homes, the TV is rarely on if nobody is watching it. Instead of using it as an electronic babysitter, parents insist that children read or play actively rather than sit in front of a screen.

The main idea of the above paragraph, the first sentence, clearly sets up the comparison/contrast pattern of organization.

In the United States today, families basically have two contrasting attitudes toward television.

The use of "two contrasting attitudes" tells us that the two types of attitudes are different from each other. In the rest of the paragraph "in contrast" and "instead of" also signal to the reader that contrasts are being emphasized.

In addition, a number of behaviors are listed for each attitude toward television. In the description of the first type of attitude, families

- Allow the television to be on at any time of the day or night
- Watch television alone or don't interact with other family members while they are watching
- Use the television for background noise
- Use the television as an electronic babysitter

In the description of the second type of attitude, families

- Strictly control when the television will be watched and what will be watched
- Watch programs together and discuss them
- Don't leave the television on if nobody is watching
- Don't use it as a babysitter, but insist that children read or play actively

## In Sentences

Writers can use comparison and contrast to tell the reader both differences and similarities. For example, a writer might explain the *similarities* in two families' TV habits as follows:

*Both* families enjoyed spending time together on Sunday afternoons watching football or baseball games on television.

In this sentence both indicates that the two families have been compared and that they have something in common—their TV habits.

On the other hand, a writer might explain the *differences* between two families' TV habits.

My family left the television on all evening, whether anyone was watching or not, *but* I noticed my best friend's family only turned the television on for special programs on PBS or the Discovery Channel.

In this sentence, the "but" tells us that the next part of the sentence will be different in meaning from the first part. The two families have very different TV viewing habits.

**Clues.**  Watch the following clues to help you recognize comparisons or contrasts in sentences or longer passages.

1. *Comparisons* use words like:
   - also
   - both
   - similarly
   - alike
   - as (e.g., the same as, as big as, as small as, etc.)
   - same
   - in comparison
2. *Contrasts* use words and phrases such as:
   - but
   - yet
   - although
   - while
   - instead of
   - in contrast
   - on the other hand
   - however
   - in comparison
   - than (e.g., more than, less than, happier than, etc.)

## In Paragraphs

In paragraphs a writer can develop many more points of comparison between two items. He or she can include a number of points that support one main idea. Consider all of the different kinds of things that are being compared in the following paragraph which contrasts the life of the slave family to that of the plantation master's family.

> While slave parents who were able to spend time with their children loved them as much as the masters loved their children, the slave family was as different from the master's family as anyone can possibly imagine. Of course, the master's family was well-fed, well-dressed and lived in beautiful homes. In contrast, the slave families lived on an absolute minimum of food, were often provided one set of clothes for a year, and lived in shacks. The master's children were waited on hand and foot by slave mothers, while their own children had no one to tend to them. The chances were that the master's family was a nuclear family, which lived together until the children grew up and started their own families. In contrast, the slave family could be broken up at any time by the sale of the father, mother or children.

The main idea of this paragraph appears in the second half of the first sentence:

> The slave family was as different from the master's family as anyone can possibly imagine.

The author does recognize that there is one similarity between the families when she states that "slave parents who were able to spend time with their children loved them as much as the masters loved their children." However, if we look carefully at the rest of the paragraph, we can see the support the writer gives for the way that these families are *different*. The emphasis, then, is on the *contrast* between the two types of families. For example, the master's family was

> well-fed,
> well-dressed and
> lived in beautiful homes.

In contrast, the slave families

> lived on an absolute minimum of food,
> were often provided one set of clothes for a year,
> and lived in shacks.

The author continues to give examples of contrasts throughout the rest of the paragraph. When you look closely at this passage, you find the clue words "different from," "in contrast," "while," and "but."

| Exercise **1** | **Understanding Comparison and Contrast** |

The following excerpts all contain comparisons and/or contrasts. Read each example and then answer the questions that follow. The first one has been done for you.

1. We know much more now than we did even a few years ago about how the human brain develops and what children need from their environments to develop character, empathy, and intelligence. (Hillary Rodham Clinton, *It Takes a Village and Other Lessons Children Teach Us*)

List the two things being compared:

a. *what we know now about the human brain and children's needs*

compared to

b. *what we knew a few years ago about these topics.*

2. It is less respectable in Hispanic culture for a married woman to work outside the home than in either African-American or non-Hispanic white culture. (Robin Wolf, *Marriages and Families in a Diverse Society*)

The attitude towards married women working outside the home is being compared in:

a. _____

and

b. _____

3. "Compared to families with young children, families with adolescents have been neglected. Even for the affluent sector, little work has been done on strengthening support networks for families during the stress of the great transition from childhood to adulthood. Still less attention has gone into strengthening networks for families who live in poverty or culturally different situations. Although adolescents are moving toward independence, they are still intimately bound up with the family, which is much more important to them than is evident. This is especially true in early adolescence. For that reason, we need to pay attention to the ways in which family relationships can be utilized to help adolescents weather the conditions of contemporary life." (From David A. Hamburg, "The American Family Transformed")

This paragraph wants readers to focus on the needs of

a. families with <u>*adolescents*</u>

rather than

b. families with _____

In the middle of the paragraph, the author points out the contrast that

a. "adolescents are moving toward independence" _____

but

b. _____

## Comparisons and Contrasts in Longer Selections

To identify the comparison/contrast thought pattern in longer readings, look for the same clues that you look for in sentences and paragraphs.

### *It Takes a Village*

Hillary Rodham Clinton

*In her book* It Takes a Village and Other Lessons Children Teach Us *Hillary Rodham Clinton puts forth her ideas about the condition of American children and families today. She also makes many suggestions for what we can do to help strengthen families in our society today. As you read, look for the main idea of the whole passage and for her use of comparison and contrast.*

**bear** have

Parents bear the first and primary responsibility for their sons  1
and daughters—to feed them, to sing them to sleep, to teach them
to ride a bike, to encourage their talents, to help them develop spir-
itual lives, to make countless daily decisions that determine whom

Copyright © August 5, 1995, Baby Blues Partnership. Reprinted with special permission of King Feature Syndicate.

they have the potential to become. I was blessed with a hardworking father who put his family first and a mother who was devoted to me and my two younger brothers. But I was also blessed with caring neighbors, attentive doctors, challenging public schools, safe streets, and an economy that supported my father's job. Much of my family's good fortune was beyond my parents' direct control, but not beyond the control of other adults whose actions affected my life.

2     Children exist in the world as well as in the family. From the moment they are born, they depend on a host of other "grown-ups"—grandparents, neighbors, teachers, ministers, employers, political leaders, and untold others who touch their lives directly and indirectly. Adults police their streets, monitor the quality of their food, air, and water, produce the programs that appear on their televisions, run the businesses that employ their parents, and write the laws that protect them. Each of us plays a part in every child's life: It takes a village to raise a child. . . .

3     The sage who first offered that proverb would undoubtedly be bewildered by what constitutes the modern village. In earlier times and places—and until recently in our own culture—the "village" meant an actual geographic place where individuals and families lived and worked together. To many people the word still conjures up a road sign that reads, "Hometown U.S.A., pop. 5,340," followed by emblems of the local churches and civic clubs.

**sage** wise person

4     For most of us, though, the village doesn't look like that anymore. In fact, it's difficult to paint a picture of the modern village, so frantic and fragmented has much of our culture become. Extended families rarely live in the same town, let alone the same house. In many communities, crime and fear keep us behind locked doors. Where we used to chat with neighbors on stoops and

**fragmented** divided into separate pieces

porches, now we watch videos in our darkened living rooms. Instead of strolling down Main Street, we spend hours in automobiles and at anonymous shopping malls. We don't join civic associations, churches, unions, political parties, or even bowling leagues the way we used to.

The horizons of the contemporary village extend well beyond the town line. From the moment we are born, we are exposed to vast numbers of other people and influences through radio, television, newspapers, books, movies, computers, compact discs, cellular phones, and fax machines. Technology connects us to the impersonal global village it has created. 5

**refuge** safe place to hide

To many, this brave new world seems dehumanizing and inhospitable. It is not surprising, then, that there is a yearning for the "good old days" as a refuge from the problems of the present. But by turning away, we blind ourselves to the continuing, evolving presence of the village in our lives, and its critical importance for how we live together. The village can no longer be defined as a place on a map, or a list of people or organizations, but its essence remains the same: it is the network of values and relationships that support and affect our lives. 6

## Exercise 2 — Checking Your Understanding of Comparison and Contrast

1. State in your own words the main idea of this excerpt from Clinton's book.
2. What is Clinton comparing in paragraphs 3, 4, and 5? What clues can you find in these paragraphs?
3. What, in her opinion, are the differences between the contemporary village and the "earlier" village?
4. In what ways does she say that the definition of today's village is similar to or the same as the earlier village? *(Para. 6)*

## Exercise 3 — Making Connections

1. Who was involved in raising you? (Mother? Father? Aunts? Uncles? Churches? Social groups? Boy Scouts? 4-H clubs?)
2. Do you think that you had a strong "network of values and relationships" that supported you and that continue to support you?
3. Do you agree with Clinton's idea that "it takes a village to raise a child"? Explain why or why not.

• • • • • • • • • • • •
# Organizing to Learn
## Making Charts
• • • • • • • • • • • • • • • • • • • • • • • • • • • • • • • • • • • •

A useful way to check your comprehension after you've read a comparison/contrast paragraph or longer reading is to make a chart of the information. To do this, follow these simple steps:

- Determine the main idea.
- Decide what is being compared or contrasted.
- Put the names of what is being compared or contrasted on the top of two columns.
- Determine the points on which the items are being compared.
- List the likenesses and differences for each point under the correct columns.

Read the following paragraph about two different types of marriage systems.

> The modern system of marriage agreements is now practiced by most people in most parts of the world, but a more traditional system is still used in some places. In the modern system, each person—the man and the woman—willingly agrees to marry. Usually in this system, the man proposes to the woman, and if she accepts, they inform their parents of their engagement and hope for their parents' support. In traditional systems, on the other hand—especially in Asia—it was not necessary for the woman to agree to marry. Usually the prospective husband or his family made the marriage arrangement with the prospective bride's father or parents.

Looking carefully at what is being compared or contrasted, we can identify *marriage systems* or *marriage agreements,* and we can identify the first sentence as the main idea:

> Main idea: The modern system of marriage agreements is now practiced by most people in most parts of the world, but there is another widely followed system for marriage agreements.

Then we are ready to set up the chart with the points of similarities or differences. (In this case, of course, differences are emphasized.)

| **Modern Marriage Agreements** | **Earlier Marriage Systems (Especially in Asia)** |
|---|---|
| *The man and the woman must agree to marry each other* | *It was not necessary for the woman to agree* |
| *The man proposes and if the woman accepts, they tell the families* | *The man or his family made arrangements with the prospective bride's father, who makes the final decision* |

| Exercise **4** | **Using Charts** |
|---|---|

The paragraph below compares and contrasts some of the experiences of children in two-parent and in single-parent families. The emphasis is on single-parent families; the comparison with two-parent families is sometimes implied rather than directly stated. As you read this paragraph, watch for the different points of comparison so that you can complete the chart below.

> The family change perspective sees positive signs as well as drawbacks in one-parent families. One-parent families grant children more autonomy than two-parent families. That is, they allow children to make more decisions and have more control over their lives. This autonomy can have negative consequences when a teenager decides to put activities with peers ahead of studying. However, one-parent families also require responsibility for household chores from children of all ages. Children in one-parent families perform more housework than children in two-parent families. It has been suggested that single parents make an unspoken trade-off in which personal autonomy is granted in return for help in running the household. Moreover, children in one-parent families tend to be more androgynous than children in two-parent families, in that they learn aspects of both traditional male and traditional female roles. Boys often learn to cook, and it is not unusual for teenage girls to work on Saturdays to earn spending money. These characteristics—household responsibility and androgyny—which one-parent families tend to foster in children can be viewed as positive adaptations to new circumstances. (Robin Wolf, *Marriages and Families in a Diverse Society*)

1. Complete the following chart by listing the points of contrast in the above paragraph (half of the points have already been done for you).

| One-Parent Families | Two-Parent Families |
|---|---|
| Children have more autonomy—make more decisions (which is sometimes a problem) | Children make fewer decisions for themselves |
|  | Children have fewer household responsibilities |
| Children are more "androgynous"—learn both traditional male and female roles (e.g., boys cook) |  |
|  | Missing some of the positive things that single-parent families have |

2. Now, complete a chart for the following paragraph which you already read on page 226.

> While slave parents who were able to spend time with their children loved them as much as the masters loved their children, the slave family was as different from the master's family as anyone can possibly imagine. Of course, the master's family was well-fed, well-dressed and lived in beautiful homes. In contrast, the slave families lived on an absolute minimum of food, were often provided one set of clothes for a year, and lived in shacks. The master's children were waited on hand and foot by slave mothers, while their own children had no one to tend to them. The chances were that the master's family was a nuclear family, which lived together until the children grew up and started their own families. In contrast, the slave family could be broken up at any time by the sale of the father, mother or children.

| _____ | _____ |
| _____ | _____ |
| _____ | _____ |
| _____ | _____ |
| _____ | _____ |
| _____ | _____ |

# CAUSE AND EFFECT

Cause and effect statements answer two types of related questions. Causes answer *why* something is the way it is, and effects usually explain the *results* of some action.

## In Sentences

For example, a writer might say:

> The high rate of divorce today is caused by a lack of family values.

This writer is trying to explain *why* divorce rates are so high. He might go on to say:

> These high divorce rates have obvious effects on young people's attitudes towards marriage.

In this sentence the writer is focusing on one of the *results* of divorce. Since cause and effect are such closely related ways of thinking about things, they may be combined in the same sentence or certainly in the same paragraph. For example, the above writer might have written:

> The high rate of divorce today is caused by a lack of family values, and it has obvious effects on the attitudes of young people towards marriage.

**Clues.**     Watch for the following clues to help you recognize cause and effect statements in sentences or longer passages.

1. Statements explaining *causes* use words like:
   - because
   - since
   - the factors are
   - is caused by
   - the reason why
2. *Effects* are indicated by words and phrases like:
   - as a result
   - the effects are
   - therefore
   - consequently
   - so
   - contributes to
   - leads to
   - changes
   - influences

## In Paragraphs

Longer explanations of causes and effects may be a paragraph or more in length. Sometimes many factors contribute to one effect, and each factor needs to be examined in order to understand how a change occurs. All these factors are supporting points for the main idea of a paragraph. For example, the main idea of a paragraph might be that there is no one reason why a couple decides to divorce; rather, many issues lead to this decision. The rest of the paragraph provides the supporting points, which are the varied reasons why people choose to divorce. Also, one cause may have many effects, and each needs to be explained for the reader to understand what happened. For example, a divorce may have many effects, including economic consequences for both partners, emotional responses, a need to move residences, and the effects on children.

In cause and effect paragraphs writers may also need to analyze a "chain" of interrelated causes and effects or other complex relationships, such as the understanding of both immediate and underlying causes or immediate and long-range results. For example, in the paragraph below the author is discussing "another" factor reshaping family life; other paragraphs around this one dealt with other factors. The factor discussed here is the influx of mothers into the workplace. Then the author goes on to explain why women went into the workplace. Read the paragraph and see if you can identify three reasons why women were entering the workforce in such large numbers. Clue words have been underlined to assist you.

Another factor reshaping family life has been a massive influx of mothers into the work force. As late as 1940, less than 12 percent of white married women were in the work force; today the figure is nearly 60 percent and over half of all mothers of preschoolers work outside the home. The major forces that have propelled women into the work force include a rising cost of living which spurred many families to seek a second source of income; increased control over fertility through contraception and abortion, which allows women to work without interruption; and rising education levels, which lead many women to seek employment for intellectual stimulation and fulfillment. (James Kirby Martin et al., *America and Its People*)

## Exercise 5  Cause and Effect

1. Based on the paragraph above, list three causes why women were entering the workforce in such large numbers.

   a. _____

   b. _____

   c. _____

2. To further explain each of the causes for women entering the workplace, the author gives us a reason behind that cause. For example, the first cause you should have identified above was the rising cost of living. But this cause was effective because women needed to bring a second income into the family. What were the reasons behind the causes you listed in question 1? List them in the chart below.

| *Reasons for the cause* | *Cause* |
|---|---|
| a. *Rising cost of living* | a. *Women needed to bring a second income into the family* |
| b. | b. |
| c. | c. |

From the information in the cause and effect paragraph below, write or copy the main idea and fill in the chart that follows.

3. The status of women [in China] has been changed greatly. The marriage law promulgated in 1950 advocates equality of men and women and freedom of marriage; marriages are no longer arranged by parents. Nurseries, kindergartens, public canteens, and homes for the aged have been widely established, gradually relieving women from family work and enabling them to participate in production. (*Encyclopedia Britannica*, "China")

Main idea: _____

| Cause | Effect |
|-------|--------|
| _____ <br> _____ <br> *Nurseries, and available care for the aged* <br> _____ | *Marriages are no longer arranged by parents* <br> _____ <br> _____ |

## Making Maps for Cause and Effect

As you know, one good way to organize what you have read is to make a map of the information. These maps are sometimes called *concept maps* because they visually show the relationships among all the important sections of a reading. Maps can be drawn in many sizes and shapes depending on the information being covered. For cause and effect, for example, you probably want to indicate how they relate to each other. You want the map to clearly show how the cause leads to the effect. This can be done by the layout of the map (making it flow in a certain direction) and it can be emphasized with the use of arrows. The following map is based on the paragraph you just read for Exercise 5. In this case the box on the right is the result, and the arrows pointing to it are the three major causes for women entering the workplace. Farther to the left are the reasons behind the causes that you identified in question 2, in Exercise 5.

**Exercise 6**  **Concept Mapping**

Complete the concept map using your answers from question 2, Exercise 5.

**Why Mothers Entered the Workforce**

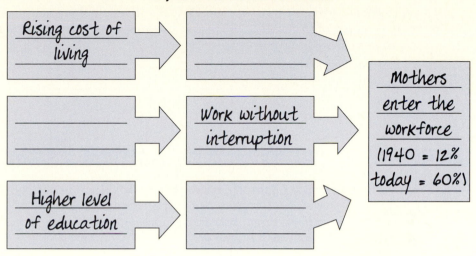

Rising cost of living →

Work without interruption →

Higher level of education →

Mothers enter the workforce (1940 = 12% today = 60%)

---

**Exercise 7** | **Identifying Patterns of Organization in Sentences**

Decide whether each of the following sentences is primarily organized by *comparison/contrast* or *cause/effect*. Write out the clues that helped you identify the pattern of organization. The first one has been done for you.

1. As a result of their parents' inability to preserve their marriages or to marry at all, almost a quarter of U.S. kids live in single-parent households, the majority headed by females. (Deborah Black, "The Single-Parent Family")

   Pattern of organization: *Cause/effect* _____

   Clues: *"As a result"* _____

   *This sentence is obviously organized by cause/effect because it states that single-parent homes are the result of parents' "inability to preserve their marriages or to marry at all." The phrase "as a result" at the beginning of the sentence gives us a definite clue that an effect will follow.*

2. Good families . . . share a common shortcoming—they can tell in a minute what's wrong with them, but they aren't sure what's right with them. (Delores Curran, "What Good Families Are Doing Right")

   Pattern of organization: _____

   Clues: _____

3. According to Dr. Jerry M. Lewis—author of a significant work on families— *No Single Thread*—healthy spouses complement, rather than dominate, each other. (Delores Curran, "What Good Families Are Doing Right")

   Pattern of organization: _____

   Clues: _____

4. If the welfare system were reformed to encourage family cohesion—or at least not discourage poor mothers and fathers from getting and staying married—many of these social problems would improve. (From Joseph Perkins, "Reform Should Make Room for Dad")

Pattern of organization: _____

Clues: _____

---

**Exercise 8** | **Identifying Patterns of Organization in Paragraphs**

For each of the following paragraphs write out the main idea on the line provided. Decide whether each paragraph is primarily organized by *comparison/contrast* or *cause/effect*. Write the clues that helped you identify the pattern of organization. The first one has been done for you.

1. The increase in divorce has contributed to the feminization of poverty, the growing impoverishment of women and their children. Female-headed families represent one-fourth of all families with children, yet they constitute over half (54 percent) of all poor families with children. Divorce often results in sharp downward social mobility for women with children. The poverty rate among single-mother families runs 45 percent, compared to a 6 percent poverty rate for two-parent families and an 18 percent poverty rate for single-father families. Although single-father families are less likely to live in poverty than single-mother families, the economic plight of all impoverished single parents and their children is a cause for concern. (Robin Wolf, *Marriages and Families in a Diverse Society*)

Main idea: *"The increase in divorce has contributed to the feminization of poverty, the growing impoverishment of women and their children."*

Pattern of organization: *Cause/effect*

Clues: *"Has contributed to," "results in"*

> *The primary thought pattern of this paragraph is cause/effect because the author's main purpose is to look at one result of increased divorce rates: poverty, particularly for women and children. Clues include "contributed" in the first sentence and "results in" in sentence 3. Most of the rest of the paragraph gives statistics to show just how severe the problem of poverty is for divorced women and their children. Don't be misled by the comparison in the last sentence, introduced by "although"; this point is more of an afterthought than the main focus of the paragraph.*

2. Even though our national rhetoric proclaims that children are our most important resource, we squander these precious lives as though they do not matter. Children's issues are seen as "soft," the province of softhearted peo-

ple (usually women) at the margins of the larger economic and social problems confronting our country. These issues are not soft. They are hard—the hardest issues we face. They are intimately connected to the very essence of who we are and who we will become. Whether or not you are a parent, what happens to America's children affects your present and your future. (Hillary Rodham Clinton, *It Takes a Village and Other Lessons Children Teach Us*)

Main idea: _____

_____

Pattern of organization: _____

Clues: _____

3. The family is the first environment where an individual encounters drug use. Parents who smoke, drink alcohol, or use other drugs, will affect the formation and development of their children, even before they are conceived or born. Studies have found that the father's exposure to harmful substances at work, smoking cigarettes, drinking alcohol and using other drugs may contribute to low birth weight and other malformations in the baby. Young women, especially of low socioeconomic status, who abuse drugs and alcohol tend to be malnourished and lack access to prenatal health care—factors which can contribute to later fetal malformations during pregnancy. Families can also be gravely damaged or destroyed by excessive use of psychoactive substances by family members. The damage can result from the immediate effects of drug use, such as violence associated with intoxication, or from long-term effects, such as economic problems, discord and breakdown in communication resulting from drug dependence and impaired health. (Lee-Nah Hsu, "Drug Use and the Family")

Main idea: _____

_____

Pattern of organization: _____

Clues: _____

4. In American society, life in many families is organized primarily around the *nuclear family*. A nuclear family is made up of parents and their children and spans only two generations. In contrast, traditional societies consider the *extended family* to be of primary importance. The extended family includes those kin who extend outward from the nuclear family, such as grandparents, aunts, and uncles. Extended kin relationships have always been central in immigrant families which are coping with a new environment, but have diminished in importance among white middle-class families. However, today, extended kin relationships are once more growing in importance. Families are increasingly likely to provide housing to extended kin who have fallen on financial hard times. One-third of African-American families and one-fourth of white families include other adults in the household. Most often this other adult is a relative. (Robin Wolf, *Marriages and Families in a Diverse Society*)

Main idea: _____

_____

Pattern of organization: _____

Clues: _____

5. Most women in the labor force work primarily because the family needs the money and secondarily for their own personal self-actualization. Because of the decline in real family income from 1973 to 1988, most families find it essential for both parents to work to support them at a level that used to be achieved by one wage-earner, and in many families two earners are required to keep the family out of poverty. Most divorced, single, and widowed mothers must work to avoid poverty. (Sandra Scarr, Deborah Phillips, and Kathleen McCartney, "Working Mothers and Their Families")

Main idea: _____

_____

Pattern of organization: _____

Clues: _____

## PATTERNS OF ORGANIZATION: SUMMARY OF CHARACTERISTICS AND CLUES

| Pattern of Organization | Characteristics | Clues |
|---|---|---|
| Examples | Gives examples | *Word clues:* "such as," "for example," "for instance," "in addition," "moreover"<br><br>*Other clues:* lists separated by commas |
| Chronological order | Organizes information by time | *Word clues:* "then," "when," "after," "before," "later," "while"<br><br>*Other clues:* dates (1942, October, etc.) |
| Definition | Answers the questions, "What is it?" or "What does it mean?" | *Word clues:* "means," "refers to," "consists of," "is"<br><br>*Other clues:* definitions are provided in parentheses between dashes, or between commas immediately after the term |

| Pattern of Organization | Characteristics | Clues |
|---|---|---|
| Comparison and Contrast | Answers the question, "How are two things similar?" | *Comparison word clues:* "also," "both," "similarly," "alike," "as," "same," "in comparison" |
| | Answers the question, "How are two things different?" | *Contrast word clues:* "but," "yet," "although," "while," "instead of," "in contrast," "on the other hand," "however," "than" |
| Cause and Effect | Answers the questions, "What happened to make something the way it is?" and "What was the consequence of something that happened?" | *Word clues for causes:* "because," "since," "the factors are," "is caused by," "the reason why" |
| | | *Word clues for effects:* "as a result," "the effects are," "therefore," "consequently" |

## Cause and Effect in Longer Selections

The clues for recognizing cause and effect patterns of organization in longer selections are the same as they are for sentences and paragraphs. Since longer selections can have a variety of thought patterns, you would identify cause and effect as the dominant thought pattern if it reflected the main idea of the selection.

## *The Single-Parent Family*

### DEBORAH BLACK

*The following essay was written by Deborah Black, an older student who returned to college, while she was raising three daughters by herself. She writes about the single-parent family and, because she is a single parent herself, she uses her own experience as an example.*

### Preparing to Read

1. What single-parent families do you know?
2. What are some of the challenges these families face?

**parity** equal level

As a result of their parents' inability to preserve their marriages or to marry at all, almost a quarter of U.S. kids live in single-parent households, the majority headed by females. David Blankenhorn, president of the Institute for American Values, a New York family-issues research group, says that as an expectation of childhood the experience of fatherlessness is approaching a rough parity with the experience of having a father.     1

**flourish** do well

Generally, children from single-parent families have more trouble while growing up and bear more scars than children from two-parent families. This is contrary to the longstanding opinion that children recover quickly from divorce and flourish in families of almost any shape. Sara McLanahan, a Princeton University sociologist who studies children of divorce as they enter adulthood, says, "Almost anything you can imagine not wanting to happen to your children is a consequence of divorce" (Magnet 44).     2

**deprived** taken away

Children in single-parent families have less than one third of the median per capita income of kids from two-parent families. Seventy-five percent of single-parent children will sink into poverty before they reach eighteen years of age, versus 20% of the kids from two-parent families. Had family breakdown not deprived many families of a male breadwinner, the child poverty rate would have declined in the 80's.     3

Growing up in a single-parent family marks not only the child's external economic circumstances, but also his or her psyche. A study from the National Center of Health Statistics has found that children from single-parent homes were 100 to 200% more likely than those from intact families to have emotional and behavioral problems and 50% more likely to have learning disabilities.     4

**magnitude** quantity

Judith Wallerstein, co-author of *Second Chances: Men, Women & Children a Decade after Divorce,* made some startling discoveries in her 15-year study of children of divorce. She was alarmed by the magnitude of pain and fear expressed by the children when their parents divorced. She believed these wounds would not heal and could be harmful years later.     5

Males in the study, even those who were bright, had difficulty learning and behaving well after divorce. Female children did much better, even better than girls from intact families. But Wallerstein found the girls' success tended to be "fragile." Says she: "These girls were on super behavior, consciously trying to be good little girls at a high inner cost" (Magnet 44). By young adulthood males and females were having equal difficulty forming loving, intimate relationships.     6

Can the single parent provide a positive role model for male and female children? Joseph White in his book *The Psychology of Blacks: An Afro-American Perspective* tells us that the single parent     7 can provide a positive role model for his or her children. He cites examples of black single-parent families who have used the extended family to help rear children who are fatherless or motherless. This extended family provides a safety net for these children of divorce and poverty. White feels that going to workshops, discussion groups, and community forums can help the single parent cope with his or her dual roles and responsibilities.

**dual** double

8    The welfare system has a new program that is a valuable resource in providing troubled families with a chance for a better future. Project Independence is a program that gives a single parent an opportunity to further his or her education, thus enabling the parent to get not just a job but a career that will allow him or her to adequately provide for the family. This program provides child care, transportation, remediation, and financial aid. Additionally, single parents in this program receive food stamps, Medicaid, and a welfare check. The people who run this program are caring, dedicated individuals who encourage participants to set realistic goals and then help them to achieve these goals.

9    Being in this program has brought many changes in my life. After my divorce, I was alone, confused, and scared. I was undereducated and had no job skills that would make me marketable for employment. Like many people I thought that going on welfare was like admitting defeat. This program eliminated this viewpoint and gave me the opportunity to start a new life.

10    Can I be both mother and father to my three girls? The answer is yes. Though I never would have chosen this path, it is the one I have to travel. Much of the time I feel like I am experiencing multiple personalities: mother, father, and college student. One of the most important things to me is to be a good role model for my children. Every day they see me studying, working, and trying to get ahead. I also try to teach them how to be self-sufficient, how to cope with life's difficulties, and how to keep the lines of communication open between us.

11    The support systems that a parent enlists can help him or her to be a successful parent. Project Independence, Success at 6, Head Start, and Families First are important programs that can help struggling families in America. The success of future generations depends on our collective willingness to recognize the problems and support the solutions to them.

## Works Cited

Magnet, M. (1992, August). The American Family, 1992. *Fortune*, pp. 42–47.
White, J. L. (1984). *The Psychology of Blacks: An Afro-American Perspective.* Englewood Cliffs, NJ: Prentice-Hall.

| Exercise **9** | **Checking Your Understanding** |
| --- | --- |

1. Choose the best main idea sentence for the reading.

   _____ a. Almost a quarter of U.S. kids live in single-parent households, the majority headed by females.

   _____ b. Even though raising a family as a single parent can be difficult, it can be done well if these parents have good support systems.

   _____ c. The author feels as if she has multiple personalities: mother, father, and college student.

   _____ d. Generally, children from single-parent families have more trouble while growing up and bear more scars than children from two-parent families.

2. All of the following are problems that children have in single-parent families, *except:*

   _____ a. Single-parent children are generally poorer.

   _____ b. Single-parent children often have more emotional and behavioral problems.

   _____ c. Single-parent children have bad parents.

   _____ d. Single-parent children can find support in the extended family.

   Identify the pattern of organization *(cause/effect, chronological order, examples, comparison/contrast,* or *definition)* and the main idea for the following paragraphs.

3. Paragraph 8

   Pattern of organization: _____

   Main idea: _____

4. Paragraph 9

   Pattern of organization: _____

   Main idea: _____

5. What kinds of support does Project Independence provide? *(Paras. 8 and 9)*

6. What supporting details from the essay tell us that Deborah Black *is* doing a good job raising her three girls alone? *(Para. 10)*

| Exercise **10** | **Making Connections** |
| --- | --- |

What are some other things that single parents can do to make their lives easier and to help them do a good job of raising their children?

**LANGUAGE TIP**

### Subordination

Sentences with comparison/contrast and cause/effect often use subordination within the sentence. Such sentences are called complex sentences and are made up of at least one independent clause and one dependent clause. As a reader, it is important for you to recognize the independent clause because it is usually the most important idea in the sentence. Remember, the independent clause can stand alone as a sentence; the dependent clause cannot. That's why it's called "dependent"; it needs to be with the other part of the sentence.

The dependent clause begins with a subordinating conjunction, such as

> although
>
> even though
>
> since
>
> while
>
> whereas
>
> because

You will recognize some of these subordinating conjunctions as "clue" words for recognizing patterns of organization.

For example, the word *although* in the following sentence is a subordinating conjunction beginning a dependent clause, and it also signals to the reader that this sentence is organized as a comparison/contrast.

> Although single-father families are less likely to live in poverty than single-mother families, the economic plight of all impoverished single parents and their children is a cause for concern. (Robin Wolf, *Marriages and Families in a Diverse Society*)

Notice that in this sentence the most important statement is that "the economic plight of all impoverished single parents and their children is a cause for concern." The idea that follows the word "Although" ("single-father families are less likely to live in poverty than single-mother families") is not as important and is therefore written as a dependent clause. It is not a complete thought by itself and needs the rest of the sentence to complete the idea.

*(continued)*

Subordinating conjunctions are especially helpful in explaining cause and effect relationships. "Because" and "since" are frequently used to begin dependent clauses. For example, in the following sentence the authors of a marriage and family text explain why they will include the experiences of various ethnic and racial groups.

Because family experiences of racial and ethnic groups vary, an examination of families in the United States would not be complete without taking into account ethnic and racial variation. (Robin Wolf, *Marriages and Families in a Diverse Society*)

The first part of the sentence—"Because family experiences of racial and ethnic groups vary"—is a dependent clause. The sentence is not complete until the result is added in the independent clause that finishes the sentence.

Dependent clauses can be found at the beginning or at the end of a sentence. In the following example, "because" begins the dependent clause in the middle of the sentence.

Most women in the labor force work primarily because the family needs the money. (Arlene Skolnick and Jerome Skolnick, *Family in Transition*)

In this case, the effect is given in the independent clause—"Most women in the labor force work"—and the reasons why women work are given in the dependent clause at the end of the sentence. A similar sentence could be written with the dependent clause at the beginning.

Because families need money, most women work.

**Exercise 11** | **Subordination**

Underline the subordinating conjunction and the dependent clause in each of the following sentences. Then, circle the independent clause (the most important clause). The first one has been done for you.

1. <u>Although stepfamilies experience a good deal of stress as family members adjust to new roles in the family,</u> most couples who remarry report that they are satisfied with their marriages.
2. Because women were able to decide when to have children, it became easier for them to work without interruptions.
3. Children can have a hard time adjusting to their parents' divorce even though children between ages 6 and 12 are generally flexible.
4. While children are taken care of by many adults in extended families, children in nuclear families must depend on only their parents.
5. Women have been forced to enter the workforce because men frequently do not earn enough money to support a family.

. . . . . . . . . . . . . . .

# Working with Words

## Word Parts: Roots

. . . . . . . . . . . . . . . . . . . . . . . . . . . . . . . . . . . . . . . .

Roots are word parts that usually provide the basic meaning of a word. They may occur at the beginning, middle, or end of a word. Roots are often combined with prefixes (see pages 213–214) and suffixes to form a word. For example, the word *monogamy* means marriage to one spouse. This word is formed from the combination of the prefix *mono*, which means one, and the root *gamy*, which means marriage.

| Exercise **12** | **Working with Words: Roots** |

Below is a list of twelve common roots, their meanings, and examples of words that use that root with that meaning. Add your own examples in the space provided.

| Root | Meaning | Example | Your Examples |
|------|---------|---------|---------------|
| aqua, aqui | water | aquarium | _____ |
| auto | self | automatic | _____ |
| bio | life | biology | _____ |
| cept | receive | reception | _____ |
| chron | time | chronology | _____ |
| cogi | think, know | recognize | _____ |
| duct | lead | aqueduct | _____ |
| gamy | marriage | polygamy | _____ |
| logy | study | sociology | _____ |
| port | carry | transport | _____ |
| vid, vis | see | vision | _____ |
| vit | life | vitality | _____ |

. . . . . . . . . . . . . . .

# Applying Your Skills

. . . . . . . . . . . . . . . . . . . . . . . . . . . . . . . . . . . . . . . .

## Reform Should Make Room for Dad

#### JOSEPH PERKINS

*The following reading was written by Joseph Perkins, a columnist for* The San Diego Union-Tribune. *Perkins addresses the question of what happens to the fathers of children who are born to teenage mothers. In it he argues that our culture and government institutions work against the father becoming involved in raising his children. He believes that these young fathers need help and encouragement so that they can become responsible parents.*

---

## Preparing to Read

Take another look at the title of this article. Based on this title, what do you think the author is going to say? Write down two opinions that you think the author will include.

**promiscuous**
having many sexual relationships

Olie Mann was only 17 years old when he got a girl pregnant.   1
At the time, the Cleveland youth hardly fit anyone's ideas of a model father. "I was in a gang," he remembers. "I sold drugs. I was very promiscuous."

2    The teen-age mother of his child was whisked away to Texas by her mother, who wanted to put as much distance as possible between her daughter and incorrigible young Olie. But Olie wanted to have his child near him.

3    He turned to the National Institute for Responsible Fatherhood and Family Development, a Cleveland-based organization that began 10 years ago as a local support program for teen fathers.

4    Since its inception, the institute has reached almost 2,000 young fathers like Olie. The program is built on expectations: That the young dads will legitimize their children by acknowledging paternity. That they'll finish school. That they'll hold down a steady job.

**acknowledging paternity** accepting being the father

5    The caseworker assigned to Olie, who himself had been through a similar experience, encouraged the young man to clean up his act. Olie went back to school and earned his high-school equivalency degree. He dropped out of the gang. He gave up drugs.

6    Now, three years later, he is married to the mother of his child. The family lives happily in Cleveland.

7    There are hundreds of thousands of young men like Olie in inner cities throughout the country. They want to be real fathers to their children, but most are unable to take advantage of the kind of program that helped Olie get on the straight and narrow.

8    While there are myriad public and private programs that provide aid and comfort to unwed mothers, there are precious few that support unwed fathers. That's because our culture tends to view the role of fathers in family life as less important than mothers.

9    Just look at television and film, says psychologist Jane Myers Drew, author of *Where Were You When I Needed You Dad?* "There often is such a sense of Dad being the fool, or not important, or that he's sort of a throwaway, or we can get along without him."

10    Ultimately, Drew says, the marginalization of fathers is detrimental to the development of children. "Dads have so much to do with building self-esteem, setting values, encouraging a child to find his or her place in the world," she says. "Without Dad there, it leaves a real gap."

**marginalization** keeping on the sidelines
**detrimental** bad for

11    This "gap" is probably even more pronounced in poor families. Not only are such families deprived of a breadwinner, they also lack a positive role model who can imbue poor young men, like Olie Mann, with character and a sense of responsibility.

12    The welfare system is no help. It tilts decidedly in favor of single mothers, at the expense of poor, young fathers. In California, for example, an unmarried mom may receive $500 to $600 a month through Aid to Families with Dependent Children, another $100 in food stamps, plus free medical care. If she has a man at home, she risks losing all of this.

13    The government's subsidy of single motherhood contributes mightily to the devaluation of fatherhood in poor families. In poor

**subsidy** financial support

**surrogate** someone who takes the place of

homes, the government acts as surrogate for the father, providing most of the family's material support. Poor children are virtual wards of the state.

The perverse irony is that by supporting unmarried mothers, 14 and thereby marginalizing fathers, the government actually perpetuates poverty. Roughly half of all poor families are headed by unmarried mothers. Such families have a staggering 650% greater probability of being poor than families with a husband and wife present.

Moreover, the diminished role of fathers in poor families al- 15 most certainly has contributed to the rise of the various social pathologies that afflict many inner-city communities.

Teen pregnancies, school dropouts, drug and alcohol abuse, 16 juvenile delinquency all are symptomatic of the breakdown of the family. If the welfare system were reformed to encourage family cohesion—or at least to not discourage poor mothers and fathers from getting and staying married—many of these social problems would improve. . . .

What welfare mothers really need are husbands and fathers. 17 Whereas one in three female-headed families is poor, only one in 20 married-couple families falls below the poverty line.

If the government provided all poor men the kind of moral and 18 material support that Olie Mann received from the National Institute for Responsible Fathers and Family Development, there would be far more stable, intact families in America's inner cities. In the long run, there would be fewer poor, too.

| Exercise **13** | Checking Your Understanding |
|---|---|

1. In your own words, state the main idea of this reading.
2. Why does Perkins say that the welfare system does not help families stay together? What supporting points does he provide to strengthen his position? *(Para. 12)*

Identify the pattern of organization (cause and effect, definition, comparison/contrast, examples, chronological order) and the main idea in the following paragraphs.

3. Paragraphs 5 and 6

    Pattern of organization: _____

    Main idea: _____

4. Paragraph 8

    Pattern of organization: _____

Main idea: _____

5. Paragraph 10

   Pattern of organization: _____

   Main idea: _____

**Exercise 14**   **Making Connections**

1. Do you know any young dads who don't live with their children?
2. Do you think there should be programs to help them as Perkins argues in this article?
3. Do you think the fathers of children born out of wedlock should somehow be forced to pay child support? How could this be done?

**Exercise 15**   **Organizing to Learn**

Complete the following cause/effect map which is based on information in paragraphs 14, 15, and 16.

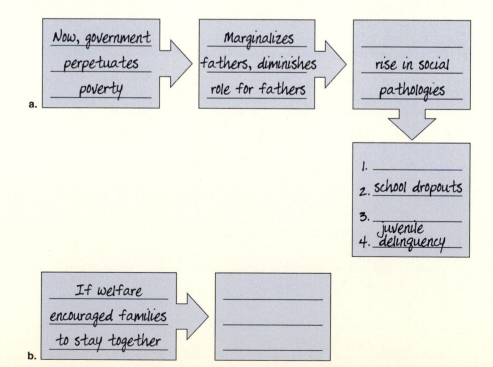

a. Now, government perpetuates poverty → Marginalizes fathers, diminishes role for fathers → rise in social pathologies →

1. _____
2. school dropouts
3. _____
4. juvenile delinquency

b. If welfare encouraged families to stay together →

| Exercise **16** | **Working with Words** |
|---|---|

Choose three words from the article whose prefixes and/or roots you can identify. Then provide the following information for each word.

| Word | Its Prefix and Meaning of Prefix | The Root and Meaning of Root | The Meaning of Your Word |
|---|---|---|---|
| _____ | _____ | _____ | _____ |
|  | _____ | _____ | _____ |
| _____ | _____ | _____ | _____ |
|  | _____ | _____ | _____ |
| _____ | _____ | _____ | _____ |
|  | _____ | _____ | _____ |

## *Chapter Review*

• • • • • • • • • • • • • • • • • • • • • • • • • • • • • • • • • • • • • • • • • • • • • • •

| Exercise **17** | **Skills Review** |
|---|---|

Alone or in your class group, fill in the blanks below about patterns of organization without looking at page 240. When you finish, check your chart against the one in the text to find out if you missed any information.

| Pattern of Organization | Characteristics | Clues |
|---|---|---|
| _____ | _____ | *Word clues:* "such as," "for example," "for instance," "in addition," "moreover" |
|  | _____ | *Other clues:* lists separated by commas |
| Chronological order | Organizes information according to time | *Word clues:* "then," "when," "after," "before," "later," "while" |
|  |  | *Other clues:* _____ |
| _____ | Answers the questions, "What is it?" or "What does it mean?" | *Word clues:* _____ |

| Pattern of Organization | Characteristics | Clues |
|---|---|---|
| | _____ _____ _____ | *Other clues:* definitions are provided in parentheses between dashes, or between commas immediately after the term |
| Comparison | Answers the question _____ _____ | *Comparison word clues:* _____ _____ |
| Contrast | Answers the question _____ _____ _____ | *Contrast word clues:* "but," "yet," "although," "while," "instead of," "in contrast," "on the other hand," "however," "than" |
| _____ | Answers the questions, "What happened to make something the way it is?" and "What was the consequence of something that happened?" | *Word clues for causes:* "because," "since," "the factors are," "is caused by," "the reason why" *Word clues for effects:* _____ _____ _____ |

## Exercise 18   Writing

Write a paragraph or a short essay explaining what you think makes a successful family. Be sure to support your opinion with examples.

## Exercise 19   Collaborative Activity

Answer the following question and prepare to discuss it in your class groups.

What do you think makes a successful family? What are the most important things that families should do in your opinion? Why is each of these important? Fill out the questionnaire in your groups.

### Suggestions for a Successful Family

**Things Families Should Do**                    **Reasons**

1. _____         _____
2. _____         _____
3. _____         _____
4. _____         _____

**Exercise 20** | **Extension Activity**

Interview the oldest person you know (a grandparent, great-grandparent, neighbor, etc.). Ask that person what life was like in his or her family when he or she was young. You might ask things like (1) Where did you live, in the city or in the countryside? (2) Who were the members of a typical family household? (3) Who did what kinds of work in and out of the home? and (4) What was the role of men and women in raising the children?

Write a paragraph or short essay in which you summarize what you learned about family life in the past.

## *Unit* *Review*

## *What Good Families Are Doing Right*

### DELORES CURRAN

*No matter what kind of family you have—nuclear, extended, single-parent—it is not easy to maintain a strong and healthy family today. The following article by Delores Curran outlines some of the most important things that good families can do. Probably most important of all is to keep lines of communication open.*

### Preparing to Read

1. How do you feel about how your family works? What do you like about your family relationships? What kinds of things would you change?
2. Think about your own family and other families that you are familiar with as you read the article.

1     I have worked with families for fifteen years, conducting hundreds of seminars, workshops, and classes on parenting, and I meet good families all the time. They're fairly easy to recognize. Good families have a kind of visible strength. They expect problems and work together to find solutions, applying common sense and trying new methods to meet new needs. And they share a common shortcoming—they can tell me in a minute what's wrong with them, but they aren't sure what's right with them. Many healthy families with whom I work, in fact, protest at being called *healthy*. They don't think they are. The professionals who work with them do.

2     To prepare the book on which this article is based, I asked respected workers in the fields of education, religion, health, family counseling, and voluntary organizations to identify a list of possible traits of a healthy family. Together we isolated fifty-six such traits, and I sent this list to five hundred professionals who regularly work with families—teachers, doctors, principals, members of the clergy,

scout directors, YMCA leaders, family counselors, social workers—asking them to pick the fifteen qualities they most commonly found in healthy families.

While all of these traits are important, the one most often cited 3 as central to close family life is communication: The healthy family knows how to talk—and how to listen.

"Without communication you don't know one another," wrote 4 one family counselor. "If you don't know one another, you don't care about one another, and that's what the family is all about."

"The most familiar complaint I hear from wives I counsel is 5 'He won't talk to me' and 'He doesn't listen to me,' " said a pastoral marriage counselor. "And when I share this complaint with their husbands, they don't hear *me,* either."

"We have kids in classes whose families are so robotized by 6 television that they don't know one another," said a fifth-grade teacher.

Professional counselors are not the only ones to recognize the 7 need. The phenomenal growth of communication groups such as Parent Effectiveness Training, Parent Awareness, Marriage Encounter, Couple Communication, and literally hundreds of others tells us that the need for effective communication—the sharing of deepest feelings—is felt by many.

**reveal** to make known

Healthy families have also recognized this need, and they 8 have, either instinctively or consciously, developed methods of meeting it. They know that conflicts are to be expected, that we all become angry and frustrated and discouraged. And they know how to reveal those feelings—good and bad—to each other. Honest communication isn't always easy. But when it's working well, there are certain recognizable signs or symptoms, what I call the hallmarks of the successfully communicating family.

## The Family Exhibits a Strong Relationship Between the Parents

According to Dr. Jerry M. Lewis—author of a significant work on 9 families, *No Single Thread*—healthy spouses complement, rather than dominate, each other. Either husband or wife could be the leader, depending on the circumstances. In the unhealthy families he studied, the dominant spouse had to hide feelings of weakness while the submissive spouse feared being put down if he or she exposed a weakness.

Children in the healthy family have no question about which 10 parent is boss. Both parents are. If children are asked who is boss, they're likely to respond, "Sometimes Mom, sometimes Dad." And, in a wonderful statement, Dr. Lewis adds, "If you ask if they're comfortable with this, they look at you as if you're crazy—as if there's no other way it ought to be."

11    My survey respondents echo Dr. Lewis. One wrote, "The healthiest families I know are ones in which the mother and father have a strong, loving relationship. This seems to flow over to the children and even beyond the home. It seems to breed security in the children and, in turn, fosters the ability to take risks, to reach out to others, to search for their own answers, become independent and develop a good self-image."

## The Family Has Control over Television

12    Television has been maligned, praised, damned, cherished, and even thrown out. It has more influence on children's values than anything else except their parents. Over and over, when I'm invited to help families mend their communication ruptures, I hear "But we have no time for this." These families have literally turned their "family-together" time over to television. Even those who control the quality of programs watched and set "homework-first" regulations feel reluctant to intrude upon the individual's right to spend his or her spare time in front of the set. Many families avoid clashes over program selection by furnishing a set for each family member. One of the women who was most desperate to establish a better sense of communication in her family confided to me that they owned nine sets. Nine sets for seven people!

13    Whether the breakdown in family communication leads to excessive viewing or whether too much television breaks into family lives, we don't know. But we do know that we can become out of one another's reach when we're in front of a TV set. The term *television widow* is not humorous to thousands whose spouses are absent even when they're there. One woman remarked, "I can't get worried about whether there's life after death. I'd be satisfied with life after dinner."

14    In family-communication workshops, I ask families to make a list of phrases they most commonly hear in their home. One parent was aghast to discover that his family's most familiar comments were "What's on?" and "Move." In families like this one, communication isn't hostile—it's just missing.

15    But television doesn't have to be a villain. A 1980 Gallup Poll found that the public sees great potential for television as a positive force. It can be a tremendous device for initiating discussion on subjects that may not come up elsewhere, subjects such as sexuality, corporate ethics, sportsmanship, and marital fidelity.

16    Even very bad programs offer material for values clarification if family members view them together. My sixteen-year-old son and

his father recently watched a program in which hazardous driving was part of the hero's characterization. At one point, my son turned to his dad and asked, "Is that possible to do with that kind of truck?"

"I don't know," replied my husband, "but it sure is dumb. If 17 that load shifted . . ." With that, they launched into a discussion on the responsibility of drivers that didn't have to originate as a parental lecture. Furthermore, as the discussion became more engrossing to them, they turned the sound down so that they could continue their conversation.

Parents frequently report similar experiences; in fact, this use 18 of television was recommended in the widely publicized 1972 Surgeon General's report as the most effective form of television gatekeeping by parents. Instead of turning off the set, parents should view programs with their children and make moral judgments and initiate discussion. Talking about the problems and attitudes of a TV family can be a lively, nonthreatening way to risk sharing real fears, hopes, and dreams.

## The Family Listens and Responds

"My parents say they want me to come to them with problems, but 19 when I do, either they're busy or they only half-listen and keep on doing what they were doing—like shaving or making a grocery list. If a friend of theirs came over to talk, they'd stop, be polite, and listen," said one of the children quoted in a *Christian Science Monitor* interview by Ann McCarroll. This child put his finger on the most difficult problem of communicating in families: the inability to listen.

It is usually easier to react than to respond. When we react, we 20 reflect our own experiences and feelings; when we respond, we get into the other person's feelings. For example:

*Tom, age seventeen:* "I don't know if I want to go to college. I don't think I'd do very well there."
*Father:* "Nonsense. Of course you'll do well."

That's reacting. This father is cutting off communication. He's 21 refusing either to hear the boy's fears or to consider his feelings, possibly because he can't accept the idea that his son might not attend college. Here's another way of handling the same situation:

*Tom:* "I don't know if I want to go to college. I don't think I'd do very well there."
*Father:* "Why not?"
*Tom:* "Because I'm not that smart."
*Father:* "Yeah, that's scary. I worried about that, too."
*Tom:* "Did you ever come close to flunking out?"

*Father:* "No, but I worried a lot before I went because I thought college would be full of brains. Once I got there, I found out that most of the kids were just like me."

22    This father has responded rather than reacted to his son's fears. First, he searched for the reason behind his son's lack of confidence and found it was fear of academic ability (it could have been fear of leaving home, of a new environment, of peer pressure, or of any of a number of things); second, he accepted the fear as legitimate: third, he empathized by admitting to having the same fear when he was Tom's age; and, finally, he explained why his, not Tom's, fears turned out to be groundless. He did all this without denigrating or lecturing.

**denigrating**
putting someone down

23    And that's tough for parents to do. Often we don't want to hear our children's fears, because those fears frighten us; or we don't want to pay attention to their dreams because their dreams aren't what we have in mind for them. Parents who deny such feelings will allow only surface conversation. It's fine as long as a child says, "School was okay today," but when she says, "I'm scared of boys," the parents are uncomfortable. They don't want her to be afraid of boys, but since they don't quite know what to say, they react with a pleasant "Oh, you'll outgrow it." She probably will, but what she needs at the moment is someone to hear and understand her pain.

24    In Ann McCarroll's interviews, she talked to one fifteen-year-old boy who said he had "*some* mother. Each morning she sits with me while I eat breakfast. We talk about anything and everything. She isn't refined or elegant or educated. She's a terrible housekeeper. But she's interested in everything I do, and she always listens to me—even if she's busy or tired."

25    That's the kind of listening found in families that experience real communication. Answers to the routine question, "How was your day?" are heard with the eyes and heart as well as the ears. Nuances are picked up and questions are asked, although problems are not necessarily solved. Members of a family who really listen to one another instinctively know that if people listen to you, they are interested in you. And that's enough for most of us.

| Exercise **1** | **Checking Your Understanding** |

1. Choose the best main idea statement for the article.
   _____ a.  Most good families have certain characteristics in common.
   _____ b.  Good families can tell you what's wrong with them but are not sure what is right with them.

_____ c. Good families have control over television viewing habits.

2. According to Curran, communication is key to a healthy family. List the supporting examples that she gives. *(Paras. 3–6)*

a. _____

b. _____

c. _____

d. *Families are so robotized by television that they don't know one another.*

Identify the pattern of organization (cause and effect, definition, comparison/contrast, examples, chronological order) and the main idea for the following paragraphs.

3. Paragraph 9

Pattern of organization: _____

Main idea: _____

4. Paragraph 12

Pattern of organization: _____

Main idea: _____

5. Which of the following reasons are *not* given by the author to support her position that families should have control over television? *(Paras. 12–18)*

_____ a. It takes up too much time.

_____ b. It has educational programs.

_____ c. People are often out of one another's reach when they are in front of the television.

6. Which of the following reasons are given by the author to support her position that the television can be used positively within the family?

_____ a. It can start interesting discussions in the family.

_____ b. It can lead to discussions about values within the family.

_____ c. It can keep people company who are at home alone.

**Exercise 2    Working with Words**

Choose three words from the reading on pages 255–259 whose roots you can identify. Then provide the following information for each word.

| Word | Its Root and Meaning of Root | The Meaning of Your Word |
|------|------------------------------|--------------------------|
| 1. _____ | _____ | _____ |
| 2. _____ | _____ | _____ |
| 3. _____ | _____ | _____ |

**Exercise 3**   **Making Connections**

Which points from this article do you think are most important for what good families are doing right? Explain your answer.

**Exercise 4**   **Organizing to Learn**

Read the following paragraphs and identify the pattern of organization and the main idea. Then, on a separate sheet of paper, design a map, chart, time line, or outline that you think best visually represents the information.

1.  The healthiest families I know are ones in which the mother and father have a strong, loving relationship. This seems to flow over to the children and even beyond the home. It seems to breed security in the children and, in turn, fosters the ability to take risks, to reach out to others, to search for their own answers, become independent and develop a good self image.

    Pattern of organization: _____

    Main idea: _____

2.  It is usually easier to react than to respond. When we react, we reflect our own experiences and feelings; when we respond, we get into the other person's feelings.

    Pattern of organization: _____

    Main idea: _____

# UNIT
# 5
# Our Community and Workplace

*Inferences and Facts Versus Opinions*

*No man is an island.*

John Donne

### Preparing to Read

1. What kind of work do you think the group of people in this picture has been doing? Why?
2. The people appear to be happy working together to accomplish some common goals. Why do you think a number of them are wearing the same T-shirt with the words "Food from the Hood"?
3. What do you think the quote means? What does it have to do with the picture?

## UNIT OBJECTIVES/SKILLS TO LEARN

In this unit you will learn how to

- Recognize inferences and clues that inferences are based on
- Distinguish between facts and opinions
- Draw your own conclusions after comparing the opinions of others

In the process of acquiring these skills, you will read and use information about

- The problems of growing up for our young people and some solutions to those problems
- Community issues and community successes
- Careers for the twenty-first century

### Key Terms and Concepts

**inference**   reasonable assumptions based on available information
**fact**   information that most people would accept as true
**opinion**   someone's interpretation of facts
**visual aids**   pictures, charts, graphs that help the reader understand the material
**community**   a group of people who work together with common goals
**resolving conflicts**   solving problems between people in the community
**career**   a profession or occupation for which you need education and training

• • • • • • • • • • • • •

# Raising Issues
## Living in Communities

• • • • • • • • • • • • • • • • • • • • • • • • • • • • • • • • • • • • • • •

We live in many communities. Increasingly, as we move toward the year 2000, we realize that we live in a *world* community. All the peoples of the earth are connected by concerns for international trade, protecting our environment, and peace between nations. Music, movies, media, and Internet links connect us as never before. We are also, of course, members of much smaller groups that affect our everyday life: our families, our neighborhoods, our schools, and our work communities. Chapters 9 and 10 will examine how we are part of our local communities—as young people growing up in neighborhoods, as adults starting careers in the workplace, and as partners of all ages helping each other to build positive communities in which to live. You will read about some of the problems of our communities and some of the positive things that we can do to take responsibility for building solutions.

## *Planting Seeds, Harvesting Scholarships*

Jonathan Alter

*The following reading from the feature article "Everyday Heroes" appeared in* Newsweek *in May 1995. It provides one example of some of the positive things that a group of teenagers did to improve their lives, their future, and their community. The photo on page 263 pictures the people of this story.*

1    It may not be history's biggest victory garden, but don't underestimate the size of the victory. Shortly after the Los Angeles riots in 1992, a group of 40 students at Crenshaw High School and their energetic biology teacher decided to reclaim the weedy quarter-acre plot that had long been abandoned behind the school's football field. The goal was simple: to create a community garden that would bring life back to one of the city's most battered neighborhoods while giving the students some hands-on science experience. They planted flowers, herbs, lettuce, collard greens and other vegetables. A colorful mural soon appeared on the back wall, with a brown hand reaching toward a white one. In the middle of South-Central L.A., an oasis bloomed. The kids donated some of the produce to needy families in South-Central and sold the rest at local farmers markets. They called their project Food From the 'Hood.

2    And the ideas kept on sprouting. Buoyed by their success and aided by a growing roster of adult volunteers, the Crenshaw students decided to diversify. They had the herbs, they had the lettuce—what could be a better accompaniment than salad dressing? The Food From the 'Hood members created their own recipe and designed their own label for the brand called Straight Out 'the Garden. Local business leaders helped with the marketing and manufacturing, and now the dressing is sold, for $2.59 a bottle, in more

than 2,000 stores in 23 states. The burgeoning enterprise has cata-
pulted the student farmers into student owners; they expect to earn
$50,000 in profits this year, which will go toward funding college
scholarships. Ten of the 15 seniors in Food From the 'Hood have
been accepted at four-year colleges—a remarkable record for an
inner-city public school. "When a kid gets an acceptance letter to
college, that's our immediate payoff," says Melinda McMullen, a
marketing consultant who worked with teacher Tammy Bird to
steer the kids toward produce and profits.

Even more important than the money is the sense of accom-    3
plishment that has grown out of Food From the 'Hood. "We
showed that a group of inner-city kids can and did make a difference," says freshman Terie Smith, 15. The students run all aspects
of the business—from weeding and harvesting to public relations
and computer logs. They've received inquiries from across the
country about duplicating their business plan, and they may fran-
chise their logo to a group of New York kids who hope to sell apple-
sauce. Food From the 'Hood members also have set up a mentor
system and an SAT preparatory program. "We all try to help each
other in everything," says Jaynell Grayson, 17, who will attend
Babson College on scholarship next year. Grayson doesn't know
who her father is: her mother has been incarcerated most of her
life. Food From the 'Hood has been a substitute family for her.
"What comes from that garden is inspiration," says McMullen.
"From anything—even the riots—amazing things can grow."

**incarcerated** in jail

### Exercise **1**   Discussion Questions

1. What was the original goal of the group when they planted the first garden behind the football field?
2. How did the project grow and expand?
3. Why is the title of the article "Planting Seeds, Harvesting Scholarships"?

### Exercise **2**   Making Connections

1. Why is the students' sense of accomplishment more important than the money?
2. Have you yourself or has anyone you know ever been involved in a community project with other people? What did you or they do?

# Growing Up in Our Neighborhoods

## INFERENCES

## RECOGNIZING INFERENCES

Often writers (and speakers) do not state everything directly. Instead, they give you clues—pieces of information—so that you can make some reasonable assumptions or guesses about what they are trying to say. To understand this kind of communication, you must infer, or "read between the lines," and think about what is being said. A writer or speaker who says something indirectly is *implying* meaning, and the reader or listener is *inferring* the meaning from the clues that are given.

We make inferences in everyday life when speaking to our friends. The clues for these inferences are often the things that are happening or have happened around us that we both know about. As an example, let's say you have a baseball team, the bases are loaded, and the team member who is up to bat strikes out. She says, "Oh, that's just great!" We can reasonably infer that she means, "That's just terrible!"

You base your inference on clues in the situation and on your own experience in similar situations. From the context clues—having just struck out while the bases were loaded—we know that she is upset and that she is using the word *great* to mean the opposite, *terrible*. You no doubt received extra visual clues from the expression on her face and from the way she acted. She probably looked upset instead of happy, and her body language probably showed disappointment instead of triumph.

Sometimes our inferences can help us to predict what will happen next in a situation or a story. For example, if your boss has just observed you arriving 20 minutes late for work for the third time this week, and he says with a frown, "Mark, see me in my office," what do you infer, or predict, he will say to you? It's not likely he's going to praise you for a job well done. You know that being on time is expected in most jobs, and the boss is also frowning, which would lead you to infer that he is unhappy with something you've done.

### Recognizing Inferences in Visual Images

It has been said that "a picture is worth a thousand words." Many people think pictures can communicate information to us more quickly and efficiently, and perhaps more accurately, than long wordy readings can. We can infer a lot of information from the images presented. For example, study the following picture which shows a woman working in a community.

What clues does the picture provide?

> *a van loaded with tools*
> *a ladder on top of the van*
> *a woman dressed to go out on the job*
> *tools slung over the woman's shoulder and strapped around her waist*

What can you reasonably infer from these clues?

> *This woman is ready to go to work.*

Can you tell from this picture what kind of job she has?

> *Her job is in a technical field that requires using lots of tools.*

Can you infer what company she works for?

> *No. From a combination of the clues in the picture and your own experience, you might reasonably infer that she works for the telephone company, cable company, or a gas and electric company. However, there is no logo on her shirt or visible lettering on the van to tell us exactly who her employer is.*

Does she like her job and feel confident about her ability to do it?

> *Yes. She is smiling confidently and she appears comfortable carrying the equipment.*

Did this picture surprise you in any way or contradict what you would expect from your own experience? What kind of inference about work can you draw from this?

> *You may have been surprised to see a woman dressed for this kind of work because, in our society, men have traditionally held the jobs that required more physical labor. You may infer, then, that the photographer is trying to suggest that women are moving into technical jobs that were chiefly held by men in the past and that they are probably enjoying their work.*

Exercise **3**    **Recognizing Inferences in Visual Images**

For the following pictures, some reasonable inferences are provided for you. Write down the information or clues in each picture that support that inference. The first one is done for you.

1.

Reasonable inference: *The elderly man is demonstrating how to build a model house, and both he and the child are enjoying the activity.*

Clues: *The man appears to be placing a roof made of tongue depressors on the top of a model house.*

*The child is leaning in close, paying careful attention, and smiling happily.*

2.

Reasonable inference: *The young man the police are talking to and the children in the foreground are quite comfortable with the police in their neighborhood.*

Clues: _____

_____

_____

3.

Reasonable inference: *This is a photograph of a high school hallway.*

Clues: _____

_____

Reasonable inference: *Different taggers, or writers of graffiti, have been there.*

Clues: _____

_____

_____

4.

Reasonable inference: *Everybody in this neighborhood is happy to see the soldier come home.*

Clues: _____

_____

_____

Reasonable inference: *The girl on the left is hoping the soldier will notice her.*

Clues: _____

_____

_____

## Making Inferences from Reading

Writers use inferences in many ways. Sometimes they present us with a lot of detailed information and then expect us to reach the same conclusions they did by using inferences. You did this in Chapters 3 and 4 when you learned how to identify unstated main ideas in what you read. Read the following excerpt from a news story to see what you might reasonably infer.

> WASHINGTON—[In Washington, D.C.] police have no gasoline for their cruisers. Health clinics have run out of drugs. Six blocks from the White House, firefighters ride trucks with no ladders and buy their own boots.
>
> Potholes blister Embassy Row. The decrepit water-treatment plant threatens to spew sewage into the Potomac. Earlier this year, inmates set fire to their cells after the prison ran out of food. (Lori Montgomery, *The San Diego Union-Tribune*)

What can we reasonably infer from this information?

*Washington, D.C., is having serious trouble maintaining regular city services.*

In this case this inference would also be the main idea for this passage. It is unstated, but the details, or clues, in the article add up to this conclusion.

What clues do we have to make this inference?

*(1) Police don't have gasoline, (2) health clinics don't have drugs, (3) firefighters don't have ladders, (4) the streets have potholes, (5) the water-treatment plant is too old, and (6) prison inmates ran out of food. This long list of examples shows that things are falling apart in that city.*

You can also infer that these conditions are disgraceful. This understanding is implied more subtly. The writer states that "six blocks from the White House" firefighters don't have the proper equipment. The firefighters' problems are no doubt true all over the city, but it looks worse when we realize how close this is to the home of the president of our country. Also, it's emphasized that potholes are on Embassy Row. If there are potholes in those streets—where ambassadors from countries all over the world reside—there are probably potholes everywhere. This makes the condition of the streets even more embarrassing. From the details the writer included and the way she stated them, we can probably also conclude that she thinks we should do something to remedy these problems in our nation's capital.

---

**Exercise 4**    **Recognizing Inferences in Passages**

Read the following passages and choose the reasonable inferences that you can make from the information and clues presented there. Each of these passages discusses issues of public safety and growing up in our communities. Circle or underline the clues in the passage that helped you to arrive at these inferences. Place a check mark in front of each statement that you decide is a reasonable inference. The first one has been done for you.

1. Even celebrities sometimes quietly give of themselves behind the scenes. In Joe Dumars's life, <u>basketball and community responsibility came together</u>

early on. The Detroit Pistons' guard grew up in Natchitoches, La., the youngest of seven children. One day his father, a truck driver, cut an old door in half, nailed a bicycle rim to it and transformed the neighborhood. "We had the biggest yard, a basketball hoop, and it was just a magnet for all the kids in the area," he remembers. "It was always crowded, but everyone was made to feel welcome. My mother, Ophelia, made sure of that." (Jonathan Alter, "Everyday Heroes")

✔ a. Dumars's father made a basketball hoop and a backboard out of an old door and a bicycle rim.

____ b. Joe Dumars was the youngest of seven children.

____ c. Dumars's father knew his son would be a basketball star when he grew up.

✔ d. Dumars's yard became a kind of neighborhood center.

*Statements a and d are the only reasonable inferences from the information provided in the paragraph. We are told that Dumars's father "cut an old door in half" and "nailed a bicycle rim to it." In the next sentence we discover that there was a basketball hoop in the yard, and we infer that this must have been what his father built. Statement d is supported by the hints "transformed the neighborhood," "a magnet for all the kids in the area," and "it was always crowded, but everyone was made to feel welcome." Statement b is not an inference because it is a fact directly stated in the paragraph. There is not enough information in the paragraph to support statement c. His father might have hoped that Dumars would become a basketball star, but no information in the paragraph tells us that.*

2. In Denmark, a small Scandinavian country, parents have an interesting attitude towards teenagers and alcohol. Most families allow their teenagers to drink small amounts of alcohol at family dinners and at social occasions. This practice seems to make the consumption of alcohol a normal part of life, and Danish parents believe that if alcohol is not forbidden to their children, their children will not sneak off to drink alone. In addition, families, schools and Danish society in general all participate in an interesting tradition. When a group graduates from *gymnasium* (high school), they celebrate by visiting each of the classmate's homes to have a drink. Of course, after visiting between 15 and 30 classmate's homes, you can imagine the condition of the students! To ensure the students' safety, the school organizes the activity by providing the class with a bus and a chauffeur to drive it.

____ a. Teenagers are probably in fewer drunk driving accidents in Denmark than in the United States.

____ b. Danish teenagers are different from teenagers in other parts of the world.

____ c. Danish high school graduates get terribly drunk during their graduation ceremony.

____ d. Probably not many accidents in Denmark are caused by drunk students who are celebrating their high school graduation.

3. Frequently the children in middle and upper middle class suburbs are busy people. They often leave school to be driven hurriedly to soccer or lacrosse practice three times a week and then to a game once a week on the weekend. They also very often take music lessons once a week near their home or across town, but they need to practice in between lessons, of course. In addition, they may study judo, karate, sewing, or they may be active in church youth organizations.

_____ a. These children are probably driven around by their parents.

_____ b. These children probably take the bus to all these activities.

_____ c. There's a good chance that these children don't have very much free time to play.

_____ d. These children study whenever they're not at organized activities.

4. When Rural Studio was called on to help Mattie Hogan, they gave her more than just a comfortable home. They gave Hogan her family back. Because her trailer home was substandard, Hogan had been unable to be reunited with her children, who had been put in foster care. Then the students stepped in. "They gave me new windows and stopped my leaks, and they did my plumbing," Hogan told me. "The ceiling was falling in, the floor was caved in." Today, the trailer has a comfortable, finished look, and the Hogan family is back together. "It cost about $500 for the materials," Teresa Costanzo told me. "Weigh that against the thousands and thousands of dollars that foster care would cost." (Michael Ryan, "Houses from Scratch")

_____ a. Rural Studio is a group of students who do home repairs.

_____ b. Mattie Hogan was not a good mother to her children.

_____ c. The students helped Mattie Hogan because they probably had to do volunteer service at their college.

_____ d. The Hogan family can live in the trailer now because the repairs completed by the volunteers brought the trailer up to the required standards.

5. Everything seemed fine for Camara when he came to this country from Kingston, Jamaica, several years ago. He was living with his mother and step-father, taking tough courses and getting top grades at Thomas Jefferson. But after a bitter fight with his parents, he found himself out on the street. For four days, he lived and studied on the subway at night, getting off to go to school during the day.

This would throw most kids for a loop. Even if they're not getting on well with their mothers and fathers, young people depend on parents to provide food and shelter and a certain degree of emotional support and stability. But after people at Thomas Jefferson helped Camara get settled in a homeless shelter, he pulled his grades back up, studied for his SATs, and applied for college admission. Rather than devastating him, the experience of being alone, with nowhere to spend the night but a subway car, seems to have strengthened Camara's resolve to study and make something of himself. (Albert Shanker, "A Real Role Model")

_____ a. Camara's parents knew he could do well out on his own so they threw him out of the house while he was still in high school.

_____ b. Camara had a special kind of inner drive and determination to be successful in school despite the circumstances of his life.

_____ c. Most young people who have the same problems as Camara are not as successful as he was.

_____ d. Camara's parents were unable to take care of him.

• • • • • • • • • •

# Organizing to Learn

## Separating Personal Opinion from Reasonable Inferences

• • • • • • • • • • • • • • • • • • • • • • • • • • • • • • • • • • • • • • •

It is important to be able to distinguish between what the author is implying, or reasonable inferences, and your own personal opinion related to the subject. For example, in number 5 Exercise 4 on page 276 the author writes:

> But after a bitter fight with his parents, he found himself out on the street. For four days, he lived and studied on the subway at night, getting off to go to school during the day.

What was your opinion about these events? It might have been something like one of the following:

1. Parents should never throw their children out, no matter how big the disagreement.
2. He should have *showed* his parents; he should have just hid out for a while, so they could worry about him.
3. Why should he still worry about school? Even his parents don't care what happens to him.
4. I know what it is like to be on the streets when you are a kid; it can really be tough.

You may have had many other opinions about these sentences and that's fine. As you learned in the PRO reading system, you should always be involved with what you read. You should reflect on what you've read, make connections with your prior reading and experiences, and form your own opinions about it. The only caution is to not confuse your opinions with inferences suggested by the author.

For any reasonable inference that you make, be sure that there are clues that lead to that inference in the reading.

| Exercise **5** | Identifying Personal Opinion or Reasonable Inference |

Read the following paragraph. Then write "O" for opinion or "I" for reasonable inference. Remember, a reasonable inference has supporting clues in the passage itself. The first two have been done for you.

> Authorities have become convinced that reformatories have failed as rehabilitation centers and instead have become crime schools in which teenagers learn how to become more effective criminals. A study conducted by the U.S. Department of Justice in 1987 showed that 49.7 percent of all juveniles in detention facilities had been arrested six or more times. Half of that number had been arrested eleven or more times. Acting on this belief, the Commonwealth of Massachusetts closed all five of its reform schools in 1972 and placed its young criminals in small, community-based programs. (David Newton, *Teen Violence: Out of Control*)

1. __*I*__ The number of juveniles who are repeatedly arrested and returned to reformatories indicates that reformatories are failing to achieve their goal of deterring young people from returning to crime.

   *This inference is reasonably based on the clues: "49.7 percent of all juveniles in detention facilities had been arrested six or more times"; half of those people "had been arrested eleven or more times"; and "reformatories have failed as rehabilitation centers."*

2. __*O*__ It's obvious that many of these juveniles cannot be helped, and they should simply be treated as adults in the courts.

   *Although the paragraph clearly seems to say that reformatories do not keep the majority of youths from committing additional crimes, there are no clues that prove that they simply cannot be helped by any means, and there is no mention of adult courts. This statement is clearly an opinion based on other data and experience.*

3. _____ The community-based programs in Massachusetts are definitely the best way to deal with youthful offenders.

4. _____ The Commonwealth of Massachusetts believed that placing young criminals in small, community-based programs would be more effective than placing them in reform schools.

5. _____ The State of New York has the best reform schools in the country.

## IDENTIFYING INFERENCES IN LONGER PASSAGES

Inferences in longer passages are sometimes easier to identify because we are given more information. You still go through the same process: add up the information you are given directly in the piece, consider all the clues you are given about what is implied, and then answer the questions based on inferences. Many times in a longer piece that is a narrative, or story, you will be asked to predict what will happen next. Based on what has already happened, on the character of the people in the story, and on your own experiences, you should be able to answer such questions quite accurately.

## Codes of Conduct

### GEOFFREY CANADA

*The following reading tells the story of how Geoffrey Canada and his brothers learned how to resolve a conflict with some other boys in their neighborhood. Canada's mother taught her children an important lesson on the day he describes. As you read, see if you can predict how the conflict will be resolved. What do you think his mother wanted her children to learn from this experience? Mark some clues as you read.*

1    Down the block from us was a playground. It was nearby and we didn't have to cross the street to get there. We were close in age. My oldest brother, Daniel, was six, next came John who was five, I was four and my brother Reuben was two. Reuben and I were unable to go to the playground by ourselves because we were too young. But from time to time my two oldest brothers would go there together and play.

2    I remember them coming inside one afternoon having just come back from the playground. There was great excitement in the air. My mother noticed right away and asked, "Where's John's jacket?"

3    My brother responded, "This boy . . . this boy he took my jacket."

4    Well, we all figured that was the end of that. My mother would have to go and get the jacket back. But the questioning continued. "What do you mean, he took your jacket?"

5    "I was playing on the sliding board and I took my jacket off and left it on the bench, and this boy he tried to take it. And I said it was my jacket, and he said he was gonna take it. And he took it. And I tried to take it back, and he pushed me and said he was gonna beat me up."

6    To my mind John's explanation was clear and convincing, this case was closed. I was stunned when my mother turned to my oldest brother, Daniel, and said, "And what did you do when this boy was taking your brother's jacket?"

Daniel looked shocked. What did he have to do with this? And 7
we all recognized the edge in my mother's voice. Daniel was being
accused of something and none of us knew what it was.

Daniel answered, "I didn't do nuthin; I told Johnny not to take 8
his jacket off. I told him."

My mother exploded. "You let somebody take your brother's 9
jacket and you did nothing? That's your younger brother. You can't
let people just take your things. You know I don't have money for
another jacket. You better not ever do this again. Now you go back
there and get your brother's jacket."

My mouth was hanging open. I couldn't believe it. What was 10
my mother talking about, go back and get it? Dan and Johnny were
the same size. If the boy was gonna beat up John, well, he certainly
could beat up Dan. We wrestled all the time and occasionally hit
one another in anger, but none of us knew how to fight. We were all
equally incompetent when it came to fighting. So it made sense to
me. If my mother hadn't had that look in her eye, I would have
protested. Even at four years old I knew this wasn't fair. But I also

**signified** meant

knew that look in my mother's eye. A look that signified a line not to
be crossed.

My brother Dan was in shock. He felt the same way I did. He 11
tried to protest. "Ma, I can't beat that boy. It's not my jacket. I can't
get it. I can't."

My mother gave him her ultimatum. "You go out there and 12
get your brother's jacket or when you get back I'm going to give
you a beating that will be ten times as bad as what that little thief
could do to you. And John, you go with him. Both of you better
bring that jacket back here."

The tears began to flow. Both John and Dan were crying. My 13
mother ordered them out. Dan had this look on his face that I had
seen before. A stern determination showed through the tears. For
the first time I didn't want to go with my brothers to the park. I
waited a long ten minutes and then, to my surprise, John and Dan
triumphantly strolled into the apartment. Dan had John's jacket in
his hand.

| Exercise **6** | **Checking Your Inferences** |
|---|---|

Use the clues you identified in the story to support your answers to each of the
following questions.

1. Why did the boys' mother send them back to get the jacket themselves?
2. Why did she make the oldest son, Daniel, get the jacket even though it wasn't
   his?

3. Why were the boys scared about going back to the playground?
4. How do you think they got the jacket?

## *Codes of Conduct (Continued)*

GEOFFREY CANADA

*The following passage explains how the boys got John's jacket back.*

1    My mother gathered us all together and told us we had to stick together. That we couldn't let people think we were afraid. That what she had done in making Dan go out and get the jacket was to let us know that she would not tolerate our becoming victims. I listened unconvinced. But I knew that in not going with Dan and John I'd missed something important. Dan was scared when he left the house. We were all scared. I knew I could never have faced up to that boy. How did Dan do it? I wanted to know everything.

2    "What happened? How did you do it? Did you have to fight? Did you beat him up?" I asked. Dan explained that when he went back to the playground the boy was still there, wearing John's jacket. He went up to him and demanded the jacket. The boy said no. Dan grabbed the jacket and began to take it off the boy. Dan was still crying, but the boy knew it was not from fear of him. A moment of resistance, but Dan's determination prevailed. The boy grew scared and Dan wrestled the jacket free. He even managed a threatening "You better never bother my brother again" as the boy fled.

3    Dan's description of the confrontation left me with more questions. I was trying to understand why Dan was able to get the jacket. If he could get it later, why didn't he take it back the first time? How come the boy didn't fight? What scared him off? Even at four years old I knew I needed to know these things. I needed some clues on which I could build a theory of how to act. Dan's story couldn't help me much. It took many years of playing and hanging on the streets of the South Bronx before I began to put together the pieces of the theory. The only real lesson I learned from the jacket episode was if someone takes something from you, tell your mother you lost it, otherwise you might be in danger of getting your face punched in by some boy on the streets of New York City. This was a valuable bit of understanding for a four-year-old in the Bronx.

| Exercise **7** | **Checking Your Inferences** |
|---|---|

Use the clues you identified in the story to support your answers to each of the following questions.

1. Why did the author's mother tell her boys that she didn't want people to think they were afraid?
2. Why did the boy let Dan get the jacket back without a fight?
3. Why do you think Dan was crying if it was not from fear of the boy?
4. Why did the author infer at that time that if someone takes something from you it is better to tell your mother that you lost it?

• • • • • • • • • • • • •

# Working with Words

## Language of Imagery
• • • • • • • • • • • • • • • • • • • • • • • • • • • • • • • • • • • • • • •

Good writers and good speakers often use language that helps make their ideas stronger by affecting our senses. Their use of language can make us see pictures in our minds or to imagine how something feels or smells. Sometimes the writer uses a colloquial, or slang, expression to create this picture. For example, in "Codes of Conduct" Canada writes:

My mother *exploded.* "You let somebody take your brother's jacket and you did nothing?"

He was trying to explain how upset she was when the boys said they did nothing about their brother's coat being stolen. Everyone knows she didn't actually "blow up"; she was just very angry at the boys' lack of action. The word *exploded* gives us a strong visual image, or picture, of how she looked and talked at that instant.

Sometimes, also, writers do not make their point directly. The reader has to picture the images to figure out exactly what is being said. For example, what do you think teenagers in a gang mean when they say:

"I would rather be *judged by twelve* than *carried by six.*"

What are the clues and visual images (pictures formed in your mind) in the sentence?

"Judged by twelve" means face a trial (there are twelve people on a jury)

"Carried by six" refers to being in a coffin. Six people (pallbearers) carry the coffin.

The entire statement means that I would rather be arrested for a crime (even murder) than be killed.

**Exercise 8    Understanding the Language of Imagery**

In the following sentences, some examples of language that use imagery have been italicized. Explain (1) what visual images are formed when we read these words, and (2) what the words actually mean in the sentence.

1. They called their [garden] project Food From the 'Hood. And the *ideas kept on sprouting*. . . . "From anything—even the riots—amazing things can grow." (Jonathan Alter, "Planting Seeds, Harvesting Scholarships")

   Visual image: _____

   Meaning: _____

2. For four days, he lived and studied on the subway at night, getting off to go to school during the day. This would *throw most kids for a loop*. (Albert Shanker, "A Real Role Model")

   Visual image: _____

   Meaning: _____

3. *An Eye for an eye. A tooth for a tooth. (The Bible)*

   Visual image: _____

   Meaning: _____

4. [I lived] on a quiet, tree-lined street where voices raised in anger were scarcely ever heard. The telephone, *like some grim umbilical*, kept me connected to the old world with news of death, imprisonings and misfortune. (Brent Staples)

   Visual image: _____

   Meaning: _____

5. "We had the biggest yard, a basketball hoop, and it was just *a magnet for all the kids in the area*," he remembers. (Jonathan Alter, "What Works")

   Visual image: _____

   Meaning: _____

6. My mother gathered us all together and told us *we had to stick together*. (Canada, "Codes of Conduct")

   Visual image: _____

   Meaning: _____

7. But I also knew that look in my mother's eye. *A look that signified a line not to be crossed.* (Canada, "Codes of Conduct")

Visual image: _____

Meaning: _____

## Beacon Schools: A Model for Community Development

### GEOFFREY CANADA

*Geoffrey Canada has spent most of his life working with young people who are at risk of joining gangs and selling drugs and who do not know appropriate ways of dealing with the problems and conflicts in their lives. In Canada's opinion, these young people's families and communities need support. In the following excerpt from his book* FistStickKnifeGun, *he describes the program in which he is involved that he believes addresses wider community issues as well as juvenile violence prevention.*

### Preparing to Read

1. Preview the following reading selection. Write down what you think will be Canada's general approach to working with young people.
2. Write two reader's questions that you think will be answered in this selection.

When dealing with the issue of young people and violence in our country, it's clear that we can't separate violence from all of the other problems that plague our youth: educational failure, teenage pregnancy, drug and alcohol abuse, lack of employment, crime, AIDS . . . the list goes on and on. And we know we cannot design a few small demonstration projects and expect to have any real impact on any of these issues. We can't expect to make a difference unless we are willing to talk about comprehensive services for massive numbers of children *and* their families. The Beacon Schools program is one model to accomplish this. 1

The Beacon Schools concept is fairly simple; the most complicated part was getting government to make the investment to start the program. It was the mayor of New York City, David N. Dinkins, 2 who decided in 1991 to turn a crime prevention plan from one that merely hired more police to one that invested in children. Story has it that Mayor Dinkins had to decide between a prison barge to handle the overcrowding in city jails or Beacon Schools. He chose Beacons. . . .

3      The Beacon sites are places that combine comprehensive services with activities based on a youth development model. Schools are a natural place to house Beacon programs because when designed correctly, a Beacon is more than just a bunch of services for children and families, it is a community development strategy. We have realized that you cannot save children without saving families and you cannot save families without rebuilding communities. Beacons work on all of these issues at the same time, and schools are designed to handle the large numbers of people that must be involved in order to rebuild communities. . . .

4      What we did was to have several performances by a theatre company right on the block. People heard the laughing and music and began to open their windows to find out what was happening. Slowly they began to come downstairs, and when they did they saw a first-rate theatre group. People naturally started to talk to one another and to get to know others who lived on the block. This was the beginning of a strategy to get the community's residents to meet one another and to become aware of what we at Rheedlen [the agency that helps set up community programs] were trying to do.

**strategy** long-range plan

5      Another key component to involving the community was the creation of a block association on 144th Street. We encouraged the adults to come together and decide what they wanted for the children on their block, and we said we'd help them to do what *they* wanted. They decided they wanted a "play street." You have to be a New Yorker to understand why this is an extremely difficult thing to get accomplished in New York City. It's not because of the city permit required, or the community board approval process. It's because of parking. New Yorkers are required to move their cars to alternate sides of the street on alternate days so the streets can be cleaned. This requires everyone to double-park, and is a huge hassle. A play street means that no cars are allowed on the block at all from 8:00 A.M. until 4:00 P.M., which means that not only do you have to worry about double-parking, you have to do it on someone else's block.

6      There was a huge debate about the play street on 144th Street. People with cars were upset. Where were they supposed to park? What if someone broke into their cars while they were on some other block? Others pleaded for the children, asking car owners to make the sacrifice for them. In the end the block decided to open the play street. Now in the summer when you look down 144th

Street you can see children engaged in all kinds of activities—and a smug look on the faces of adults who know they are doing the right thing for the children even if it hurts.

One critical strategy of the Beacon Schools program is provid-   7
ing activities designed for adolescents during the late evenings and weekends. Typically poor communities like Harlem offer few services to children after school hours; where services are offered, they usually end by 6:00 P.M. and are hardly ever available on weekends. When we surveyed what was available for children in our Central Harlem neighborhood we identified approximately five thousand children who needed late-evening activities on the weekend. If we didn't include the children we were serving at our Beacon school, we could only find services elsewhere for approximately fifty of those children. If we expect our young people to engage in positive activities, we must provide them the places and the structure to do so. Leaving thousands of them on street corners with nothing to do only invites trouble.

Rheedlen's Beacon school is designed to provide activities be-   8
yond those for children and adolescents. We discovered long ago that we cannot save children without making just as strong an effort to help their parents. Our Beacon offers a range of programs for adults, including education classes, support groups, aerobics, African dance, and targeted workshops in areas that parents select. We also have trained social workers on site to provide more intensive counseling and referral if parents need it.

**unanticipated**
unexpected

One of the unanticipated results of having so many parents in-   9
volved in our Beacon program is that it has reduced the level of violence in the school itself. When we began to think about it, this made sense. Young people are less likely to act violently in a setting where their mother, or their friend's mother, might be. As the Countee Cullen Community Center involved more and more of the community, adults and children, the school and the center took on more of the values of the larger community and fewer of the values of the adolescents in that community. Knowing someone's mother could be walking down the hallway or be in a nearby classroom, the children became less likely to yell curses or engage in violent behavior.

Rheedlen's Beacon program at Countee Cullen is designed to  10
help rebuild the Central Harlem community that surrounds it, but it is also designed to help support the education of the young children that attend the elementary school. Rheedlen staff have become directly involved in working with these students. They have helped with counseling, instruction, and bridging the gap between school and home. It is often obvious that a child having a difficult

time in school has a problem at home. Schools today don't have the ability or training to go to a child's home when a parent will not come to the school. Rheedlen staff will make that home visit and work with that parent and the entire family. In this way the home and school connection can be strengthened and teachers can get support dealing with even the most difficult children.

11     Safety is so important when you have a large building like Countee Cullen, with its five floors, one that stays open so many hours, especially late evenings. Rheedlen has a security force that makes sure the message received at the front door is that we expect good manners, and no violence. The young men and women who make up our security team really like the children and don't try to intimidate them. When there's a problem they try to reason, but they are firm. They don't believe in using force or bad language, or in bending the rules, which get enforced fairly by all the members of the team. If there is a problem, members of the security team use their walkie-talkies to converge on the problem site and diffuse the situation before it can get out of hand. If someone is really aggressive and refuses to obey the security team, the police are called to expel that person. The police, as we've seen, are not well loved by young people in Harlem, so we use them sparingly. We have had to call the police only a few times in the years we have been open, and we maintain a good relationship with our community police officer.

12     Rheedlen's Beacon school is having its desired effect. Over the course of a week more than a thousand children and adults come to our programs. The whole community benefits from so many people just being outside walking in the community on their way to or from healthy activities. The teenagers have begun to exert real control over their lives. For example, they decided that a huge billboard on 144th Street, one that was right across from the school and had advertised cigarettes or alcohol their whole lives, needed to be changed. Our Teen Youth Council fought to have the usual ad replaced by one for the United Negro College Fund. Now, instead of the children on that block and in the school seeing a compelling reason to drink or smoke, they see a picture of Martin Luther King, Jr., compelling them to go to college.

13     The Teen Youth Council has also decided to improve the physical conditions on 144th Street. They have regularly cleaned the block and painted over graffiti, and this last winter they got trees planted up and down the whole block. They've led hunger drives for the homeless, clothing drives for poor people, voter registration drives aimed at nonvoters, and antiviolence demonstrations to get the message out that, in a world where they have felt their odds of surviving to adulthood to be shrinking, they want to opportunity to grow up.

There are many exciting things occurring at our Beacon 14 school, and people have come from near and far to observe what we are doing there. I have to constantly remind people that this is just the fourth year of a ten-year developmental model. We still have a long way to go—but we all feel we are off to a great start.

---

**Exercise 9**  **Checking Your Understanding**

1. List some of the causes of problems for U.S. youth that Canada mentions. *(Para. 1)*
2. Why did Mayor Dinkins choose to fund the Beacon Schools? *(Para. 2)*
3. Why did they have theater performances on the street? *(Para. 4)*
4. What is a "play street"? What problems did the members of the block association on 144th Street have to work out to have one? *(Paras. 5 and 6)*
5. Why did the Beacon School encourage so much parent participation? What were some of the positive effects of this idea? *(Paras. 8 and 9)*
6. What have been some of the positive effects of the Rheedlen's Beacon School? *(Paras. 12 and 13)*

---

**Exercise 10**  **Checking Your Inferences**

1. What reasons can you infer for Canada's statement, "We have realized that you cannot save children without saving families and you cannot save families without rebuilding communities?" *(Para. 3)*
2. The author states, "If we expect our young people to engage in positive activities, we must provide them the places and the structure to do so. Leaving thousands of them on street corners with nothing to do only invites trouble." *(Para. 7)* What kind of trouble is the author implying young people might get into?
3. What are some reasonable inferences about the statement, "The school and the center took on more of the values of the larger community and fewer of the values of the adolescents in that community"? *(Para. 9)*
4. What can you safely infer from the author's last statement, "We still have a long way to go—but we all feel we are off to a great start." *(Para. 14)*

---

**Exercise 11**  **Making Connections**

1. Do you think that programs like the Beacon School would be good for other communities? Explain your answer.

2. Do you know of any community programs in your neighborhood? Describe them.

• • • • • • • • • • • • • •

# Applying Your Skills

• • • • • • • • • • • • • • • • • • • • • • • • • • • • • • • • • • •

## *Fighting Tradition*

JOHN L. MITCHELL

*The following article introduces some ways to teach young people a different code of behavior for the future, one that moves toward resolution of conflicts and more peaceful communities rather than violent solutions.*

### Preparing to Read

1. Preview the following article. What do you think the author will be suggesting for the "New Rules of Manhood."
2. The article describes ways that fathers are thinking about teaching their sons today. What do you think were the rules that fathers learned about getting along in a tough neighborhood when they were growing up?

1    As young boys, they were raised under a simple code of manhood: Be the aggressor, don't let anyone push you around, and if someone is coming at you, get in the first lick.

2    Now they are fathers, trying to teach the rules of aggression to their own sons and finding that the lessons are complex and confusing: Avoid conflict if you can. If someone demands your money, there are times you give it up. Be tough, but not too tough—it can get you killed.

3    Sunday will bring reflections on the changing role of fathers, and little has changed more in large cities like Los Angeles than the way boys are taught to stick up for themselves. Fathers are being

forced to define manhood in a way that is sharply at odds with what they experienced growing up.

Look at the way the ritual has changed through Nathaniel 4 Howard's eyes.

"It seemed like almost every day someone was chasing me 5 home from school," recalls Howard, who grew up in Oklahoma and South-Central Los Angeles. "I didn't have time to open the screen door, so I just dived in through a hole in the screen and cut up my clothes. One day my mother forced me out of the house. She dragged me by the chest and put me back outside. She said, 'You can fight him or fight me.' "

Now 43 and living in the West Adams district west of down- 6 town, Howard says he can't imagine giving his 14-year-old son, Timothy, the same advice. One of Timothy's friends was shot to death after winning a fistfight with another boy.

"Children today don't have the same set of values," Howard 7 says wearily. "They don't play by the rule 'May the best man win.' "

In Howard's boyhood, tears were looked upon with scorn by 8 men like his dad, who taught him how to box. Fathers might have preached the art of turning the other cheek, but they would quietly praise and reward sons who refused to back down. Toughness was a valued trait to be passed on, a tool of survival.

**ethic** values system

That ethic has faded dramatically as the streets become more 9 dangerous and hair-trigger tempers turn innocent skirmishes into gun deaths.

There is also far more social awareness of the consequences 10 of male aggression, human behavior experts say, and a backlash against the macho mentality of previous generations.

Men like Howard, who were allowed to roam their neighbor- 11 hoods all day in their youth, now find themselves chauffeuring their children to keep them out of danger. Fathers who recall the days

**toe the line** follow the rules

when any parent on the block could make a child toe the line now live in communities that have grown fearful of teenage boys.

Howard says Timothy is vulnerable to the age-old tradition of 12 responding to stress with aggression. Since his mother died about two years ago, he has gotten into several fights and has been suspended from school.

"Any time someone says something about his mother, he is 13 ready to fight," Howard says. "His mother is his weak spot, and other children can be cruel when it comes to picking on weak spots."

And so Howard did something his father, a Korean War vet- 14 eran, never would have done. He enrolled his son in counseling, and he himself joined a weekly gathering of about a dozen fathers at Children's Institute International in Los Angeles.

15      Recently, the fathers in the group spent an evening on the question of how to teach their sons to protect themselves in today's world. It was a double-edged discussion that swung from laughter over the scrapes they had experienced growing up to fear about what their sons would face.

16      David Zubia, a 38-year-old print shop manager, had more than his share of street scuffles growing up in Los Angeles. He is determined that his son Devon, 12, will not grow up the same way.

17      Zubia said he began teaching his son how to defend himself when some of his classmates began taunting him, sneaking up behind him and pulling down his gym shorts in class. But "defending" in this era meant getting the boy more involved in sports, building his confidence.

18      "He needs to be more diplomatic, more verbal in resolving conflicts," Zubia said. "That's how you survive today."

**diplomatic** able to avoid conflicts

19      Survival also means keeping a close eye on your child.

20      "I try to know where he's at at all times, day or night," Zubia said. "I pick him up and drop him off. He doesn't have the freedom to run the streets the way that I did. There is too much danger out there. That's where the odds are against them."

21      "You can't tell your son today to go fist-to-fist with someone," echoed Melvin Johnson, 59. "You don't know what the other kid has in his pocket."

22      The clinical psychologist who runs the sessions, Hershel K. Swinger, 59, said he was raised the same way as most of the men in the room while growing up in rural Kansas.

23      "I remember my mother telling me to go out and fight. I did, and the fighting got good to me, and I started chasing the boy down the street," he said. "I could hear my mother running after me saying, 'Come back here.' "

24      Swinger, who is black, said he faced a different reality about 10 years ago when police stepped up a crackdown on street gangs, and virtually all young black males seemed to be the target of suspicion.

25      "I didn't know which was worse, the gang members or the police," he said. "So I bought my way out. I sent my son to an expensive school in Northern California."

26      Ronald Levant, a Harvard professor who has written about the changing rules of manhood and grew up in Southern California, said the need for toughness was more immediate in the lives of men who survived the Depression of the '30s and World War II.

27      That ethic has come into conflict with more recent social changes that are conditioning men to be more communicative, he said. There are more families in which women work, putting pressure on men to be more involved in their children's upbringing.

There are more families headed by women, breaking down the dominance of male values. And there is more pressure on fathers to practice what they preach.

"We need to rethink the roles of men in our society and help 28 our children to develop skills that we weren't given as a matter of course," Levant said. "Children need to learn how to anticipate dangerous situations and resolve them or avoid them."

Levant said his father, a printer with an eighth-grade educa- 29 tion, was ill-equipped to give such advice when he was raising his family in South Gate.

**ill-equipped** not prepared

"My dad was as tough as they come, a man with few words," 30 Levant recalled. "He would show disgust" if Levant came home having lost a fight.

Many of the fights grew out of the prejudice that some felt 31 against the Levants, one of the few Jewish families in South Gate.

"I was called a kike," Levant recalled. "At some point I realized 32 this was a fighting word, and I couldn't back down. My father told me to fight."

"Would I raise a son like that?" Levant asked. "Hell, no." 33

---

**Exercise 12**   **Checking Your Understanding**

1. State the main idea of paragraph 1 in your own words.
2. State the main idea of paragraph 2 in your own words.
3. What does "the art of turning the other cheek" mean? *(Para. 8)*
4. What do fathers like Howard do now to keep their children out of trouble? *(Paras. 11–14)*
5. What did Swinger's mother tell him to do? *(Paras. 22–23)*
6. What did Swinger do to keep his son out of trouble? *(Para. 25)*

---

**Exercise 13**   **Checking Your Inferences**

Write a reasonable inference on each of the following points from the article based on the clues provided there.

1. Levant says he would not raise a son the way he was raised. Why? What will he do differently?
2. Zubia says of his son, "He needs to be more diplomatic, more verbal in resolving conflicts. That's how you survive today." How is he suggesting things have changed?

3. "Survival also means keeping a close eye on your child." What kinds of things must parents do to accomplish this?
4. "There are more families in which women work, putting pressure on men to be more involved in their children's upbringing." How, according to the author, must men be more involved?

## Exercise **14**   Organizing to Learn

Based on the information in paragraphs 12 to 14, write "I" if the statement is a reasonable inference or write "O" if the statement is an opinion unsupported by clues in the paragraphs.

1. _____ Boys should always fight if someone is insulting their mother.
2. _____ Responding to stress with aggression is not always the best thing to do.
3. _____ Children were acting cruelly when they said things about Timothy's mother who had died.
4. _____ Howard thinks his son can learn some alternatives to fighting by attending counseling.
5. _____ Howard thinks he can learn to put up with his son's fighting by going to a weekly gathering of fathers at the Children's Institute International.

## Exercise **15**   Working with Words

Make a list of five to seven words from the article "Fighting Tradition" that you think are important for you to learn. Using either the context clues or the dictionary, for each word you've chosen (1) write the word, (2) write the appropriate definition of the word, and (3) write a sentence using the word.

## Exercise **16**   Making Connections

1. How were you raised to deal with conflict? Were there times when you were a teenager that you avoided getting into fights? Did you get into fights? Explain.
2. What are some more things that fathers and families can do to keep their children safe? Make a list of ideas.
3. If you had teenagers today what precautions would you take to make sure *they* were safe?
4. What are the rules of conduct for young men now?

5. What are the rules of conduct for young women now?
6. What do you think the rules of conduct should be for young men and women?

# Chapter Review

| Exercise **17** | **Skills Review** |

1. What does making an "inference" mean?
2. Why is it important as a reader to be able to make reasonable inferences?
3. Individually, or in your class group, complete the following outline on how to make inferences.

### Making Inferences

*Inferences* are based on

a. _____

b. _____

In stories, *inferences* help us *predict* what will probably happen based on

a. _____

b. _____

c. _____

| Exercise **18** | **Writing** |

Write a short essay in which you describe a hypothetical neighborhood and some of its specific problems. Then explain the types of solutions you have for the problems you identified.

| Exercise **19** | **Collaborative Activity** |

In your group, imagine that you will be the people to develop a plan to improve the sense of community in a neighborhood. (If you wish, you can share your answers from Exercise 18).

**Step 1** Describe your neighborhood. It can be any kind of neighborhood you wish. Describe the problems in your neighborhood that you want to solve.

**Step 2** Describe your plan for activities and programs in the neighborhood that will help solve the problems that you identified in step 1.

**Exercise 20**     **Extension Activity**

Find an article in a local newspaper or magazine about a community group that is working to improve your neighborhood or wider community. What community *problem,* or issue, is this group trying to solve? What work are they doing to create a solution? What steps have they already completed? What do you think still needs to be done?

CHAPTER

# 10

# *Work and the Community*

## FACTS VERSUS OPINIONS

### RECOGNIZING FACTS AND OPINIONS

One way to evaluate what you are reading is to examine the information, or evidence, you are given. Is the information based on facts? Or is the information based on opinions?

A *fact* is information that most people would accept as true. It is something that can easily be verified. Recognized experts in a field would be able to determine whether a stated fact is true or not. For example, if someone says, "One dollar equals 98 cents," you would immediately recognize this as an incorrect statement. The correct statement of fact is, "One dollar equals 100 cents."

An *opinion* is someone's interpretation of facts. For example, if someone's grandfather says, "Five dollars is a lot of allowance for a young person," his grandchild may disagree. They may have different understandings of what five dollars will buy today and different expectations about what allowance should be used for. You may or may not agree with an opinion that is stated. As another example, if your brother says, "Brand Q shampoo is the best shampoo to buy," you may or may not agree with him; you do not simply accept his opinion as fact. You will probably make your own decision—based on your own experience, the ingredients printed on the label, price, friends' recommendations, etc.—about which shampoo to buy.

Read the following paragraph and see if you can determine which are statements of fact and which are opinions.

Managers at Quickie's Fast Food work a minimum of 40 hours a week. They are responsible for hiring employees, scheduling work hours, training and supervising workers, maintaining a suitable work environment, upkeep of the physical plant, ordering supplies, keeping track of sales and expenses, and any other tasks necessary in the operation of the business. They are not paid nearly enough for the work they do. The amount of work they have to do is too much for one person; assistant managers should be hired at all restaurants that have more than five employees.

This paragraph is obviously a combination of facts and opinions. Look at each sentence separately and write "F" before statements of fact and "O" before statements of opinion.

1. _____ Managers at Quickie's Fast Food work a minimum of 40 hours a week.
2. _____ They are responsible for hiring employees, scheduling work hours, training and supervising workers, maintaining a suitable work environment, upkeep of the physical plant, ordering supplies, keeping track of sales and expenses, and any other tasks necessary in the operation of the business.
3. _____ They are not paid nearly enough for the work they do.
4. _____ The amount of work they have to do is too much for one person; assistant managers should be hired at all restaurants that have more than five employees.

You should have identified sentences 1 and 2 as probable statements of fact. It would not be difficult to discover if these statements are true or not. The number of hours managers work could be counted. The tasks listed in the second sentence are probably all part of the manager's job description given at the time of hiring. Sentences 3 and 4, however, are statements of opinion. Based on the facts in sentences 1 and 2, did you think that changes should be made? You might not have any background in this field of work, so you may not have formed a specific opinion. The writer has decided that managers are underpaid and that an assistant manager should be hired to help with the workload. This is the writer's opinion, her interpretation of the facts, and certainly not everyone would arrive at the same conclusion. Also, she does not back up that opinion with supporting details or arguments.

## Recognizing Facts and Opinions in Visual Images

Visual images, such as advertisements, TV commercials, cartoons, and pictures express opinions as well as present facts. As a critical reader and thinker, it is important to be able to tell the difference between the two in the images you observe. Examine the following Calvin and Hobbes cartoon and decide whether it is primarily presenting facts or opinions. Notice that you will also be able to apply some of your skill for making inferences from Chapter 9.

# Calvin and Hobbes

**by Bill Watterson**

Calvin and Hobbes © 1995 by Watterson. Distributed by Universal Press Syndicate. Reprinted with permission. All rights reserved.

What facts did you observe in this cartoon?

*The main fact you might observe here is that Calvin appears to be trying to do his homework. He has a book, paper, and pencil and is sitting at his desk. From his expression and comments, we could reasonably infer that he doesn't want to do his homework.*

What opinions did you observe in this cartoon?

*Actually, all the words in the cartoon appear to be opinions. Everything Calvin says is an opinion on how hard work is and how unfair it is that he has to work at his homework and "everything" else. Hobbes's statement, "The American Dream lives on," suggests that all Americans would like to live like Calvin wants to: "I wish I could just push a button to have anything I want." We wouldn't have to work for anything; everything would just be given to us. Cartoonist Bill Watterson explained the reason for creating this particular strip this way: "As somebody said, we all want to go to heaven, but nobody wants to do what it takes to get there." (Bill Watterson, Calvin and Hobbes, Tenth Anniversary Book)*

| Exercise **1** | Recognizing Facts and Opinions in Visual Images |
| --- | --- |

Advertisements usually have a certain purpose: to convince you to want whatever they are presenting. The following ads use visual images and printed words to persuade you to choose a certain career, pick a job with their company, or enroll in their school for career training. We've identified the general purpose for each ad. Examine each ad and see if you can determine what are *facts* and what are *opinions*. You will need to use your inference skills to help you understand these ads. The "connections" questions help direct you to think critically about how the ads use a combination of facts and opinions. The first one has been done for you.

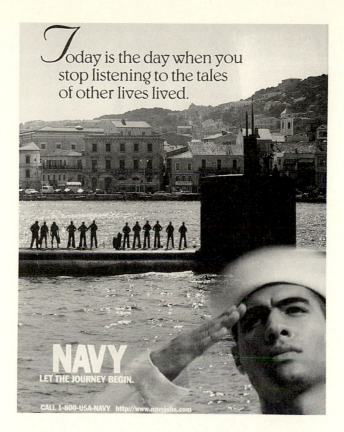

*Today* is the day when you stop listening to the tales of other lives lived.

**NAVY**
LET THE JOURNEY BEGIN.

CALL 1-800-USA-NAVY  http://www.navyjobs.com

1. Purpose: To encourage you to join the Navy.
   a. List the facts.
      the Navy's phone number
      the Navy's Internet address
      *more than a dozen people, probably members of the Navy, standing on a*
      *submarine deck, viewing a port in an attractive, somewhat exotic-looking*
      *area of the world.*
   b. List the opinions.
      *"Today is the day when you stop listening to the tales of other lives lived."*
      *The inference here is that you can embark on a life of adventure, not just*
      *listen to other people's exciting stories. It is suggested that life in the Navy*
      *is an exciting adventure.*
      *"Let the journey begin." In other words, don't hesitate. The ad makers'*
      *opinion is that you can start an exciting life with the Navy now. The phone*
      *number and the Internet address are listed immediately under this advice.*
   c. Connections.
      1. Why would life in the Navy be exciting?
         *Answers will vary. From the ad you might say that you get to travel to*
         *new and interesting parts of the world.*

2. Would life in the Navy always be exciting? Why or why not?
   *Answers will vary. Since this ad gives very little information, it's hard to tell what kind of work you would be doing or where you might be stationed. There is no guarantee included that you will even be assigned to a position that involves travel to new places.*
3. Do you think you would like to have a career in the Navy? Why or why not?
   *Answers and reasons will be different for each student.*
4. What else would you like to know before signing up for a career in the Navy?
   *You might want to know what kind of work you would be doing, how much you would be paid, and where you would be stationed.*

# TAKE THE TIME TO CHANGE YOUR FOCUS

If you're not an overnight success, you're not alone. Cymer started building the first safe, reliable excimer laser for microlithography over ten years ago. And it's still our primary focus. Today, eight out of ten excimer lasers used for microlithography are made by Cymer. We have installations around the world and set the standard for performance and reliability.

Our idea's time has come. And so has yours to leave the mundane for the extraordinary. Put your career into motion and join us as we gear up for explosive growth in the coming year with new facilities, new products and worldwide support.

---

### ENGINEERING OPPORTUNITIES

---

**COMPLIANCE/ELECTRICAL ENGINEER**

**CUSTOMER SYSTEMS ENGINEERS**

**DIRECTOR OF PRODUCT DEVELOPMENT**

**ELECTRICAL ENGINEER**

**LASER TEST ENGINEERS**

Impact the future of laser technology.
Cymer, Inc.
16750 Via Del Campo Court
San Diego, CA 92127
www.cymer.com

2. Purpose: To convince all qualified people to apply for a job with Cymer.
   a. List the facts.
   b. List the opinions.
   c. Connections.
      1. How do you think Cymer can help you "leave the mundane for the extraordinary" and "put your career in motion?"
      2. Would you be interested in qualifying for one of these positions with Cymer? Why or why not?
      3. What additional information would you like to know before applying for a position with Cymer?

*Academy alumni have been nominated for 96 Oscars, 69 Tonys and 217 Emmys.*

# Academy People

Before sitcoms, before soaps, even before silent movies, there was the American Academy of Dramatic Arts. The Academy is where many of the finest actors of this century got the training they needed. Since its founding in 1884, the Academy has been dedicated to a single purpose: to prepare actors for professional careers.

For actor training of the highest quality, investigate the American Academy of Dramatic Arts.

# American Academy of Dramatic Arts

For information about the Academy's Professional Training Program and Six-Week Summer Course, contact:

*In New York:* 120 Madison Avenue, New York, NY 10016   (212) 686-9244 / (800) 463-8990

*In California:* 2550 Paloma Street, Pasadena, CA 91107   (818) 798-0777 / (800) 222-2867

3. Purpose: If you want a career as an actor, to persuade you to apply to the American Academy of Dramatic Arts.
   a. List the <u>facts</u>.
   b. List the <u>opinions</u>.
   c. <u>Connections</u>.
      1. If you are interested in a professional acting career, why should you apply to the American Academy of Dramatic Arts rather than somewhere else?
      2. If you are interested in a professional acting career, would you like to apply to the American Academy of Dramatic Arts? Why or why not?
      3. What additional information would you want to know before applying to the academy?

## Recognizing Facts and Opinions in Printed Material

Both facts and opinions are obvious in all printed material that we read, including newspapers, magazines, Web sites, and textbooks. A writer doesn't write facts all the time; much of what we read is an *interpretation* of facts. As readers we need to recognize these opinions, or interpretations, and be prepared to challenge them if necessary.

For example, the American Academy of Dramatic Arts ad on page 301 presents both facts and interpretations of facts, or opinions. For example, the statement "Academy alumni have been nominated for 95 Oscars, 69 Tonys and 209 Emmys" is probably a fact. Certainly the information could be easily checked to see if it is accurate. On the other hand, the statement that the Academy has trained "many of the finest actors of this century" is based on opinion. We don't know what criteria are being applied to select the finest actors. Opinion statements often have this quality of requiring a judgment or evaluation. The ad also states, "For actor training of the highest quality, investigate the American Academy of Dramatic Arts." The term "highest quality" signals the reader that a judgment is being made, and other people may or may not agree with this judgment.

## *How to Get an Internship*

*Read the following passage and watch for statements of fact versus statements of opinion.*

---

**internship** short-term experience and training in a professional field

An internship is the best way to try out a profession and get 1 some experience. Here's how to land that coveted (and usually unpaid) spot:

First, target the right companies. *The Internship Bible* by 2 Samer Hamadeh and Mark Oldman lists 100,000 opportunities, more than 200 of which are available to high school students. Every two years, the National Society for Internships and Experimental Education in Raleigh, North Carolina, prints a 400-page directory of internship programs, which costs $29; ask your school guidance office to buy a copy. Or, look for the *Book of Associations* at your library. It lists every kind of industry organization you can imagine. Call an association in your field of interest, and they may be able to recommend a nearby organization where you can intern.

3      Your homework's not done yet. The main factor in getting a company interested is not straight A's or a club presidency, Hamadeh says. It's an enthusiastic letter. "Many students just copy the letter in those cover-letter books, and it's boring," he says. "Employers look for a letter from the heart."

4      In about two paragraphs, describe who you are, specifically mentioning what appeals to you about the organization, and what position you would like. If you can find a person in a supervisory position, such as the advertising manager, in the field in which you want to work, address the letter to him or her. Otherwise, send it to the human resources department. Write a few months before you'd like to start the internship, and follow up with a phone call two weeks later. Be friendly, but persistent. If an organization can't accommodate an intern for a few months, ask to come for a week. In the end, who can resist free help?

## Exercise 2 — Identifying Facts and Opinions

Read each of the following statements taken from the reading and write "F" in front of those that you think are facts and write "O" in front of those that appear to be opinions. The first two have been done for you.

1.  __O__ An internship is the best way to try out a profession and get some experience.
    *You should have identified this statement as an opinion. A reader might well question this opinion. Is an internship really the best way, especially since many of them are unpaid positions?*

2.  __F__ *The Internship Bible* by Samer Hamadeh and Mark Oldman lists 100,000 opportunities. . . .
    *This statement is probably a fact. It would be easy to verify whether there is such a book or not and whether it lists that many internships.*

3.  _____ Every two years, the National Society for internships and Experimental Education in Raleigh, North Carolina, prints a 400-page directory of internship programs, which costs $29. . . .

4.  _____ The main factor in getting a company interested is not straight A's or a club presidency, Hamadeh says. It's an enthusiastic letter.

• • • • • • • • • • • • •

# Working with Words
## Connotation and Denotation

• • • • • • • • • • • • • • • • • • • • • • • • • • • • • • • •

When you look up a new word in the dictionary, you are looking for its exact meaning, so you can distinguish it from all the similar words. The meaning that you find in the dictionary is called the *denotation* of the word. For example, if you looked up the word *work* in Webster's Dictionary, you would find it defined as "physical or mental effort or activity," "labor," and "employment or job." The denotation is the dictionary definition of the word. However, as people use words, they often also acquire a connotation as well.

*Connotations* are the positive and negative feelings, or emotions, that sometimes accompany a word. A lot of words used to describe work have positive and negative feelings attached to them. For example, the term *busy work* usually has a negative connotation. It means work that is not meaningful, work that is just done to appear busy, to fill time. Another example is the term *rewarding work,* which has a positive connotation. Most people prefer to be employed in rewarding work, work that helps us feel good about ourselves and leaves us satisfied that we have contributed something to the community in which we live.

| **Exercise 3** | **Connotations of Words** |
|---|---|

Read the following paragraph about work and decide whether each of the uses of work has a positive or negative connotation. Write a "+" if the connotation is positive and write a "−" if the connotation is negative.

> Work is a word we all use freely. It has many different connotations. We might do a "good day's work." We have people in our organization who are "workaholics" and "workhorses." We "work a problem through." We "work out" on a dance floor or athletic field. (William F. Roth, Jr., "The True Nature of Work")

1. _____ good day's work
2. _____ workaholic
3. _____ workhorse
4. _____ work a problem through
5. _____ work out

## *The Power of Popular Music*

WARREN K. AGEE, PHILLIP H. AULT, AND EDWIN EMERY

*One industry that many people would like to work in is the music industry. The following reading is an excerpt from a mass communications textbook that examines the influence of popular music in our society, especially the relationship of music to social issues. Although you might expect a textbook to be filled mostly with statements that are clearly facts, you will notice that this excerpt includes many interpretations not easily proven or disproven. Read carefully to sort the facts from the opinions. Also watch for words that have positive and negative connotations.*

1    The impact of popular recordings on the public consciousness is insufficiently recognized as a means of mass communication. Tape cassettes and compact discs form crucial channels of communication in the youth culture. Through them, desires, anger, ideas, attitudes, and fads spread around the country and across the oceans.

2    The electric guitar does not yet rank with the typewriter or word processor as a tool for distributing ideas. However, the recordings, music videos, and stage performances of such stars as Madonna and Ice-T have a strong impact on youthful thinking. For teenagers in particular, popular musicians often become role models.

3    "Hot" individual performers and groups rise from obscurity to international renown almost overnight, sometimes on the basis of only one or two recordings. They sing fervently of youth's yearnings for love, freedom from restraints, popularity, and peace. The voice of protest and defiance is prominent in the lyrics. The music is vibrant, beat-driven, insistent—and usually loud.

4    Unorthodox ideas and uninhibited language that challenge codes of conventional social conduct have found an audience through recordings. In earlier years musicians were prominent in the anti–Vietnam War movement. Today their voices are raised in the campaign against AIDS, the environmental crusade, and the women's movement. The upsurge in the popularity of rap singers has increased attention to social issues.

**uninhibited language** impolite language
**conventional social conduct** acceptable behavior

5    Some people regard popular music lyrics as seductive propaganda for a hedonistic attitude toward life that encourages the use of drugs, violence, and casual sexual relationships.

**hedonistic** pleasure-seeking

6    Although popular music is heavily oriented toward teenagers and young adults, other types of recordings have devoted followers, mostly among somewhat older groups. Heartbroken country singers with their plaintive laments sell millions of records. Jazz, blues, classical music, and the sweet saxophone sounds of the big bands lure recording customers to the cash register.

## Exercise 4    Checking Your Understanding

1. What do songs do besides entertain?
2. What is the "impact of popular recordings on the public consciousness"?
3. Which social issues are a target of popular music today?
4. What kinds of music are popular with groups other than teenagers and young adults?

## Exercise 5    Identifying Facts and Opinions

Write "F" in front of each of the following statements from the reading that appears to be based on fact and write "O" if the statement appears to be based on opinion.

_____ 1. The impact of popular recordings on the public consciousness is insufficiently recognized as a means of mass communication.

_____ 2. The recordings, music videos, and stage performances of such stars as Madonna and Ice-T have a strong impact on youthful thinking.

_____ 3. The upsurge in the popularity of rap singers has increased attention to social issues.

_____ 4. Heartbroken country singers with their plaintive laments sell millions of records.

## Exercise 6    Vocabulary: Connotations

Decide whether the following words have positive or negative connotations. Write a "+" if the connotation is positive and write a "–" if the connotation is negative.

1. _____ seductive propaganda
2. _____ hedonistic attitude
3. _____ casual sexual relationships
4. _____ heartbroken country singers
5. _____ devoted followers
6. _____ sweet saxophone sounds

## Exercise 7    Making Connections

1. Has music increased your awareness of social issues? If so, what issues have you become aware of through music?
2. Do you think music has a strong impact on your thinking? Why or why not?

## *Firms Helping to Prepare Students for Working World*

HILLARY CHURA

*Schools are looking to the business world to help prepare students for work in the twenty-first century. Corporate America has responded with school-to-work programs, internships, and other types of assistance to help ensure that students will be ready for the needs of the working world. Read carefully looking for facts and opinions.*

1    CHICAGO—Schools are looking to corporate America for help as they struggle with outdated labs, teachers who have never worked outside the classroom and graduates who can't keep a job.

2    And thousands of companies are answering the call, cooperating with districts on school-to-work programs to prepare teens for jobs in the global economy of the 21st century.

3    The help is coming just in time, says Phillip Jackson, director of inter-governmental affairs for Chicago's public schools.

4    "You have to know computers and computer technology to be an effective auto mechanic," Jackson says. "But in the auto classes, instead of state-of-the-art equipment, we have wrenches and hammers."

5    Business has noticed the deficit.

**deficit** lack

6    BellSouth learned that students in Atlanta who wanted to be graphic artists didn't know the most useful software; teens who wanted to be technicians in Key West, Fla., didn't know enough math and science to be trained.

7    So the telephone company began a school-to-work program that takes students into the field and proves the connection between homework and work.

8    "They needed more math and more science. They'd heard that from teachers, but until they got into the field and actually worked with employees who were using hand-held computers and making computations, they never were able to make the link," said Lee Doyle, BellSouth's director of corporate affairs.

9    Shell Oil has set up a Youth Training Academy that targets average students from Chicago's South Side and South Central Los Angeles. Many are middle-class but need a boost.

10    Hector Espinoza, 19, went through the Shell program in Los Angeles three years ago. He said it made him appreciate how hard his mother, a single parent, worked to pay the bills. Espinoza said

he attends college part time and works full time because of what he learned at Shell.

"Basically, I was a snobby little kid," he said. "I didn't think too 11 much of education or anything. After I joined the program, they set me straight. They would tell me I had potential—that I could go a long way."

Shell teaches about computers, resumes, work ethics and 12 money management. It helps participants get internships in fields that interest them—not just areas that pertain to Shell's balance sheet.

School-to-work initiatives are designed to improve the quality 13 of all future workers—not just the 75 percent of high school graduates who don't go to college, said J.D. Hoye, director of the National School to Work Office in the Department of Education.

Programs vary. Some target inner city schools; others work in 14 rural areas. Some teach students skills specific to a particular industry, while others opt for the more generic: computer skills, critical thinking and responsibility.

During the summer, Eastman Kodak tutors teachers in what 15 corporate America wants and offers teens apprenticeships in the basics of mechanics and electronics. It also presses local, state and federal educators to improve.

## Exercise **8**    Checking Your Understanding

1. According to this article, why do schools need the help of corporations?
2. The author says that "business has noticed the deficit" in the students' preparation. What kind of deficit does she mean?
3. What kind of program did BellSouth set up for students? What did the students learn?
4. Describe Shell Oil's program for students.
5. What does Eastman Kodak do to help both teachers and students?

## Exercise **9**    Identifying Facts and Opinions

Write "F" in front of each of the following statements from the article that you think are facts and write "O" in front of those that appear to be opinions. (Remember, if a statement is a fact, it should be easy to verify. It will not make too many "judgments" that are not supported by sufficient detail.)

1. _____ . . . teens who wanted to be technicians in Key West, Fla., didn't know enough math and science to be trained.

2. _____ Schools all have outdated labs, teachers who have never worked outside the classroom and graduates who can't keep a job.
3. _____ Shell Oil has set up a Youth Training Academy that targets average students from Chicago's South Side and South Central Los Angeles.
4. _____ Hector Espinoza, 19, went through the Shell program in Los Angeles three years ago.
5. _____ School-to-work initiatives are designed to improve the quality of all future workers.
6. _____ "Basically, I was a snobby little kid," he said.
7. _____ Shell teaches about computers, resumes, work ethics, and money management.

## Exercise **10**   Making Connections

1. How do you think your neighborhood schools could be helped by industry? Explain your answer.
2. Are there any school-to-work programs in your community? If so, what kind of assistance are they providing students? If not, how do you think your school could attract the help of large local industries?

# Organizing to Learn
## Using Visual Aids

Visual aids include charts, graphs, pictures, maps, diagrams, flowcharts—any visual image beyond the words themselves. These visual images help to clarify our understanding of the printed words. Sometimes they even add new information. They may also summarize in a single image what took hundreds of words to explain.

When you analyze a visual aid look for the following things:

1. What is the topic?
2. How does the visual aid relate to the text around it? Does it illustrate a nearby paragraph of information? Or does it show additional information—beyond anything explained in the text?
3. What are the distinct parts of the visual aid? How are the parts related to each other?
4. What is the main idea communicated by the visual aid?
5. What is the source of the information? How current is it?
6. What overall conclusions, or connections, can you reach from studying this visual aid?

## Example of a Bar Graph

Study the following graph, which is called a bar graph because "bars" are used to show the relationships between data, and read the paragraph that accompanies it.

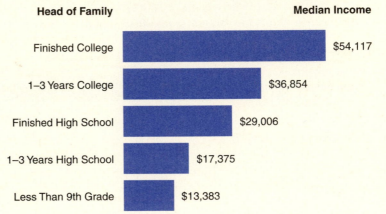

**The More Education People Have, the Bigger Their Earnings.**

*Source:* Data from U.S. Census Bureau, 1994.

Most people value the knowledge and skills transmitted by the schools because they hope to translate those skills into good jobs and money. Does education really enhance the opportunity for social mobility? The answer is apparently yes. As [the graph] . . . shows, the more education people get, the higher their incomes are. Today, due to the increasing reliance of modern industries on highly educated workers, the value of a college education has risen dramatically. In 1980 college graduates earned about 32 percent more than high school graduates, but ten years later the earnings difference had gone up to 61 percent. (Alex Thio, *Sociology*)

Now, examine how the questions for visual aids would be answered for this graph.

1. What is the topic?
   *The topic is "education and earnings." This information is given in the title of the graph.*
2. How does the visual aid relate to the text around it? Does it illustrate a nearby paragraph of information? Or does it show additional information—beyond anything explained in the text?
   *In the paragraph below the bar graph, the author refers specifically to the graph. He writes, "As [the graph above] shows, the more education people*

*get, the higher their incomes are." He does not in this case interpret all the specific elements of the graph for the reader, so you would need to study the graph more on your own.*

3. What are the distinct parts of the visual aid? How are the parts related to each other?

*First, there are two distinct parts to this graph. On the left is the heading "Head of Family" and underneath this heading are varying lengths of education, from "Finished college" on the top to "Less than 9th grade" on the bottom. This information is arranged vertically, that is, down to up. On the right is the heading "Median Income" and below it are bars varying in length with dollar amounts from "$54,117" on the top to "$13,383" on the bottom. Each bar extends horizontally, that is, left to right, to indicate the changes in median income. (It is important to recognize the difference between vertical and horizontal because many questions related to graphs use these terms.)*

*Second, ask yourself how the parts relate to each other. For example, what is the median income if the head of the family has finished high school? The answer is "$29,006." Then, what is the median income if the head of the family has finished college? The answer is "$54,117."*

4. What is the main idea communicated by the visual aid?

*The main idea summarizes the important relationships identified in the visual aid. If you study all the data provided in this graph, you will arrive at the main idea: "People who complete more education earn more money." In this graph, the main idea is already stated at the top for you: "The more education people have, the bigger the earnings." Don't expect to have this kind of statement provided in most cases. Here the main idea is printed above the graph and is restated in the paragraph of text that refers to it: "As [the graph] shows, the more education people get, the higher their incomes are."*

5. What is the source of the information? How current is it?

*The source of data for a visual aid is often printed below it in small print. Here the source is identified as "Data from U.S. Census Bureau, 1994." The date, 1994, tells you how current the information is.*

6. What overall conclusions, or connections, can you reach from studying this visual aid?

*You could respond to this question a number of ways. For this graph you might say, "Well, people had better get as much education as they can," or "I had better make sure I finish my degree."*

**Exercise 11**   **Using Visual Aids**

Study the visual aid on page 312—a table. This table lists major technical occupations, their average starting salary, and the average salary of experienced individuals in these occupations. Answer the questions that follow.

**TECHNICAL CAREERS AND INCOME FOR CAREERS THAT DO NOT REQUIRE A BACHELOR'S DEGREE**

| Occupation | Average Starting Salary | Average Salary of Experienced Individuals |
|---|---|---|
| Personnel clerk | $12,900 | $22,600 |
| Aircraft mechanic | 26,800 | 43,000 |
| Dental hygienist | 18,300 | 32,700 |
| Drafter | 15,900 | 27,300 |
| Emergency medical technician | 22,300 | 28,200 |
| Flight attendant | 13,400 | 28,400 |
| Photographer | 22,900 | 34,200 |
| Regulatory inspector | 20,400 | 28,300 |
| Respiratory therapist | 18,000 | 26,700 |
| State police officer | 23,100 | 29,700 |
| Surveying technician | 12,600 | 27,700 |

*Source:* U.S. Department of Labor, Bureau of Labor Statistics, *Occupational Outlook Handbook* (Washington, DC, May 1993); authors' extrapolations to January 1994.

1. What is the topic?
2. What are the distinct parts of the table? How are the parts related to each other?
3. Which three occupations have the highest starting salaries?
4. Which three occupations have the highest average salary for experienced individuals?
5. What is the main idea communicated by the visual aid?
6. What is the source of the information? How current is it?
7. What overall conclusions, or connections, can you reach from studying this visual aid?

# Gender Inequality: Employment

JAMES WILLIAM COLEMAN AND DONALD R. CRESSEY

*The following excerpt from a college sociology textbook looks at women's employment and the inequalities that exist between men and women in income earned and job prestige. Read to see why these differences exist and how they might be changing. Notice how the two visual aids that accompany the text help you to understand the writers' analysis.*

## Employment

1  Women's role in the work force has undergone a remarkable change. Fifty years ago, fewer than a quarter of all adult women in the United States worked outside the home. Today, that figure has more than doubled, and the number of working women continues to increase. In the next decade, six of every ten new workers in the United States are expected to be women. A similar trend is evident in Canada, where 45 percent of all workers are now women, and both North American countries are behind such European nations as Denmark, Finland, and Sweden.

2      Although the gap between men's and women's pay has narrowed in recent years, it continues to be a large one (see Figure 1). In 1975 women earned only about 60 percent as much as men, but

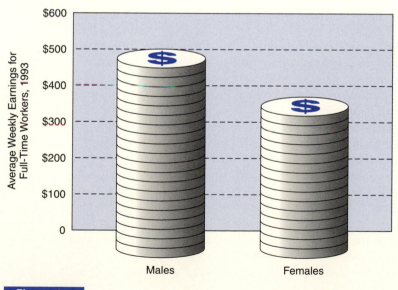

**Figure 1**

*The Income Gap*

*Source:* U.S. Bureau of the Census, *Statistical Abstract of the United States, 1993* (Washington, DC: U.S. Government Printing Office, 1993), p. 426.

by 1992, that figure was around 75 percent. Unfortunately, the reason the gap has closed is due more to a decline in men's earnings than to an increase in women's pay. An analysis by the Economic Policy Institute concluded that over two-thirds of that improvement was caused by the drop in men's wages and only a third by increasing women's wages.

Many women receive smaller paychecks than men because   3
they enter lower-paying occupations and hold lower-ranking jobs within their field. Yet there are substantial differences in pay even among men and women who do the same type of work. Women in sales earn only 56 percent as much as salesmen, and women professionals earn about 72 percent as much as their male counterparts. A *Business Week* survey found that the starting salaries of male graduates of the best MBA programs in the United States are 12 percent higher than the starting salaries of female graduates. Even when workers break out of the traditional occupational stereotypes, women still come up short. Although 94 percent of all registered nurses are female, male nurses earn about 10 percent more than their female co-workers. Women who cross the gender barrier to join the building trades, on the other hand, earn about 25 percent less than male construction workers.

**MBA** masters of business administration

Employers traditionally justified this inequality by claiming   4
that men need higher pay because they must support their families and that women just work for "extra" money. Few employers openly use such rationalizations anymore, but they nonetheless persist in paying women lower wages. Some economists explain this income gap by pointing out that the average male worker has more years of experience than his female counterpart. Others argue that women are more likely to put the demands of their families ahead of their jobs. A *Time* magazine poll, for example, found that a happy marriage was the single most important goal for most young women, while young men rated career success as their number-one objective. Although such factors are significant, sexism and discrimination are still of central importance as causes of the income gap. Employers pay women less for the same work because they can get away with it: They know that the prevailing wages are lower for women, and that their female workers probably cannot get another job at "men's wages."

Many occupations are clearly "sex-typed"; that is, they are   5
considered either men's jobs or women's jobs. Almost 60 percent of all university professors are men, as are 86 percent of police officers and 92 percent of engineers. In contrast, 75 percent of primary and secondary teachers, 84 percent of all librarians, and 98 percent of all secretaries are women. "Women's jobs" almost always have lower pay and lower status than comparable "male" positions. The nurse

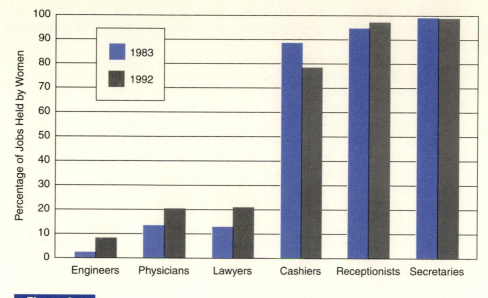

**Figure 2**

*Women's Work: Less Prestigious, Lower-Paying Jobs*

*Source:* U.S. Bureau of the Census, *Statistical Abstract of the United States, 1993* (Washington, DC: U.S. Government Printing Office, 1993) pp. 405–407.

(usually female) is subordinate to the doctor (usually male), just as the secretary (usually female) is subordinate to the executive (usually male). Jobs that are relatively autonomous are usually typed as male, as in the case of truck drivers or traveling sales personnel.

6        "Women's jobs" also offer less chance for advancement (see Figure 2). The secretary seldom becomes a top executive, nor the nurse a doctor. Although there are now far more women in middle management, they still are more likely to be in dead-end positions (such as administering affirmative action programs or supervising the hiring process) than in the production and financial posts that lead to the top corporate jobs. After years of progress at other levels, women still hold only 2 percent of top corporate positions in the United States and 6 percent of the seats on corporate boards of directors. Even governments follow this pattern of discrimination: A typical example is the Canadian federal government, in which women hold only 12 percent of the senior civil service positions. Many successful women complain about an invisible "glass ceiling"—a kind of unseen barrier that seems to block them from rising to the top levels of power. A recent survey of female attorneys in the Los Angeles area, for example, found that 60 percent felt they

received less desirable case assignments than their male colleagues, and 75 percent felt they were held to a higher standard than the men.

There are, nonetheless, some hopeful signs. As Francine D. 7 Blau and Marianne A. Ferber point out, there has been a slow but steady decrease in occupational segregation since the 1960s, and many women have managed to breach the walls that kept them out of better-paying "men's jobs." In 1960, only about 6.5 percent of U.S. physicians were women; today that number is over 20 percent. Women have made similar strides in the legal profession: in 1960, fewer than 1 out of 20 lawyers and judges was a woman, but today the ratio is more than 1 in 5.

**Exercise 12**  **Checking Your Understanding**

1. What changes have occurred in women's role in the workplace? *(Para. 1)*
2. What inequalities still exist for women in the workplace? *(Para. 2)*
3. What does it mean when the author says many occupations are "sex-typed"? *(Para. 5)*
4. What hopeful signs are there for the future? *(Para. 7)*

**Exercise 13**  **Using Visual Aids**

1. Answer the following questions based on Figure 1, "The Income Gap."
   a. What were the average weekly earnings for men working full-time?
   b. What were the average weekly earnings for women working full-time?
   c. What was the source of this information?
   d. For what year were the earnings reported?
2. Answer the following questions based on Figure 2, "Women's Work: Less Prestigious, Lower-Paying Jobs."
   a. In 1992, what percentage of physicians were women?
   b. In 1992, what percentage of secretaries were women?
   c. In which occupation did the percentage of women decrease from 1983 to 1992?
   d. By what percentage did the percentage of women lawyers increase from 1983 to 1992?

**Exercise 14**  **Making Connections**

1. Why do so few women become engineers, physicians, or lawyers?
2. What do you think can be done to remedy the problem of women's inequality in the workplace?

# DRAWING CONCLUSIONS

Drawing conclusions is "adding up" all you know about a topic and making some decisions about it. For example, in the previous reading, "Gender Inequality: Employment," the authors state that overall women have lower incomes, they tend to be limited to "women's jobs," and they hit the "glass ceiling," which keeps them from advancing. These conclusions are supported by a great deal of data and research. However, at the end of the section, the authors conclude that "there are, nonetheless some hopeful signs." They go on to support this optimistic conclusion with data that presents the positive changes that have occurred since the 1960s.

As an active reader, you need to recognize how people reach conclusions in the material you read, just as you did in the article above. Then, as a critical thinker, you need to also reach your *own* conclusions. For example, what do you think—based on your experience, reading, and studying—about Coleman and Cressey's conclusions? Do you agree with their assessment that there are hopeful signs for women's future in the workplace?

Often the conclusions that authors reach lead us to possible solutions to problems that we too may experience. Coleman and Cressey do not suggest any direct plans of action to remedy women's unequal position in the workplace; they do imply that the current situation is unfair and needs to continue to be changed. Other readings, however, like "Beacon Schools" and "Fighting Tradition" at the end of Chapter 9, discuss problems and then present definite plans for solving the problems. According to these readings, these solutions worked in their community. When you read this kind of article, ask yourself if the people in your community have the same kinds of problems? Would the authors' solutions work in your community? In this way you can critically evaluate the suggested solutions and arrive at your own conclusions.

---

**Exercise 15**  |  **Drawing Conclusions**

1. Based on the information presented in Coleman and Cressey's reading on pages 312–316 and your knowledge and experience, place a check mark next to the statement that best states your *own* conclusions about the problem of women's inequality in the workforce.

    _____ Women have made great strides towards equality since the 1960s, and they should be content to wait for their position to slowly and surely continue to improve.

    _____ Women's aggressive stance in the workplace has already caused a lot of hard feelings and problems, so they should simply do their jobs and co-operate more with their coworkers.

    _____ In order for women's equality to be achieved in the workplace, dramatic changes must be made as soon as possible in all areas of obvious inequality.

*Did you have difficulty fully agreeing with any one of these conclusions? Congratulations! You are becoming a critical reader and thinker who can confidently determine your own conclusions and solutions to the problems in your own community.*

2. Write your *own* conclusion.

## REVIEWING YOUR SKILLS

In order to examine conclusions carefully, you need to use all of the skills you have acquired so far as a reader. You must be able to use your knowledge of the reading process (prereading, active reading, and making connections) in order to:

- Figure out the main idea of a passage (stated or unstated)
- Recognize the major and minor supporting details that a writer uses to support his or her conclusion
- Understand the pattern of organization the author uses so that you can recognize how the author is framing his or her argument
- Identify important specialized vocabulary for a particular subject as well as general vocabulary that is important for your personal vocabulary plan
- Understand how to interpret visual aids
- Infer the author's assumptions about certain information that may not be stated directly
- Distinguish between facts and opinions
- Recognize the author's conclusions and decide how they will or will not be useful in your own circumstances

· · · · · · · · · · · ·

# Applying Your Skills

· · · · · · · · · · · · · · · · · · · · · · · · · · · · · · · · · · · · · ·

## *Careers for the Twenty-First Century*

LISA KALIS

*New opportunities and challenges face job seekers in the twenty-first century. The following reading explores six of the "cutting-edge" careers for the next decade and presents ways to prepare for them now.*

## Preparing to Read

1. What do you think will be some of the fastest growing careers in the twenty-first century?
2. How can you prepare for the careers of the future?

1    Welcome to the cyber-century, in which many of fastest growing careers didn't even exist a generation ago. Looking for growth and new opportunity, *Futures* has identified nine careers for the next decade. From the arts to law, technology plays a part in all but one of our choices. (That's physical therapy, which will see tremendous growth fueled by the aging population and new medical treatments.) But you don't have to be a computer techie to get on this super-job highway. Technology may add new dimensions to many careers, such as animation and online journalism, but it still stays on the sidelines. Instead, craft remains most important. So open your laptop and plug into these jobs.

**cyber** futuristic, computer-based

## Computer Animator

2    **The Payoff:** The days of the starving artist are over. Now, movie and television studios—as well as advertising, Internet, and multimedia firms—are paying top dollar for technology-versed animators. Most animators start their projects by hand drawing sketches. Then they re-create the images on a computer program and add movement and sometimes sound. There's work in both two-dimensional animation (cartoons, for example) and three-dimensional animation (think *Jurassic Park*).

3    Mimi Chung, 23, creates images for Music Pen, an interactive media company in New York City. "It's challenging to think of new ways to create something people will enjoy," she says. "And animation isn't necessarily a talent; anyone can be good if he or she tries." Salaries start around $30,000 and can exceed $100,000.

4    **What You Can Do Now:** You'll need solid knowledge of painting and drawing techniques. Try to learn programs such as Photoshop, QuarkXPress, and Illustrator. You can also get your foot in the door by trying to sell cartoons to neighborhood newspapers. Web site Yahoo! (http://www.yahoo.com/ Computers and Internet/Graphics) lists hundreds of resources and companies for animators.

5    **Next Step:** A bachelor's degree in art, computer animation, or graphics is ideal.

## Health Care Information Specialist

6    **The Payoff:** Maybe you're interested in medicine but can't stand the sight of blood. This position combines knowledge about health with computer skills—but no needles. Specialists are in charge of

patients' files in hospitals, health-maintenance organizations, and clinics. They might ponder security or legal issues when computerizing files, or create databases to analyze medical data. "I was always interested in health care, but considered myself a business person," says Ronda Shaklin, 22, a medical records supervisor in Chicago. "There are so many options. It's endless what I could do." Supervisors can earn about $30,000.

7  **What You Can Do Now:** Volunteer with a hospital or doctor's office. Knowledge of spreadsheet programs, and courses in business, computers, and life sciences are key. You can learn more online from the American Health Information Management Association at http://www.ahima.org.

8  **Next Step:** Both two- and four-year colleges offer degrees in health information management: passing a national certification exam is a must.

## Environmental Scientist

9  **The Payoff:** Saving the world is possible, and here is how to do it. Environmental technicians collect and test samples of water, soil, and air: salaries average about $30,000. Environmental engineers design ways to prevent and combat pollution and waste at about $60,000 a year. Hydrologic technician Greg Stekroat, 25, measures river levels and operates a flood warning system in New Jersey. "It can be tough, but exciting," says Greg, who spends most of his time outdoors. "You can be out during a snowstorm or a hurricane. We went out for Hurricane Bertha. That was fun, but very wet."

10  **What You Can Do Now:** Information and hot links are located at the Environmental Career Organization's Web site at http://www.cco.org. The Student Conservation Society (Box 550, Charlestown, NH 03603) offers internships for high school students in more than 20 states.

11  **Next Step:** Most technicians have a two-year degree in environmental technologies. Engineers need a four-year degree in environmental or chemical engineering.

## Physical Therapist

12  **The Payoff:** This field is booming: the U.S. Department of Labor predicts an 80 percent increase in these jobs over the next 10 years. Therapists use exercise and endurance training to treat people with muscular problems, from stroke victims to football stars. "I'm always having those 'Kodak moments,' " says Janet Wong, 34, a physical therapist in Seattle, Washington. "It's great to help people do something they thought they would never do—like walk—again." Average salaries range from $25,000 to $45,000.

13    **What You Can Do Now:** A hospital is the best place to volunteer. But opportunities are everywhere, including health centers, sports facilities, and nursing homes. Send a self-addressed envelope to the American Physical Therapy Association (APTA), Box 37257, Washington, D.C. 20013, for their career guide, *A Future in Physical Therapy,* or check out their Web site: http://www.apta.org.

14    **New Step:** Almost 150 colleges offer a four-year degree in physical therapy. After graduation, to practice, you must pass a state exam.

## Geneticist

15  **The Payoff:** Studies show you can blame genes for everything—your health, your weight, even how happy you are. And we still don't know the half of it. Less than 50 percent of the body's 80,000 genes have been found so far. Researchers are needed to identify those genes and find treatment for disease, and to study and reengineer the genetic makeup of plants and animals. Amanda Toland, 28, works with mice to study the effects of obesity on fertility, at the University of California in San Francisco. "When you make a discovery no one else has made," she says, "it's like putting a little piece in a big puzzle." Salaries start at $30,000.

16    **What You Can Do Now:** Try for an internship at a hospital, university lab, biotechnology firm, or pharmaceutical company. You can request the pamphlet *Careers in Genetics* from the Genetics Society of America, 9650 Rockville Pike, Bethesda, MD 20814.

17    **Next Step:** You'll need a bachelor's degree in biology or chemistry; more advanced degrees in genetics are helpful.

## Telecommunications Technician

18  **The Payoff:** These days, everyone needs a modem—they're logged onto networks and online services and data flies through fiber-optic cables every moment. Demand is on the rise for technicians who can install software, configure modems, and set up cables, modems, and networks. Dave Thompson, 21, received four weeks of training and now helps customers with equipment usage and repair questions for Lucent Technologies in Denver, Colorado. "It's great being part of a team, and working together to resolve problems," he says. "You learn as you go." Starting salaries are $18,000 and can go up to about $60,000 for managers.

19    **What You Can Do Now:** You will need quite a bit of basic know-how regarding computers and electrical currents. Try to get some experience in computer and Internet service companies as well as firms such as brokerage houses that need constantly updated information.

**Next Step:** No degree or license is needed to become a techni- 20
cian, but some telecommunications courses are helpful.

| **Exercise 16** | **Checking Your Understanding** |
|---|---|

1. What does the author predict will play a part in almost all of the job choices in the future?
2. What will be even more important than a knowledge of technology in preparing for future jobs?
3. Complete the following list comparing the six jobs. (1) List the six jobs. (2) Briefly describe the work done on the job. (3) List something you can do now to get started. (4) List the next step or degree you need to complete to qualify for the job. The first one has been done for you.

| Career | Work to be Done | What You Can Do Now | Next Step (Degree Needed) |
|---|---|---|---|
| 1. *Computer Animator* | *Create images on a computer program* | *Learn painting and drawing techniques, practice on software such as Photoshop* | *B.A. in art, computer animation, or graphics* |
| 2. | | | |
| 3. | | | |
| 4. | | | |
| 5. | | | |
| 6. | | | |

## Exercise **17**  Identifying Facts and Opinions

Write "F" in front of each of the following statements from the reading that you think are facts and write "O" in front of those that appear to be opinions.

1. _____ . . . craft remains the most important.
2. _____ The days of the starving artist are over.
3. _____ Now, movie and television studios—as well as advertising, Internet, and multimedia firms—are paying top dollar for technology-versed animators.
4. _____ Saving the world is possible, and here is how to do it.
5. _____ Environmental technicians collect and test samples of water, soil, and air; salaries average about $30,000.
6. _____ I'm always having those 'Kodak moments.'
7. _____ Almost 150 colleges offer a four-year degree in physical therapy.
8. _____ These days, everyone needs a modem—they're logged onto networks and online services and data files through fiber-optic cables every moment.

## Exercise **18**  Vocabulary: Connotation Versus Denotation

Decide whether the following words and phrases from the reading have positive or negative connotations. Write a "+" if the connotation is positive and write a "−" if the connotation is negative.

1. _____ cutting-edge careers
2. _____ growth and new opportunity
3. _____ computer techie
4. _____ super-job highway
5. _____ starving artist
6. _____ paying top dollar
7. _____ solid knowledge
8. _____ field is booming
9. _____ Kodak moments
10. _____ working together to resolve problems
11. _____ quite a bit of basic know-how

**Exercise 19** | Organizing to Learn

Study the table below and then answer the questions that follow it.

### CAREERS AND INCOME FOR CAREERS THAT REQUIRE A MINIMUM OF A BACHELOR'S DEGREE

| Occupation | Average Starting Salary | Average Salary of Experienced Individuals |
|---|---|---|
| Accountant and auditor | $26,100 | $47,100 |
| Actuary | 29,200 | 64,000 |
| Airline pilot | 30,000 | 110,600 |
| Architect | 28,000 | 54,200 |
| Chemical engineer | 33,300 | 52,100 |
| Chiropractor | 24,800 | 76,900 |
| Economist | 27,100 | 53,500 |
| Geologist | 24,400 | 48,500 |
| Librarian | 26,100 | 32,100 |
| Metallurgical engineer | 33,400 | 52,100 |
| Physician | 79,100 | 163,700 |
| Professor | 34,700 | 57,300 |
| Public relations | 20,900 | 52,100 |
| Securities sales | 19,800 | 98,200 |
| Social worker | 23,800 | 37,200 |
| Teacher, secondary school | 22,400 | 34,800 |
| Underwriter | 25,100 | 38,300 |
| Veterinarian | 27,900 | 57,900 |

*Source:* U.S. Department of Labor, Bureau of Labor Statistics, *Occupational Outlook Handbook* (Washington, DC 1993).

1.  What is the topic?
2.  What do the words "require a *minimum* of a bachelor's degree" mean?
3.  What are the distinct parts of the table? How are the parts related to each other?
4.  Which three occupations have the highest starting salaries?
5.  Which three occupations have the highest average salary for experienced individuals?
6.  Which two careers show the greatest increase in salaries from the average starting salary to the average salary of experienced individuals?

7. What is the main idea communicated by the visual aid?
8. What is the source of the information? How current is it?
9. What overall conclusions, or connections, can you reach from studying this visual aid?

## Exercise 20   Making Connections

1. Are you interested in any of the careers described in this reading? Why or why not?
2. What career do you want to pursue? How can you prepare for it?

# Chapter Review

## Exercise 21   Skills Review

1. What is a fact?
2. What is an opinion?
3. How can you tell the difference between facts and opinions?
4. What should you look for when you study a visual aid?
5. What's the difference between connotations and denotations of words?
6. Individually, or in your group, complete the list below of the skills you need to use to consider conclusions carefully.

**Drawing Conclusions**

a. *Find the main idea (stated or unstated)* _____

b. _____

c. _____

d. _____

e. *Interpret visual aids* _____

f. _____

g. _____

h. _____

## Exercise 22   Writing

Visit your campus career center and find some information about one career that particularly interests you. Write a brief report answering the following questions:

1. What are the job's basic duties or responsibilities?
2. What is the salary range?
3. What is the employment outlook—will there be jobs available in this field? Where will the available jobs be located?
4. What are the minimum qualifications for hiring? How much education and experience are required?
5. Why are you interested in this particular career? How does it match your special talents, interests, and goals?

| Exercise **23** | **Collaborative Activity** |
| --- | --- |

Share your career plans with other members of your group. Create a list of your group's career goals comparing the following: duties, salary, minimum qualifications, and job outlook. (For job outlook, you might rate the job one to ten, with ten being a job with many openings, in the area you wish to live.)

| **Job Title** | **Duties** | **Salary** | **Minimum Qualifications** | **Job Outlook** |
| --- | --- | --- | --- | --- |
| 1. _____ | | | | |
| 2. _____ | | | | |
| 3. _____ | | | | |
| 4. _____ | | | | |

After you have completed the list, discuss these questions: Why do you think this career is especially well-suited to you? How do you plan, step-by-step, to pursue a job in your chosen career?

**Exercise 24**     **Extension Activity**

Interview someone in your family or community who is currently employed in the career you would like to pursue. Ask what his or her greatest satisfactions are working in this field. If there were anything that he or she could change about the job, what would it be, and why? Ask at least three other questions you would like to have answered about the career.

You might also ask if his or her company has a "job shadowing" program, so you could follow the worker through an actual work day. Many industries have now begun such programs as part of their school-to-career efforts.

•••••••••••••••••••••••••••••••••••••••••••••

## Unit Review

•••••••••••••••••••••••••••••••••••••••••••••

### *Houses from Scratch*

MICHAEL RYAN

*Architecture students at Auburn University have found a way to complete their apprenticeships and to solve many housing problems in the Hale County community at the same time. Their "Rural Studio" project has become a model of school and community involvement.*

### Preparing to Read

1. As a student, are you involved with community programs?
2. What ways might schools and communities work together to improve both?

Shephard and Alberta Bryant, both in their 70s, lived with their     1
three grandchildren in a shanty in Hale County, Ala., that was literally on the verge of collapse. "You could look down through the floorboards and see the dogs and the chickens underneath the house," Shephard told me.

Now the Bryants have a new, modern home [pictured on     2
page 329] that was built with supplies costing only $16,500 and with labor and design provided by students participating in a program called Rural Studio. By scavenging items like construction rubble and old bottles to mix in with concrete, plus road signs and used timbers, the students also were able to build a smokehouse for Shephard, who makes his living fishing the Black Warrior River. The Bryants had never had such a fine home.

I wanted to see this small masterpiece and the other buildings     3
the young architects had built in the area. But most of all, I wanted to learn how a group of energetic apprentice architects and their distinguished mentor at Auburn University were using their talents to build beautiful homes for people who had never known decent housing in their lives.

"What we do is simply use the knowledge we have to do     4
something that has a practical value in people's lives," Bruce Lanier

Shephard and Alberta Bryant lived in a run-down home on the verge of collapse. Their new home, shown here, is roofed with acrylic and built mostly of hay and stucco. It has plumbing, electricity and even a smokehouse. Total cost of materials: $16,500. Labor: $0.

told me. Bruce is one of dozens of architecture students who have spent time over the last three years in Rural Studio, an Auburn program that is slowly changing the face of the impoverished areas around Greensboro, Ala., the Hale County seat. I soon discovered that Rural Studio students have done more than just indulge their artistic interests. Using whatever materials they can get their hands on—from hay bales to used tires—these eager young students have built homes and a noteworthy chapel in the county. They have designed a new family resource center, restored trailers and even built a warm, dry room for a 95-year-old man in danger of freezing in his tumbledown shack. Rural Studio has been given Hale County's Hero Award, a major civic distinction.

5      Rural Studio came into being five years ago, when Samuel Mockbee was asked to teach at Auburn. A native of Mississippi, Mockbee had graduated from Auburn and gone on to become a prize-winning architect with his own firm. He also held several different teaching appointments, including one at Yale, in addition to his work at Auburn. Mockbee designed huge buildings, but his passion was affordable housing. Frustrated in attempts to build

rural housing in his hometown of Canton, Miss., he began to discuss his ideas for affordable housing with D. K. Ruth, then head of Auburn's Department of Architecture. When Ruth raised a $500,000 endowment, Mockbee jumped at the chance to put his ideas into action, and the Rural Studio program began. "The heart of being an architect is to build houses," Mockbee told me. "It's every architect's dream."

6    Mockbee approached Teresa Costanzo, director of Hale County's Department of Human Resources, and told her his plan. Each quarter, he would bring 15 students down from Auburn to live in Greensboro. He wanted to find projects that would allow them to use their newly acquired skills in the real world. Above all, he wanted to find projects that would help people.

7    He had gone to the right person. "We have 1700 substandard homes in this county," Costanzo told me. Quickly, she identified one family that needed immediate help—the Bryants. Mockbee unleashed his students, and within weeks they came up with a design that would give Shephard and Alberta Bryant their first home with modern plumbing.

8    When Rural Studio was called on to help Mattie Hogan, they gave her more than just a comfortable home. They gave Hogan her family back. Because her trailer home was substandard, Hogan had been unable to be reunited with her children, who had been put in foster care. Then the students stepped in. "They gave me new windows and stopped my leaks, and they did my plumbing," Hogan told me. "The ceiling was falling in, the floor was caved in." Today, the trailer has a comfortable, finished look, and the Hogan family is back together. "It cost about $500 for the materials," Teresa Costanzo told me. "Weigh that against the thousands and thousands of dollars that foster care would cost."

9    Not everything the Auburn students build is housing. On a bluff above a wooded valley outside Greensboro stands what may be their most remarkable achievement—a rural chapel, sunk into the earth and set to catch the full glory of the sun. The walls are made of used tires.

10   It may be that some buildings that come out of Rural Studio, like the chapel, will be remembered for years to come. The people who have decent homes for the first time will certainly never forget the work these students have done.

11   But time may prove that the studio's greatest legacy is the change it makes in the careers of some of tomorrow's most promising architects. "They're learning things they would never learn anywhere else," said Teresa Costanzo. "They see social problems we deal with, problems they've never been exposed to before. We try to explain why they happen. When they leave here, they'll be able to apply what they're learning."

## Exercise **1**    Checking Your Understanding

1. What is the Rural Studio program?
2. How was the Rural Studio program started?
3. What did Sam Mockbee hope to achieve for students, and for Hale County, by starting the Rural Studio program?
4. List two projects that the students completed. Explain how each project benefited the people involved.
5. What does the author think Rural Studio's "greatest legacy" will be?

## Exercise **2**    Making Inferences

1. What can you infer from the author's statement "He had gone to the right person" when he explained that Mockbee had approached Teresa Costanzo?
2. What can you infer from the statement in the last paragraph: "But time may prove that the studio's greatest legacy is the change it makes in the careers of some of tomorrow's most promising architects"? What kinds of changes might there be?

## Exercise **3**    Identifying Facts and Opinions

Write "F" in front of each of the following statements from the article that you think are facts and write "O" in front of those that appear to be opinions.

1. _____ . . . a group of energetic architects . . . were using their talents to build beautiful homes for people who had never known decent housing in their lives.
2. _____ Each quarter, he would bring 15 students down from Auburn to live in Greensboro.
3. _____ What we do is simply use the knowledge we have to do something that has a practical value in people's lives.
4. _____ On a bluff above a wooded valley outside Greensboro stands what may be their most remarkable achievement—a rural chapel.
5. _____ Now the Bryants have a new, modern home that was built with supplies costing only $16,500 and with labor and design provided by students participating in a program called Rural Studio.

## Exercise **4**    Working with Words

1. **Connotations and Denotations**
   Decide whether the following words and phrases from the article have positive or negative connotations. Write a "+" if the connotation is positive and write a "–" if the connotation is negative.

_____ a.  beautiful homes

_____ b.  impoverished areas

_____ c.  decent housing

_____ d.  ingenious students

_____ e.  prize-winning architect

_____ f.  run-down home

2. **Using Imagery**

For each of the following italicized groups of words, explain (1) what visual images are formed when we read these words, and (2) what the words actually mean in the sentence.

a.  Rural Studio, an Auburn program that is slowly *changing the face* of the impoverished areas around Greensboro.

Visual image: _____

_____

Meaning: _____

b.  Mockbee *unleashed his students*, and within weeks they came up with a design.

Visual image: _____

_____

Meaning: _____

c.  The *heart* of being an architect *is to build houses.*

Visual image: _____

_____

Meaning: _____

**Exercise 5**   **Making Connections**

1.  How do you think the students benefited from their participation in the Rural Studio program?
2.  What are some projects that students at your school and community members might do together to improve the community?

**Exercise 6**   **Organizing to Learn**

1.  What do you observe in the picture that accompanies this article that supports the main ideas that the author presents? List specific details.
2.  Which paragraph of the text relates specifically to this visual aid?

# BIBLIOGRAPHY

Adler, Mortimer J., and Charles Van Doren, *How to Read a Book*. New York: Simon & Schuster, 1972.

Agee, Warren K., Phillip H. Ault, and Edwin Emery, *Introduction to Mass Communication*, 11th ed. New York: HarperCollinsCollegePublishers, 1994.

Alter, Jonathan, "What Works," *Newsweek*. May 29, 1995.

Althen, Gary, *American Ways: A Guide for Foreigners in the United States*. Yarmouth, ME: Intercultural Press, 1988.

*The American Heritage Dictionary, Second College Edition*. Boston: Houghton Mifflin, 1983.

Black, Deborah, "The Single-Parent Family," in Elizabeth Penfield, *Short Takes: Model Essays for Composition*, 5th ed. New York: HarperCollinsCollegePublishers, 1996, pp. 188–190.

Boskin, Warren, *Health Dynamics*. Saint Paul, MN: West Publishing, 1990.

Byer, Curtis O., and Louis Shainberg, *Living Well, Health in Your Hands*. New York: HarperCollinsCollegePublishers, 1995.

Canada, Geoffrey, *FistStickKnifeGun*. Boston: Beacon Press.

Carson, Benjamin, *Think Big*. Grand Rapids, MI: Zondervan Publishers, 1992.

Cavan, Ruth Shonle, "Family," *The New Best Book of Knowledge*. Danbury, CT: Grolier, 1982.

Chenoweth, Karen, and Cathy Free, "Homeless Children Come to School," *American Educator*. Fall 1990.

"China," *Encyclopedia Britannica*, 15th ed. Chicago: Encyclopedia Britannica, 1984, p. 296.

Chura, Hillary, "Firms Helping to Prepare Students for Working World," *San Diego Union Tribune*. March 31, 1997, p. D–3.

Clinton, Hillary Rodham, *It Takes a Village and Other Lessons Children Teach Us*. New York: Simon & Schuster, 1996.

Cohen, Daniel, *Re: Thinking*. New York: M. Evans and Company, 1982.

Coleman, William James, and Donald R. Cressey, *Social Problems*, 6th ed. New York: HarperCollinsCollegePublishers, 1996.

Curran, Delores, "What Good Families Are Doing Right," *McCall's*. March 1983, pp. 458–459.

Eshleman, J. Ross, Barbara G. Cashion, and Lawrence A. Basirico, *Sociology*. New York: HarperCollinsCollegePublishers, 1993.

*Futures*, Scholastic Inc., Spring 1997, p. 18.

Garraty, John, *The American Nation*, 8th ed. New York: HarperCollinsCollegePublishers, 1996.

Gay, Kathlyn, *Garbage and Recycling*. Hillside, NJ: Enslow Publisher, 1991.

Glazer, Nona, "Family," *The World Book Encyclopedia*. Chicago: World Book, 1993.

Golden, Daniel, "Building a Better Brain," *Life*. July 1994, pp. 63–70.

Gray, Paul, "Teach Your Children Well," *Time*. Fall 1993, p. 68.

Hamburg, David A., "The American Family Transformed," *Society*. Jan.-Feb. 1993, vol. 30, no. 2, p. 60.

Harris, Louis, "2001: The World Our Students Will Enter," in William Vesterman and Josh Ozersky, *Reading for the Twenty-First Century*. Boston: Allyn and Bacon, 1994.

"Homestreet, USA," *Greenpeace*. 1991 Oct.-Dec., pp. 8–18.

Hong Kingston, Maxine, *The Woman Warrior*. New York: Vintage International, 1989.

Hsu, Lee-Nah, "Drug Use and the Family," *World Health*. Nov.-Dec., 1993, vol. 46, no. 6, pp. 21–24.

Hubler, Shawn, "Fledging Teacher Gets Tough Lessons, Unexpected Rewards," *Los Angeles Times*. June 16, 1996.

Jewler, A. Jerome, and John N. Gardner, *Your College Experience*. Belmont, CA: Wadsworth Publishing Company, 1993.

Jordan, Michael, *I Can't Accept Not Trying*. San Francisco: HarperCollins, 1994.

Joseph, Elizabeth, "My Husband's Nine Wives," *The New York Times*. May 23, 1991.

Kalis, Lisa, "Careers for the 21st Century," *Futures*. Scholastic Inc., Spring 1997, pp. 14–18.

Kean, Patricia, "Blowing Up the Tracks," in William Vesterman and Josh Ozersky, *Readings for the Twenty-First Century*. Boston: Allyn and Bacon, 1994.

Keller, Helen, *The Story of My Life*. New York: Bantam, 1990.

Martin, James K., et al., *American and Its People,* 2nd ed. New York: HarperCollinsCollegePublishers, 1993.

Klein, Joe, "The Education of Berenice Belizare," *Newsweek*. August 9, 1993.

Kozol, Jonathan, *Illiterate America*. Garden City, NY: Anchor Press, 1985.

Lamanna, Mary Ann, and Agnes Riedmann, *Marriages and Families*. Belmont, CA: Wadsworth Publishing Company, 1994.

Lampton, Christopher, *Endangered Species*. New York: Franklin Watts, 1988.

Lemonick, Michael D., "What's Wrong with Our Sperm?" *Time*, March 18, 1996, p. 78.

Levine, Deena R., and Mara B. Adelman, *Beyond Language*. Englewood Cliffs, NJ: Regents/Prentice Hall, 1993.

Mings, Turley, *The Study of Economics: Principles, Concepts, and Applications,* 5th ed., Guilford, CT: Dushkin Publishing Group, 1995.

Mitchell, John L., "Fighting Tradition." *Los Angeles Times*. June 16, 1996.

Mohr, Nicholasa, in Foreword to *Latinas: Women of Achievement*. Diane Telgen and Jim Kamp, eds., Detroit: Visible Ink, 1996.

Montgomery, Lori, "Short of Funds, the Nation's Capital Is Falling Apart," *The San Diego Union-Tribune*. March 16, 1996.

Mujica, Barbara, "Bilingualism's Goal," *New York Times*. February 26, 1984.

Newton, David, *Teen Violence: Out of Control*. Springfield, NJ: Enslow Publishers.

O'Neill, Mary, *Water Squeeze*. Mahwah, NJ: Troll Associates, Vanwell Publishing, 1991.

Perkins, Joseph, "Reform Should Make Room for Dad," in *The Rocky Mountaining News,* June 23, 1993, p. 203.

Pierpont Gardner, David, "If We Stand, They Will Deliver," *New Perspectives Quarterly*, 1990.

Raven, Berg, and Johnson, *Environment,* Fort Worth, TX: Saunders College Publishing, 1993.

Roth, William F., Jr., "The True Nature of Work," *Work and Rewards*. Westport, CT: Greenwood Publishing, 1989.

Ruggiero, Vincent Ryan, *The Art of Thinking,* 4th ed. New York: HarperCollins, 1995.

Ryan, Michael, "Houses from Scratch," *Parade Magazine*. April 6, 1997, p. 15.

Saign, Geoffrey C., *Green Essentials*. San Francisco: Mercury House, 1994.

Samovar, Larry, *Oral Communication: Speaking Across Cultures*. Madison, WI: Brown and Benchmark, 1995.

Scarr, Sandra, Deborah Phillips, and Kathleen McCartney, "Working Mothers and Their Families," in Arlene S. Skolnick and Jerome H. Skolnick, *Family in Transition,* 8th ed. New York: HarperCollinsCollegePublishers, 1994, p. 412.

Shanker, Albert, "A Real Role Model," *On Campus*. September 1996.

Sherry, Mary, "In Praise of the F Word," *Newsweek*. May 6, 1991.

Skolnick, Arlene, and Jerome Skolnick, *Family in Transition,* 8th ed. New York: HarperCollins, 1994.

Stempleski, Susan, *Focus on the Environment.* Englewood Cliffs, NJ: Prentice Hall.

Thio, Alex, *Sociology,* 4th ed. New York: HarperCollinsCollegePublishers, 1996.

Waitley, Denis, *The Psychology of Winning,* New York: Berkeley Books, 1979.

Walther, Daniel R., *Toolkit for College Success.* Belmont, CA: Wadsworth Publishing, 1994.

Waterson, Bill, *Calvin and Hobbes, Tenth Anniversary Book.* Kansas City: Andrews and McMeel, 1995.

Williams, Brian, *Healthy for Life.* Pacific Grove, CA: Brooks Cole, 1994.

Wolf, Robin, *Marriages and Family in a Diverse Society.* New York: HarperCollinsCollegePublishers, 1996.

X, Malcolm, *Autobiography of Malcolm X.* New York: Random House, 1965.

# PHOTO CREDITS

Unless otherwise acknowledged, all photographs are the property of Addison-Wesley Educational Publishers, Inc.  Abbreviations: (R) right, (L) left.

**Page 1:** F. Martinez/PhotoEdit
**Page 23:** Copyright © Vince Rodriguez
**Page 33:** Franco Salmoiraghi, Courtesy of Knopf
**Page 54:** Rhoda Sidney
**Page 63:** (L) AP/Wide World
**Page 63:** (R) Frank Scherschel/LIFE Magazine, TIME Inc.
**Page 111:** Everett Collection
**Page 127:** UPI/Corbis-Bettmann
**Page 145:** AP/Wide World
**Page 149:** John Chiasson/Gamma-Liaison
**Page 173:** Illustration by John Bindon, from "Water Squeeze," by Mary O'Neill, page 18, Copyright © 1991, Vanwell Publishing Limited, Ontario, Canada
**Page 178:** Courtesy of The New York Historical Society, New York City
**Page 184:** Kathlyn Gay
**Page 189:** Tony Freeman/PhotoEdit
**Page 207:** Corbis-Bettmann
**Page 217:** Deborah Kahn Kalas/Stock Boston
**Page 229:** Copyright © August 5, 1995, Baby Blues Partnership. Reprinted with special permission of King Features Syndicate.
**Page 248:** Carol Palmer
**Page 263:** Lester Sloan/Gamma-Liaison
**Page 268:** Hazel Hankin/Stock Boston
**Page 270:** Norma Morrison
**Page 271:** Howard Lipin/The San Diego Union-Tribune
**Page 272:** Copyright © Jonathan Chester/Extreme Images
**Page 273:** Reprinted by permission of the Norman Rockwell Family Trust Copyright © 1945 the Normal Rockwell Family Trust
**Page 298:** CALVIN AND HOBBES © 1995 by Watterson. Distributed by UNIVERSAL PRESS SYNDICATE. Reprinted with permission. All rights reserved.
**Page 299:** U.S. Navy
**Page 300:** Courtesy, Cymer, Inc.
**Page 301:** Courtesy, American Academy of Dramatic Arts, LUBOW Advertising
**Page 329:** Courtesy, Timothy Hursley

# TEXT CREDITS

*The American Heritage Dictionary*, 2nd College Edition. Copyright © 1991 by Houghton Mifflin Company. Reproduced by permission.

*The American Nation*, 8th Edition by John Garraty. Copyright © 1996 by John Garraty. Reprinted by permission of Addison-Wesley Educational Publishers.

*The Art of Thinking*, 4th Edition by Vincent Ryan Ruggiero. Copyright © 1995 by Vincent Ryan Ruggiero. Reprinted by permission of Addison-Wesley Educational Publishers.

*The Autobiography of Malcolm X* by Malcolm X with Alex Haley. Copyright © 1964 by Alex Haley and Malcolm X. Copyright © 1965 by Alex Haley and Betty Shabazz. Reprinted by permission of Random House, Inc.

*Beyond Language: Cross Cultural Communication*, 2nd Edition by Levine, Deena R., and Mara B. Adelman, Copyright © 1993. Reprinted by permission of Prentice Hall, Upper Saddle River, NJ.

"Building a Better Brain" by Daniel Golden in *Life*: July 1994. Copyright © 1994 by Time, Inc. Reprinted by permission.

"Careers for the 21st Century" *Futures*, Spring 1997. Copyright © 1997 by Scholastic, Inc. Reprinted by permission of Scholastic, Inc.

"The Education of Bernice Belizaire" in *Newsweek*, August 9, 1993. All rights reserved. Reprinted by permission of Newsweek, Inc.

*Endangered Species* by Christopher Lampton. Copyright © 1988. Reprinted by permission of Grolier Publishing.

*Environment* by Peter H. Raven, Linda R. Berg, and George B. Johnson. Copyright © 1993 by Saunders College Publishing. Reprinted by permission of the publisher.

"Everyday Heroes" in *Newsweek*, May 29, 1995. All rights reserved. Reprinted by permission of Newsweek, Inc.

"Exposure to Chemicals and the Ability to Have Normal Children," by Dr. Ruth Markowitz Heifetz. Reprinted by permission of Dr. Ruth Markowitz Heifetz, M.D., M.P.H., Senior Lecturer, Department of Family and Preventative Medicine, School of Medicine, University of California, San Diego.

"Fighting Tradition," by John L. Mitchell in *The Los Angeles Times*, June 16, 1996. Copyright © 1996.

"Firms Helping to Prepare Students for Working World," by Hillary Chura in *San Diego Union Tribune*, March 31, 1997. Reprinted by permission of the Associated Press.

*Fist Stick Knife Gun* by Geoffrey Canada. Copyright © 1995 by Geoffrey Canada. Reprinted by permission of Beacon Press, Boston.

"That Good Familites Are Doing Right," by Delores Curran as it appeared in *The New York Times*. Copyright © 1983.

*Garbage and Recycling* by Kathlyn Gay. Enslow Publishers, Inc., 44 Fadem Rd., Springfield, NJ. Copyright © 1991 by Kathlyn Gay.

*Health Dynamics: Attitudes and Behavior* by Warren Boskin, *Graf and Kreisworth.* Copyright © 1990 by West Publishing Company. All Rights reserved.

*Healthy for Life: Wellness and the Art of Living* by Brian K. Williams and Sharon Knight. Copyright © 1994 by Brooks/Cole Publishing Company.

"Home Street USA" *The Greenpeace Quarterly*, Oct./Nov. 1991. Copyright © 1991 by Greenpeace. Reprinted by permission.

"Houses from Scratch," by Michael Ryan published in *Parade.* Copyright © 1997 by Michael Ryan. Reprinted by permission of the author and the author's agents, Scovil Chichak Galen Literary Agency, Inc., 381 Park Avenue South, New York, NY 10016.

*How to Read a Book* by Mortimer J. Adler and Charles Van Doren. Copyright © 1940 by Mortimer J. Adler. Copyright renewed © 1967 by Mortimer J. Adler. Copyright © 1972 by Mortimer J. Adler and Charles Van Doren. Reprinted with the permission of Simon & Schuster.

*I Can't Accept Not Trying* by Michael Jordan. Copyright © 1994 by Michael Jordan. Reprinted by permission of HarperCollins Publishers.

*Illiterate America* by Jonathan Kozol. Copyright © 1996 by Jonathan Kozol. Used by permission of Doubleday, a division of Bantam Doubleday Dell Publishing Group.

*Introduction to Mass Communications,* 11th Edition by Warren K. Agee, Phillip H. Ault, and Edwin Emery. Copyright © 1994. Reprinted by permission of Addison-Wesley Educational Publishers.

*Latinas! Women of Achievement.* Foreword by Nicholas Mohr. Edited by Jim Kamp and Diane Telgan. Copyright © 1996 by Visible Ink Press. All rights reserved. Reproduced by permission.

*Living Well, Health in Your Hands* by Curtis O. Byer and Louis Shainberg. Copyright © 1995. Reprinted by permission of Addison-Wesley Educational Publishers.

*Marriages and Family Diversity in Society* by Robin Wolf. Copyright © 1996. Reprinted by permission of Addison-Wesley Educational Publishers.

"My Husband's Nine Wives," by Elizabeth Joseph in *The New York Times*, May 23, 1991 (Op-Ed). Copyright © 1991 by The New York Times Co. Reprinted by permission.

*Oral Communication: Speaking Across Cultures* by Larry Samovar. Copyright © 1995. Reprinted by permission of The McGraw-Hill Companies.

"In Praise of the F Word," by Mary Sherry in *Newsweek,* May 6, 1991. Reprinted by permission of the author.

*RE: Thinking: How to Succeed by Learning How to Think* by Daniel Cohen. Copyright © 1982 by Daniel Cohen. Reprinted by permission of the publisher, M. Evans & Co., Inc., New York, NY, USA.

"Reform Should Make Room for Dad," by Joseph Perkins as it appeared in *The Rocky Mountain News,* June 23, 1993. Copyright © 1993.

"The Single Parent Family," by Deborah Black as it appeared in *Short Takes: Model Essays for Composition,* 5th Edition by Elizabeth Penfield. Copyright © 1996.

*Sociology,* 4th Edition by Alex Thio. Copyright © 1996 by Alex Thio. Reprinted by permission of Addison-Wesley Educational Publishers.

*SOS Planet Earth Water Squeeze* by Mary O'Neill. Copyright © 1991. Reprinted by permission of Vanwell Publishing.

*Special Problems,* 6th Edition by James William Coleman and Donald R. Cressey. Copyright © 1996. Reprinted by permission of Addison-Wesley Educational Publishers.

*The Story of My Life* by Helen Keller. New York: Bantam, 1980.

*Styles of Thinking* by Allen F. Harrison and Robert M. Bramson. Copyright © 1982 by Allen F. Harrison and Robert M. Bramson. Used by permission of Doubleday, a division of Bantam Doubleday Dell Publishing Group.

*Teen Violence: Out of Control* by David E. Newton. Enslow Publishers, 44 Fadem Rd., Springfield, NJ. Copyright © 1995 by David E. Newton.

*The Psychology of Winning* by Denis Waitley. Copyright © 1979. Reprinted by permission of Nightingale-Conant Corp.

*Think Big* by Ben Carson, M.D., with Cecil Murphey. Copyright © 1992 by Benjamin Carson, M.D. Used by permission of Zondervan Publishing House.

*Toolkit for College Success* by Daniel Walker. Copyright © 1994. Reprinted by permission of Wadsworth Publishing Company.

*The Woman Warrior* by Maxine Hong Kingston. Copyright © 1975, 1976 by Maxine Hong Kingston. Reprinted by permission of Alfred A. Knopf, Inc.

*Your College Experience* by A. Jerome Jewler and John N. Gardner. Copyright © 1993. Reprinted by permission of Wadsworth Publishing Company.

# INDEX